OFF TRACK PLANET'S
SOUTHEAST ASIA

TRAVEL GUIDE FOR THE

YOUNG SEXY & BROKE

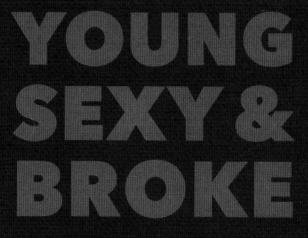

The Editors of Off Track Planet

Anna Starostinetskaya and Freddie Pikovsky

RUNNING PRESS
PHILADELPHIA

Running Press
Hachette Book Group
1290 Avenue of the Americas, New York, NY 10104
www.runningpress.com
@Running_Press

Printed in China

First Edition: August 2019

Published by Running Press, an imprint of Perseus Books, LLC, a subsidiary of Hachette Book Group, Inc. The Running Press name and logo is a trademark of the Hachette Book Group.

The Hachette Speakers Bureau provides a wide range of authors for speaking events. To find out more, go to www.hachettespeakersbureau.com or call (866) 376-6591.

The publisher is not responsible for websites (or their content) that are not owned by the publisher.

Print book cover design by Freddie Pikovsky.
Interior design by Corinda Cook.
Photograph credit information is on pages 243–244.

Library of Congress Control Number: 2018958306
ISBNs: 978-0-7624-6390-9 (paperback), 978-0-7624-6389-3 (ebook)

1010

10 9 8 7 6 5 4 3 2 1

CONTENTS

INTRODUCTION

THE BEST WAY TO DESCRIBE SOUTHEAST ASIA IS THAT IT IS A FEAST, AND ONLY PARTIALLY in the traditional sense. Of course, you will hit every street-food stall you can, sitting on rickety plastic stools and eating things you may have not thought were edible. But your eyes will also feast on towering ancient architecture, sculptures, and art, while your ears will take in a cacophony of street sounds generated by the bustle of city life. In the countryside and on remote islands, the feast will take the form of nature in abundance, with expansive caves, gushing waterfalls, thick jungles, and pounding ocean waves.

We hope this guide will serve as an appetizer in the multicourse feast that is Southeast Asia and make you hungry for more. You will inevitably stumble across the metaphorical Banana Pancake Trail, where many visitors end up because locals have tailored their offerings to suit Western tastes. But be wary of staying on the tried-and-tested path for too long. We find that the best adventures await—in this region and beyond—when you allow yourself to get a little off track.

HOW THIS BOOK IS ORGANIZED

From putting salt on watermelon to drinking beer in the shower, we've always been a little unconventional. While many travel guides are organized by country, ours is divided by interests—because we believe that following your passions will always lead you to someplace interesting. Whether you're into ripping waves from dusk 'til dawn, eating yourself into a food coma in every place you visit, gawking at obscure artifacts, or fist-pumping late into the night, you'll find something in our main section that'll stir your wanderlust.

In the second part, we lay out all the basics you need to know to get you on the road. You couldn't pay us enough to make you a bullet-point packing list, nor are we interested in holding your hand while you fill out your passport renewal forms. What you'll find here are tips on how to avoid the dreaded food-induced shits, where you can get the most beers for your buck, and how to avoid scams—plus other practical stuff mixed in.

Our last section is all about using your time abroad for good. There you'll find volunteer, study, and intern opportunities broken down by areas of interest. Many countries in Southeast Asia are struggling economically and politically, some still recovering from years of brutal warfare and environmental disasters, with new conflicts arising simultaneously. In this section, we urge you to get involved in causes such as helping children, animals, or the environment, addressing human-rights violations, and dampening the impact of disease and disaster. As a bonus, immersing yourself in a culture in this way allows you to live like a local, opening up myriad off-track opportunities.

You will notice that some destinations are more thoroughly covered than others. That's because we're not interested in spoon-feeding you everything about Southeast Asia—the internet is there for that. Instead, we want to present you with a sampling of the things we genuinely think you should do, even if that means you'll read a lot about Thailand and not so much about Myanmar (an undoubtedly beautiful place where a brewing genocide makes it hard for us to suggest jovial travel). We're hoping our recommendations push you in the direction of exploring other locales, events, and destinations inspired by—even if not covered in—this book. In other words, take OTP on the road with you as a friend who gently pushes you outside your comfort zone, not as a printed GPS device.

PART I

GET INSPIRED

Instagram, be damned! Southeast Asia might look pretty in pictures, but getting into the jungle-covered thick of it is the only way to truly understand this magical place. Your itch for adventure gets a satisfying scratch from the expansive limestone karsts jutting upward through the outskirts of Vietnam; Bali's famed beaches and jungle welcome you to become your best Bohemian self; and the monsoon-pounded Indonesian coastline creates monster waves that attract the world's top surfers. Cambodia's ancient past is laid out for you at Angkor Wat, where nature has beautifully eaten what man once made. Exploring the island nations of Southeast Asia is equal parts physical and spiritual, resulting in a truly transformative trip. With complex cuisines to spice up your palate, plenty of places to rage the night away (plus restorative coconut water waiting for you on the hungover side of things), and a region-wide cultural identity that cruxes on hospitality and collaborative living, Southeast Asia is on every backpacker's bucket list for many reasons, all of which you will soon discover.

Adventure, Sights, and Sports

THE EMERALD GREENERY FOUND JUST OUTSIDE THE BUSTLING CITY CENTERS OF Southeast Asia will lure you into its vast expanse, showering you with waterfalls, challenging your quads to push higher uphill, and testing the strength of your lungs as you blissfully soar into its cavernous depths. Miles of sea beckon deeper exploration, where the rarest aquatic life—from coral formations to almost-extinct dolphins—dwells. Climb through the beautifully ruined remains of Angkor Wat in Cambodia, trek through the hidden streams of the world's largest cave in Vietnam, and battle the ocean's herculean strength as you surf Indonesia's most unforgiving waves. Fear is your friend, even when it feels like he hates you.

THE GRANDDADDY OF TEMPLES: ANGKOR WAT (CAMBODIA)

When they stumbled upon Angkor Wat in the 1500s, many Euro explorers claimed that this temple complex was filled with impossibly beautiful, ornate structures that put Rome to shame. The now-extinct Hindu-Buddhist Khmer Empire built Angkor Wat to fulfill its lofty goals of showing the rest of the world that it was the boss of art and architecture. In the eighth century, King Jayavarman II established a foothold in the Siem Reap region, and his successors built it into a city of intricate temples that eventually included the masterful Angkor Wat. The fall of the Khmer in the fifteenth century meant these structures were left abandoned for decades, during which the surrounding jungle began to crawl over the complex, engulfing it and transforming it into a work of art no human could ever re-create. Now a holy tourist attraction, the beautifully decomposing temple is filled with towering statues, expansive terraces, and views that will transform your idea of architecture into a twisted fantasy.

What Is Wat?

The twelfth-century complex, built to represent the universe, is punctuated by five towers (the largest of which is nearly seven hundred feet high) that represent the peaks of the mythic mountain Meru. From the beginning of the long causeway entrance, Angkor Wat resembles a lotus bud. Dedicated to the supreme Hindu deity Vishnu, the temple took more than thirty-seven years to build and is the biggest attraction (in both number of tourists and sheer size) in the area. The tiered, 402-acre complex is covered in more than twenty-six hundred bas-reliefs—or sculptures carved into walls—which are all meant to be viewed from left to right. They depict Hindu funeral rituals, hand-to-hand battle scenes, five-headed serpents, mourning monkeys, and fantastical deities. The best example of Khmer art in the world, the structure has mostly survived the forces of nature for hundreds of years thanks to groups of Buddhist monks that moved in and worked to preserve it after the Khmer peaced out.

What About Thom?

While Angkor Wat is absolutely worth a visit, it is often hard to slip into a state of serene bliss when surrounded by five thousand tourists taking selfies. When the crowd proves to be too much, there's Thom: another network of temples nearby and surrounded by a moat that is said to have kept the crocodiles at bay when more than one million people occupied "The Great City" back in the day. Each of the temple's gates is flanked by fifty-four statues of deities on one side and fifty-four statues of demons on the other—an ancient devil-and-angel shoulder scenario. Onsite you will find majestic ruins of the dead and very little annoyance from the living. A few notable sites include:

PRASAT BAYON

A representation of the intersection of heaven and earth, the Bayon stands smack-dab in the middle of Angkor Thom, and its stone towers are covered with eerily large faces of god-king Jayavarman VII.

BAPHUON TEMPLE

A decrepit yet fascinating structure (which is currently being rebuilt to give tourists an idea about what the original looked like), the Baphuon is a three-tiered temple mountain that was built in honor of Hindu god Shiva in 1066.

THE TERRACE OF THE ELEPHANTS

A viewing tower built for royals, the terrace is covered in carvings of life-sized elephants and of the garuda—a mytho-logical creature often described as the king of birds.

TERRACE OF THE LEPER KING

Originally thought to be dedicated to a royal who perished of leprosy, this plat-form—covered in sculptures of demons and other funerary symbols—is now believed to have gotten its name because, when it was discovered, its central structure was covered in moss. Alternate theories suggest that the figure was that of Yama (the god of death), and that the terrace served as a crematorium.

PHIMEANAKAS TEMPLE

This three-tiered pyramid was dedicated to legendary mount Meru, and it can (and should be) climbed for breathtaking views of surrounding structures.

BONUS: TA PROHM

While technically not located inside the walled Angkor Thom complex, this temple is a must-visit, as it features huge silk and strangler fig trees swallowing its structures whole with their crawling roots. If it looks familiar, that's because parts of the 2001 film *Tomb Raider* were shot here.

OTP Tip

You will need to get a day pass to enter Angkor Wat ($37). A tuk tuk (from Siem Reap) to get around to other ruins will cost about $20-25. Hitting every single one of the sites here will make you feel like a speck in the grand scheme of things—which we promise will be a humbling experience filled with ancient-ruins-framed sunsets you'll never forget.

INDIANA JONESIN' AROUND:
OTHER TEMPLES IN SOUTHEAST ASIA

If you've been searching for that Temple of Doom since 1984, we've got just the thing. Southeast Asia is dotted with temples that will stir your Jonesin' spirit and make you break out that whip—and your best young Harrison Ford swagger.

PURA ULUN DANU BRATAN
(Bali, Indonesia)
This aquatic temple sits on the shore of Bratan Lake and was built in honor of water goddess Dewi Danu in 1663. The temple looks best at sunrise, with the morning mist rolling along the mountain range in the background.

CEBU TAOIST TEMPLE
(Cebu, Philippines)
We're big nerds for replicas, and the entrance to this temple resembles the Great Wall of China (much smaller, but no less great). The temple welcomes Taoist devotees and tourists alike, and has a gift shop within its Disneyland-like quarters.

WAT ARUN
(Bangkok, Thailand)
Who doesn't love gold? This shining temple (dedicated to the sun god Aruna) is best seen by boat, cruising by on the Chao Phraya River at night when its gilded spires are illuminated in all their glory.

SRI MARIAMMAN TEMPLE
(Singapore)
The oldest Hindu temple in Singapore, this one is a bit garish—with cartoonish statues stacked into six tiers—but you can pay all your respects to the deities, and, if you visit in October or November, partake in a fire-walking ceremony that'll make you appreciate your toes.

BOROBUDUR
(Java, Indonesia)
The largest Buddhist temple in the world, this three-tiered, 2,690-square-foot masterpiece is composed of a mix of square and circular platforms. It used to house 504 Buddha statues until nature and thieves had their way with them, leaving more than 300 damaged and more than 40 missing.

THEAN HOU TEMPLE
(Kuala Lumpur, Malaysia)
This Chinese temple dedicated to the sea-faring goddess Mazu—with all its beautiful red lanterns and six tiers—is a must-see in the Malay capital.

SHWEDAGON PAGODA
(Yangon, Myanmar)
If spiky, golden (like, real gold) pagodas are your thing, this place is for you. The nearly four-hundred-foot structure is crucial to the city skyline and is rumored to be home to eight of the hairs that adorned the body of Siddhartha Gautama (the Buddha that created Buddhism).

WAT RONG KHUN
(Chiang Rai, Thailand)
This all-white temple might seem like a dream, except that it's the real deal. Less of a religious thing and more of an art exhibit, the White Temple (as it is known to tourists), adorned with clean white serpents, dragons, and pointy pagodas, opened to the public in 1997 and looks like something from an icy fairy tale.

CROSS-COUNTRY MOTORBIKING
(VIETNAM)

Dotted with sprawling vistas, emerald-green landscapes of countryside villages, and miles of bright-blue coastline, and where winding roads turn into unforgettable experiences, Vietnam is a beautiful country to explore via motorcycle. Here's how to check off your Vietnam motorbike bucket list with confidence.

Start Smart

Though most crashes occur in metropolitan areas, on average, road-traffic accidents kill approximately fourteen thousand people in Vietnam every year and are the leading cause of death among those aged fifteen to twenty-nine. Motorcyclists account for more than half of the vehicular fatalities in the country. This is why Vietnam is not the place to *learn* how to ride a motorbike. If you're not already a motorbike rider, take a beginner's riding course in your hometown so you can get in there with some confidence. While insurance isn't legally required, considering the accident rate, it can sure come in handy even for seasoned riders. Now that we've got all the scary death warnings out of the way, let's get you on a motorbike, make some plans, and have some fun!

The Bike

There's really only one bike you should consider for trippin' in Vietnam, and that's the Honda Win—which will cost you no more than a mere 400 bucks. It's the most widely used, affordable, practical, and reliable bike there is in these here parts. Broke down in the middle of a rice paddy? Someone with Honda Win spare parts will be nearby to help, and it won't cost you an arm and a leg (unless you've had yourself a spill). Regardless, it's likely you'll end up needing some repairs along the way—which will usually be very inexpensive, some-where from $5 to $10. Purchasing your bike from a local mechanic and selling it back at the end of the journey is very common practice and has many advantages. For one, you'll have no time constraints and all the freedom to ride as long as you like without the pressure of adhering to a return date. Second, renting means putting down a large deposit, whereas buying lets you recoup close to what you paid for the bike. Make sure your ride comes with its "blue card," which is like a pink slip (certifi-cate of title) in the States. It will have a Vietnamese name on it, but as long as you possess it you are the owner of the vehicle.

OTP Tip

Don't get bamboozled! If you purchase a bike, do your homework first so you don't end up with a lemon. For starters, make sure the tires are in good shape and all the lights are working. Ask how often the oil has been changed; make sure the engine starts with ease and is free of strange noises. Look for leaks around the engine; if the engine covers are spray-painted, it's often a sign of a cover-up job. And lastly, go for a test spin—make sure it shifts smoothly, black smoke doesn't come out of the tailpipe, and the bike stays straight when you let go of the handlebars.

Pick a Route

Now that you've got your wheels, all that's left to do is ride. Commit to a timeline and take to the road, where endless possibilities abound.

THE QUICKIE: HUE TO HOI AN, ONE DAY

This beginner-friendly route is considered the best day trip not only in Vietnam, but in all of Southeast Asia. If you want an adventurous taste of motorbiking Vietnam without making a big commitment, then this is the itinerary for you. You will cruise through modern Vietnam while seeing hints of the traditional, getting a glimpse of hyperlocal life complete with lush green rice fields dotted with those iconic cone hats, mountain views, secluded beaches, and fishing villages. Make sure you stop for some locally made pho to soothe your soul.

THE CLASSIC: SAIGON TO HANOI, TWO TO FOUR WEEKS

Equal parts historical landmarks and off-the-beaten-path treks, this popular route lets you kill two birds with one stone. You will pass through beach resort Mui Ne, quirky province Dalat, coastal city Nha Trang, riverside town Ninh Binh, and bustling Hoi An. Along the way, you will experience the glory of zooming along the mountainous Hai Van Pass, the coastal little roads north of Hue, and the main thoroughfare, Ho Chi Minh Road. Take a breather at the Phong Nha Caves, where spectacular limestone karsts (the oldest rock formations of their kind in all of Asia) have been dwelling for more than four hundred million years.

THE BEACH BUM: SAIGON TO HANOI BY COASTLINE, TEN DAYS TO THREE WEEKS

If you're forever in search of that secluded beach from *The Beach*, this coastal route will tickle your sand-loving toes. The course hugs Vietnam's expansive coastline, where you will ride from beach towns to fishing villages on an eight-hundred-mile repeating cycle. You can hop off and socialize at more populous beaches such as Mui Ne and Nha Trang, and find delicious desolation at lesser-known local hangs like Phan Rang, Cam Ranh, and Quy Nhon. At night, seek out beach parties, or just relax and let the waves of the majestic sea lull you to sleep.

THE WORLD'S LARGEST CAVE: SON DOONG (VIETNAM)

Son Doong quietly loomed in a lush corner of north central Vietnam for two to five million years before a local man discovered it in 1991—which we're thinking feels like finding a $20 bill in your pocket on laundry day . . . times infinity. The cave was too steep for the dude to just jump right in, and in fact it wasn't until 2009 that the cave was properly explored by a British research team he led there. Now, a select few can experience this impressive site that's basically Disneyland for *Jurassic Park* lovers.

Glory of the Cave

This cave is so massive that a Boeing 747 could fly through its largest passage, and a forty-story skyscraper could fit into its cavernous, five-and-a-half-mile-long belly. Not only is it home to a full-on jungle, but there's a legit river running through it

with more stalagmites (the pointy rocks on the floor) and stalactites (the same pointy rocks, but on the ceiling) than you can possibly imagine. Entering the cave is no walk in the (Phong Nha National) park; it's a climbing adventure that lasts for 80 meters (262 feet). To get out of Son Doong, visitors must scale another 90 meters (that's pushing 300 feet) up the calcitite Great Wall of Vietnam. Suffice it to say, you'll need to be in good physical shape to notch this cave on your belt.

Spelunk the F*ck in There

It costs a pretty 300,000 pennies (that's $3,000 for you math whizzes) to tour the cave, and space is super limited because nature hates being stomped on by humans. Since 2016, Oxalis Adventures—the only tour company that the government has authorized to operate here—has taken brave cavers on a four-day, three-night expedition through Son Doong with one night of accommodations at a nearby village before and after the thrilling trip (presumably so travelers can freak out

and recover, respectively). If you're a photo geek, Oxalis also hosts extended photography tours complete with powerful LED lights to illuminate whatever remote cave corner you want to shoot.

Conquering the Cave

Once inside, your perception of the natural world shifts—ferns grow bigger as they reach for sunlight, and massive sinkholes (one adorably called Watch Out for Dinosaurs) take your breath away. During the expedition, visitors wash in the river, eat provided meals with the crew, explore ancient fossils and rolling fields of algae, wander through the underground jungle, investigate hidden caverns and waterfalls, and camp near the cave's unique structures—such as Hand of the Dog, which is shaped like an enormous paw. Newly discovered cave critters, including white spiders, novel shrimp species, flying foxes, and monkeys, make the journey even more thrilling.

Caves for Days

Son Doong is undoubtedly exciting, and very few have the bragging rights of having been inside it for four days. However, the rest of the region also has much to offer those seeking adventure. Several slightly more accessible caves abound in the Phong Nha region—not to mention charming villages and destinations for water sports. The Tu Lan Cave system comprises ten different crevices—complete with lakes—that require a hot jungle trek to access. If you want to test how prone you are to claustrophobia, check out the small, narrow Hang Va cave, filled with calcite cones jetting out from its shallow waters. Its sister cave (Hang En) is the third largest in the world. Although the discovery of Son Doong was pretty incredible, the mysterious Ruc tribe, which calls Vietnam's cave kingdom home, likely knows about a few others we will never see.

GET YOUR ASS KICKED IN BANGKOK (THAILAND)

We all idolized Van Damme growing up, and now's your chance to kick some ass—or likely get yours badly beaten—in the name of sportsmanship. Muay Thai (or Thai boxing) is a national sport in Thailand and quite the spectacle to behold—or, if you're brave, participate in. Be warned: these men are not fucking around when it comes to dishing out the ass whoopings—and the women are just as ruthless. However, if you can stand the heat, Frank Dux won't have nothin' on you.

Beatings Backstory

While its exact origins are debated, forms of Muay Thai have been recorded as far back as the 1500s, when kings would recruit the best fighters as their bodyguards and have them brawl for entertainment. The sport is known as the "art of the eight limbs," as it relies on eight points of contact—the fists, elbows, feet, and knees—as opposed to just the two points used in traditional boxing. Muay Thai—of which there are at least eight styles—was used in warfare before the modern era made hand-to-hand combat obsolete. As the martial art became more of a spectator sport in the early twentieth century, gloves replaced rope-wrapped hands, fighters began wearing protective gear on their sensitive bits, and official rings opened to host matches.

Muay Try

Let's get one thing straight: this is going to hurt. It doesn't matter if you won your state's CrossFit competition or if you're a Tough Mudder muthafucka . . . it will hurt. Remember how Dhalsim (that one long-limbed guy in *Street Fighter*) would just fly around and put you on your ass every time? This is that, except not Indian. Muay

Thai gyms are scattered throughout Thailand, with a high concentration in Bangkok, and you can drop in for just one lesson (which runs as little as $15) or train for months (the cost of which depends on the school you choose). The most hyped place for a tourist to try the sport is Master Toddy's Muay Thai Academy—run by the guy who trained Tito Ortiz and other greats. What does one lesson entail? You will do a shit-ton of conditioning training such as jumping rope, body resistance exercises, abdominal strength reps, and sometimes weight lifting. You will not be treated as a novice; you will get in the ring to learn some of the hundreds of techniques Muay Thai fighters bust out during a fight, then brawl 'til it burns. The heat is constant and water breaks are short. Nonetheless, you will walk out feeling like Bruce Lee's Thai cousin and will want to come back for more—except the next morning, you'll likely feel like an elephant gnawed on your limbs.

Watch and Learn

The first official Muay Thai ring was established in 1921 at Suan Kulap College in Bangkok, and the sport has become an international sensation since. The most renowned place to watch a match is Lumpinee Stadium on the outskirts of Bangkok, but catching a fight at the Rajadamnern Boxing Stadium—the city's other major venue—won't disappoint. Just promise us you won't get sucked in by scalpers trying to sell backpackers VIP tickets: those are bogus. Fighters will honor the sport, their school, and their teachers with a prayer called Wai Khru Ram Muay before proceeding to reduce their opponents to a bloody pulp. Even if you're the nonviolent type, watching people consensually beat the shit of each other for sport is pretty fun, and certain rules in Muay Thai make this particular sport the most cutthroat of martial arts to view. For example, whereas referees separate American boxers if they get into a clinch, Muay Thai actually favors the move (called a "neck clinch"), as it gives fighters a chance to throw elbows and knees more effectively. Between blows, you will notice fighters wearing armbands (Pra Jiad) and headbands (Mongkol), the latter of which are blessed by a Buddhist monk prior to battle for good luck—which should bring back sad memories of Ray Jackson's Harley-Davidson headband.

OTP Tip
If you want to see women go at it (they are not allowed to fight in larger stadiums), hit up the MBK shopping center, where fights take place right outside every Wednesday night and feature some tough-ass female fighters.

SURFING FOR ROOKIES TO RIPPERS (INDONESIA)

Sure you've seen those Aussie bro (nay, mate) types, bronzed and with perpetual salty beach hair, but did you know that Indonesia is the surfing capital of Asia? Here, you will find thirty-four thousand miles of coastline to rip—or to get your ass whipped by the waves if you're just putting your little toe in the water for the first time. No matter your surf know-how, you can hit up Bali with the best of 'em, as well as drag your board around Indonesia's more than 17,500 islands. Go between April and October for some major waves, or between November and March when the waves are less abundant and steady but the rainy season keeps the ocean tourist-free.

Best for Beginners

Bali boasts more than a hundred surfable spots, and, given its tourist population, is accommodating to noobs like you. Bali's Playgrounds is a shallow-enough reef break near Nusa Lembongan that will help you learn the ropes. In Sumbawa, a large island just east of Bali, Yo-Yo's cove houses the Wedge and the Hook—two tiny waves

where you can splash around until the sun goes down. For longboarders, Ekas Inside on Lombok Island is a smooth, long ride that will inspire you to get more time in the water under your belt.

OTP Tip

If you're on Lombok during dry season, when famed Desert Point fires up its rare left-handed breaks, you will be in the company of hundreds of surfers looking to catch a ride. Snuggle up to them for a firsthand lesson in hard knocks.

Pound the Middle Ground

So you've worked up some core strength, and your legs are no longer noodly? Congrats! Now is the perfect time to give those barrel waves a try. The A-frame Dreamland Beach in Bali is a great place to get your barreling bearings, while Medewi (on the western coast) is a serene escape if you're self-conscious about your form and don't feel like butting boards with others. If you can handle a rough start, Pitstops on the Mentawai Islands of Sumatra is tops. While sheer bravery is key to upping your surfing game, repetition is an important element of any craft. For a reliable ride, Uluwatu in Bali has a comfy wave that rolls in on schedule, all the time—kind of like that German guy you met back at the hostel.

Rip the Tide

Some surf sports in Indonesia are reserved for advanced rippers, and for good reason. When the Indian Ocean gets angry, only those with enough gusto can handle her wrath. In Sumatra, the E-Bay (left-hand) and Bank Vaults (thick right-hand) are known to be treacherous, freight-train fast, and unpredictable, while Lance's Table flows over what is known as the "surgeon's table"—a shallow reef that'll feel worse than a shark bite if you get too close. The same goes for Napalms in Java, where your untucked bits will transform into fish bait in one fell swoop. While you don't need to be kamikaze-surfer level to ride Bali's Padang Padang, you damn well better know what you're doing as these are some of the best left-handed breaks in the world.

OTP Tip

If you're serious about surfing, you won't want to fly home before hitting East Java's Grajagan Bay (known, with no sexual connotation, as G-Land). Legendary surfers have ripped these waters, which feature a four-break wave that blankets a reef and jets at unforgiving speeds across the horseshoe-shaped Plengkung Beach.

Surf and Turf

While some of Indo's islands are best for the business of surfing, a few key spots offer a balancing turf side that will help you mend the brutal wounds dealt by the sea with a few beers, hammocks, and backpacker buds. Bali's Kuta Beach is where all the beginners funnel in for an easy ride. Surf camps and schools are aplenty, the waves won't kick your ass too hard, and the dry side of the shoreline has great food, accommodations, and nightlife. To cut the tourist encounters in half and hang with surfers instead, head to Sumbawa, where you can wax your board while praising Poseidon for saving you from fast-moving Scar Reef (a wave that is as bad as it sounds).

SACRED MONKEY FOREST, BALI

Sitting square in Ubud is the Sacred Monkey Forest Sanctuary, where the Balinese monkey (also known as the macaque) is king. The forest boasts approximately six hundred primate residents that live in divided groups—like some sort of simian *Game of Thrones* spin-off. The groups sometimes battle each other when they cross paths, and females are quite protective of their young. Monkeys inhabit the forest temples, cemeteries, and every spot in between. Tourists can swing around with this community of nonhumans, but the sanctuary serves primarily as a research facility where scientists observe the monkeys' social behavior and monitor the rare plants in the area. The sanctuary operates on the Hindu principle of Tri Hita Karana, or "three ways to reach spiritual and physical well-being," which focuses on the relationships between humans and humans, humans and their environment, and humans and the Supreme God. Come here to meditate with monkeys and observe the Ngelawang moving art festival, which celebrates the victory of dharma (good) over adharma (evil). Your photos from here are guaranteed to be Instagramable AF.

VOLCANIC RICE PADDIES (INDONESIA)

A vista that you won't see back home is terraced rice paddies near the flanks of active volcanoes. The two are actually environmentally intertwined. Indonesia's landscape is dominated by volcanoes (some of which are on the bubbly verge of eruption) and dotted with rice paddies that thrive on the volcanic soil. Trekking around the country is a treat for the eyes, and a feast for the belly if you like your rice of the not-a-roni variety.

Volcano Heaven

Welcome to the Pacific Ring of Fire—which may sound like some sort of *Ninja Warrior* obstacle course but is a real region covered in volcanoes of which Indonesia forms a large part. There are currently 127 active volcanoes in the area, with the most active ones, Kelud and Merapi, located in Java. While there are many popular places to almost singe your eyebrows and give your quads a push (including super-touristy Mount Bromo), the following three 'canos are all the rage.

MOUNT IJEN

If you're into glowing, misty craters, this mount is your jam. Ijen is home to the largest acidic crater lake in the world, and its fumes will dropkick your lungs if you're not wearing a gas mask. At night, the waters are luminescent with blue sulfur flames that leap from the lake.

The entrance to this East Java mountain's base camp opens at 2:30 a.m. Bring a walking stick, and be prepared to hike for two hours or so.

MOUNT KERINCI

Is getting high on hiking more your speed? Jutting up more than twelve thousand feet over the island of Sumatra, Kerinci is the highest volcano in Indonesia and will take you several days to ascend. Camping within the freezing national park—with Sumatran tigers and rhinos roaming around—is both exhilarating and terrifying. You will hike through the surrounding forest, get stuck in rain, and run out of snacks, but it will all be worth it at the top— where a large crater filled with green water and a view of surrounding cities (and, on a clear day, the Indian Ocean) await.

MOUNT AGUNG

The highest point in Bali, this volcano last erupted (a bunch of times) in 2018 and is perfect for seekers of the kind of adventure that can give you third-degree burns. The hike up to Agung's dangerously steamy top takes about seven hours and requires a guide. On the volcano's southern slope lies the sacred Besakih Temple (Mother Temple), at which you can pay thanks to the gods that spared your magma-loving ass from becoming a fossil.

OTP Tip

If you want to see the sunrise from the top, you'll have to start hiking at midnight. Either bring a good flashlight or make sure your night vision is Predator-level!

Paddies for Days

The great thing about volcanoes—aside from their being totally badass—is that volcanic remnants feed the surrounding soil, creating a fertile habitat for crops, particularly rice. The country is the third-largest producer of rice in the world, and the paddies where the lovable little white grains are harvested are a sight to be seen. Lush, rolling, green steps spiral through vast valleys of paddies in Bali, welcoming you to get into the glutinous thick of it. What follows are some of the best rice-related sites.

TEGALLALANG

This rice terrace is the most popular tourist destination in Bali as it's easy to access from downtown Ubud. The sprawling paddies are owned by an old local farmer who will treat you to some green coconut drank and take a photo with you. Don't be stingy—give the guy a few bucks for being awesome. The surrounding craftsman village of Pakudui is filled with wares from local artisans, such as wooden vases and totem poles carved with animals and mythical creatures like the sacred garuda (aka the "king of birds").

SIDEMEN

Looking to become an expert in all things rice? Head to Sidemen in East Bali, where walking tours through the paddies will take you across rivers and hillsides as local farmers share their know-how of organic food production. This region is also known for its traditional weavings (*songket*), which are loomed by hand and printed with panoramic landscapes of its iconic rice paddies.

OTP Tip

If you want to get some thrill into your rice-paddy chill, neighboring village Rendang will get you near Telaga Waja: Class II and III white-water rapids blasting over what was once a hot lava bed formed by the eruption of Mount Agung.

PUPUAN

While rice is nice—and this village has plenty of paddies to check out—the famers here cultivate aromatic cloves (which you can see drying in the sun), coffee, and cocoa as well. This region of West Bali is also known for its tropical fruit trees, so you can get up close and personal with exotic fruits such as mangosteen and foot-funky durian. If you can finagle your way off the main path, you may find secret waterfalls and streams.

MORE PADDIES AND 'CANOS
IN SOUTHEAST ASIA

If Indonesia's expansive rice paddies and volcanoes have you itching for more adventure, similar locales in other parts of Southeast Asia will scratch you in all the right places.

RICE, RICE BABY
SAPA (VIETNAM)

The best-known rice terraces in all of Southeast Asia are found in Sapa, an area where many villages offer homestays and tour guides to the surrounding hillsides. You will trek through mud, meet a bunch of backpackers, and be floored by the beauty beneath your feet.

BAAN PA BONG PIANG (THAILAND)

This paddy sits more than 3,000 feet above sea level in the Mae Chaem district in Chiang Mai and you should visit during the growing season (June and July) to witness the local tribe cultivating rice, corn, and vegetables on these expansive rolling grounds. Stay in the remote wooden bungalows here to get fully immersed into the emerald green fields.

SOME LIKE IT HOT
MOUNT PINATUBO (PHILIPPINES)

This volcano is a serene hiking spot that is a symbol of both beauty and destruction.

It killed 722 people (and caused global temperatures to rise) when it erupted in 1991 after sitting still for six hundred years. It's now a hiking spot—complete with a crater lake—that both tourists and locals visit to remind themselves of the power of nature.

MOUNT MAYON (PHILIPPINES)

The most active volcano in the country, Mount Mayon has erupted fifty times in the previous five hundred years—most recently in 2018 when more than fifty thousand villagers had to be evacuated. Luckily, nobody was injured or killed. We'd suggest messing with a less angry volcano, such as the Taal (the Philippines' second largest), where the surrounding weather is nice and the chances of you getting covered in lava are lower.

turns them into nature's waterpark (Raging Waters be damned!). Trekking to the top through rice paddies and jungly brush will put you in position to plunge down nearly a hundred feet of falls—which drop you off a cliff at an alarming angle—before hitting a sparkling pool. Wait thirty minutes after you eat to do this one or face some butter-flies-turned-vomit discomfort.

DO GO CHASING WATERFALLS (INDONESIA)

If you've ever closed your eyes in the shower to pretend you're under a water-fall, only to be reminded that you're surrounded by porcelain once you look down at the hair-clogged drain, we've got just the solution for you: go find an actual waterfall in Bali, where nature's drains know no bounds. Waterfalls here are the kind you see on screensavers, and they make for some of the most Instagram-worthy shots, #nofilter.

The Slide: Aling-Aling, Sambangan

Waterfalls are wonderful in their own right, but adding a slip 'n' slide element

The Holy Grail: Sekumpul, Buleleng

If you're like us, you love a good deal, and these falls are a seven-for-one bulk buy. Why stare at one measly dripper when you can have a whole week's worth of waterfalls at once? You'll have to cross a few streams and trek along dirt roads to get here, but once you find your way, the Sekumpul falls will treat your eyes to a series of six or seven (depending on dry- or wet-season aftermath) cascades running down through lush bamboo forests.

OTP Tip

Like to watch from a distance? There are several gazebos in the area where you can relax and watch the falls without any of the backsplash.

The Panty Dropper: Singsing, Lovina

These falls are known to be the most romantic in the region and offer a tranquil atmosphere with smooth stone surroundings and birds chirping love songs in unison. Here's what you do: soak in the lava pool while doing that couples pose that Insta-grammers often strike—you know, the one where you look like synchronized flamingos covered in body oil despite the fact that both of you snore and drool at night. The best time to go is during the wet season, from October to April, when the waterfall is gushing at full blast.

The Big Kahuna: Nungnung, Nungnung

If thrilling heights are your jam, the Nungnung clocks in as the highest-altitude waterfall in Bali at almost three thousand feet above sea level. The fall sits in the middle of a quaint village by the same name, and its sheer magnitude will shock

and awe your senses. The five hundred steps it takes to get to this majestic cascade means that a number of weaker-than-thou tourists are unable to make the trek, leaving you free to enjoy the fall's expansive pool all by your lonesome.

The Baby Falls: Peguyangan, Nusa Penida

A miniature anything—such as a horse, poodle, or pig—is adorable, and a tiny, bite-sized waterfall is no exception. You will feel as though you're living in a diorama once you're in the thick of Peguyangan, where the miniature waterfalls will stir Godzilla-like feelings in your soul. Getting to the ravine where the waterfalls flow means performing *Cliffhanger* maneuvers around a rock wall on the island of Nusa Penida. The payoff: an infinity pool that overlooks said cliff with bubbling springs that massage out (some of) your kinks.

The Danger Cave: Tukad Cepung, Bangli

If you're jonesin' for a cavernous experi-ence, this underexplored cave-waterfall combo delivers. Contained in a circular cutoff of a hard-to-find cliff, this waterfall is unique in that it does not dump into a sea or stream. Instead, it does its own thing by just trickling through the cliffs. Watching water fall from the sky inside a cave is a trip worth taking. Don't go during a monsoon unless you're prepared to be trapped waist deep in accumulated cliff water.

OTP Tip
While there is no entrance fee to get to Tukad, tipping locals for giving you the deets to this hidden gem is a nice move.

The Lounger: Tegenungan, Gianyar

Sometimes, the ease of sitting in some water without putting all that much effort into doing so is the best. The closest waterfall to central city Ubud, this fall is nice to observe from the comfort of the sparkling plunge pool beneath. Lounge in the water until your skin turns grandma-esque, and dip your head under every now and again to hear the beat of the waterfall above. The entrance fee is less than a dollar, and you can spend hours exploring the extent of your utter laziness.

The Double Bubble: Banyumala, Buleleng

The Buleleng region is home to 90 percent of Bali's waterfalls, including this twin-fall attraction that's quite a sight. Come here to mingle with other backpackers, to get your swimming laps in around the sixty-five-foot-wide pool, or to listen to the hiss of hundreds of gallons of clean spring water filling said pool, which is surrounded by lush greenery that makes for plenty of photo ops. The pool is only about seven feet at its deepest, so feel free to float around without fear of sinking too far down.

The Hidden Treasure: Desa Musi, Gerokgak

Getting to this one requires some know-how, and the best way to learn the path is to ask a local. In Musi Village, ask around for the waterfall and prepare to be led to a cavernous landscape where water jumps from cliff to cliff—and where you can, too. Once nightfall approaches, hang with those same villagers to hunt down ancient Hindu temples and brush up on local culture.

The Soul Quencher: Jembong, Buleleng

This is a place where spiritual cleansings are a dime a dozen, and you enter the area by walking through an expanse of cocoa trees (if chocolate is not a Zen experience, we don't know what is). The falls themselves are more horizontal than most, running along rocks and trickling through jungle leaves. Bathe in the holy waters here to cleanse yourself of worldly sins (and other grime).

THE DRAGONS OF INDONESIA

Dragons are majestic creatures often relegated to the world of fantasy. However, real dragons *do* exist if you seek them out among the islands of Indonesia. Established in 1980, the Komodo National Park protects the lizard kings who call the islands home. Pack up your *Game of Thrones* dragon

fantasies and head to the island of Komodo, where the (unfortunately flightless) dragons roam free.

Enter the Dragon

The Komodo dragon is not your typical aquarium lizard. These guys grow up to twelve feet long and weigh as much as three hundred pounds (that's less like a gecko and more like a loveseat). The largest land-dwelling lizard, the Komodo feasts on a number of animals you would have trouble taking down on your own, including pigs, buffalo, horses, and dogs. While its sheer strength is impressive, the Komodo's real power comes from its septic saliva, which kills prey within a few hours of the creature's biting it. Komodo dragons—of which there are approximately five thousand left—are limited to the park's islands and to certain areas of Australia, and you can find them lounging near the beach during warm and dry summer days. Don't bring a bacon (or horse) sandwich unless you want your arm chomped off.

Underwater Adventure

The island park isn't just an on-land destination. The waters surrounding Komodo are part of the Coral Triangle and contain some of the most diverse marine species on the planet. Positioned between the Indian and Pacific Oceans, the park is in the migration path of crustaceans, and it is filled with coral reefs and expansive mangrove forests. Diving deep, you will be privy to a thousand species of fish and marine mammals, such as whale sharks, dolphins, and dugongs—which are pretty much frowny-faced manatees. At the southern tip of Komodo Bay, you will find a dive entry point locally referred to as the Alley, where manta rays wave you deeper into the water and giant trevally swim about with their mean silvery mugs. Just watch your back as you enter the aquatic expanse because Komodo dragons will stalk their prey in the water, and if your legs resemble those of a deer (ooh la la), you could lose them to the carnivorous beast.

OTP Tip

If you're a fan of colorful reef fish, a rainbow of sea life lives off of Crystal Rock within the park, where you will see scorpion fish, schools of brightly colored anthias, and moray eels.

Trek Lightly

The park can handle a maximum of sixty thousand curious tourists per year, and it is generally just about maxed out. The most coveted profession in the area is in the fishing industry, and many fishermen are targeted by authorities for being jerks to the environment. Fishing bombs are a common tool employed to literally blast fish out of the coral with a mixture of fertilizer and kerosene stuffed into a beer bottle. Ever since the region was designated in 1986 as a UNESCO World Heritage site, many officials have targeted illegal fishermen—who have retaliated by throwing fish bombs their way. Keep an ear to the ground and an eye on the water.

ISLAND HOPPING HA LONG BAY LIKE A BOSS (VIETNAM)

If you hail from a landlocked state (or even if you don't), Ha Long Bay in the Gulf of Tonkin will take your breath away, with thousands of limestone islands topped with forested hairdos jutting out of the teal water into the aquamarine sky. Cruise along and ponder the millions of years of tropical history that have shaped these islets and crevices, then pop onto a fluffy beach or into a floating village to see what livin' off the land (er, water) is like.

Dragon Tales

This geographical wonder has been around in its current form for more than eighteen thousand years, and the Vietnamese have a great origin story for the region. It is believed that during the formation of Vietnam as a country, the residents had to fight invading forces from China and Mongolia, so the Jade Emperor sent help their way in the form of a mama dragon and her dragon babies. Ha Long (which translates to "descending dragon") was formed when the dragon team fought off invaders by spewing emeralds, which landed in the water to form some sixteen hundred to two thousand islands and islets.

The foam on the islands' pristine beaches is said to be drummed up by the dragons' tails, presumably wagging vigorously from the joy of living here as opposed to, say, rural North Dakota.

Bay Breakdown

Similar to that childhood game of making shapes out of clouds, geological features in Ha Long have mostly been named for what they look like, and they come with romantic (and tragic) backstories. Here are just a few of the 980 named places in the bay. Pick your favorite and venture on.

HON GA CHOI ("FIGHTING COCK")

This one is pretty much two forty-foot rock towers that face each other and look like they're going to either fight or make out.

CON COC ("FROG ISLET")

A rock formation that looks like a toad, sitting there in the water, just waiting for rain. According to an ancient tale, farmers across Vietnam believe that when a toad grinds its teeth, the gods will bestow the country with rain.

KIM QUY ("GOLDEN TURTLE")

A cave named after a heroic turtle that fought marine monsters from the South China Sea with a holy sword before perishing from exhaustion inside the cave.

HANG TRONG AND HANG TRINH NU ("MALE CAVE" AND "VIRGIN CAVE")

The story goes that a beautiful young woman fell in love with a fisherman who was skipping town soon. The lady was exiled by some powerful dude and turned into a stone statue after starving to death while awaiting her fisherman. In a sort of Romeo and Juliet twist, the fisherman heard about his love's predicament and turned into a nearby islet.

THIEN CUNG ("HEAVENLY GROTTO")

A "dead" cave (meaning water no longer drips through it) where it is said that a young girl married a dragon in order to (somehow) save the village from drought. We know you were hankering for more dragon tales, so there you go.

People of the Bay

Tucked away between sunken mountains lie floating villages: collections of colorful houseboats that once served as homes, schools, and police stations, strung together to fight the elements. Most of these self-contained societies of fishermen and pearl farmers are being evacuated due to a government directive to move locals inland due to environmental concerns. As we're writing this, four floating villages still exist. A beautiful one is Cua Van, which has approximately seven hundred residents, some of whom offer homestay. Tour boats pass by to show land dwellers what life is like on the water. Brace your sea legs, friends!

BAY THE RIGHT WAY

Getting to Ha Long is about a three-hour road trek from Hanoi, and then it's all junk boats (not crappy boats, just the name of these particular boats) from there. Tourism over the years has desecrated some of the islands as visitors love to leave behind garbage, and much of the area's mangroves and seagrass beds have been cleared to accommodate docking wharves for tour boats. Game fishing has also depleted some of the islands' unique fish populations. To avoid further fucking this magical place, seek out ecotours—such as Eco Friendly Vietnam and Indochina Junk—that aim to reduce the impact on the region's natural resources.

OTP Tip

Hop over to Cat Ba Island—where you can find nightly accommodations—to explore its expansive national park. You may spot a golden-headed langur, the most endangered primate in the world. From Cat Ba, you can venture on to Lan Ha Bay, a less touristy water world that is technically part of more popular Ha Long but way too far for most day-trippers. Kayak trips here start at about 25 bucks a pop.

WHALE-SHARK DIVING (THAILAND)

If you smash a whale and a shark together, you get what is cleverly called a whale shark, or the largest fish in the world. The gentle giants roam the oceans near Australia, Mexico, and Thailand. Diving deep to see these mythic creatures is an experience that will put your Cancun snorkeling adventure to shame. However, actually encountering a whale shark on a dive is not a given—and you'll be one of a lucky few if you do.

Finding Nemo

You'd think that because they grow up to forty feet in length, whale sharks would be easy to spot. However, these fierce-looking but mellow monsters are fairly rare, and getting near one is mostly all up to chance. In Thailand, the shark has been spotted in places around the Similan Islands, most frequently near Richelieu Rock during high season in April. Hin Daeng (Red Rock), another good bet for shark sightings, is covered with soft coral that serves as a plankton buffet for whale sharks. Remember that wall of silver fish in *Finding Nemo*? Those are schools of trevally, and you will find them here while looking for sharks. Other designated dive spots exist around Thailand, including the slightly misleadingly named "Shark Point" in Phuket—where you will more likely see a manta ray than a whale shark.

OTP Tip

If you do encounter a whale shark creepily lurking about, don't be scurred. They believe that humans are friends, not food, and will likely never turn *Jaws* on you.

Raise the Stakes

There are a few ways to increase your chances of seeing a whale shark—none better than booking a live-aboard cruise. Phuket and Khao Lak are common port cities for live-aboards, and trips (which often include a stopover at Richelieu Rock) range from three nights to a full week. The *Dolphin Queen* is an affordable option at $750 for a four-night cruise, but you can take a Chinese junk boat (priced at $1,800 per six-night trip) for a pricier adventure. Once aboard, you will have the opportunity to dive a number of times, upping your chances of coming face-to-fin with a whale shark. Accommodations vary depending on the boat, but most will have sunning decks, nightly events, and plenty of like-minded sharkseekers.

Hands Off

We understand the urge to pet whale sharks, but keep your cute-aggression at bay. Your grimy human hands, covered in oils and particles, are not great for the marine animal, so maintain your distance. However, whale sharks are often known to swim near divers, and if one does, giving her a little wetsuit body snuggle won't hurt. Swimming with these beasts of the sea is becoming rarer as fishermen in the Philippines hunt whale sharks for meat that they sell to wealthy fishmongers in China and Taiwan as a delicacy. If luck falls on your side, feel free to old-man brag about your encounter, *Big Fish*-style.

OTP Tip

Never support places that keep these roaming creatures in captivity. Part of the adventure is not knowing when you'll bump into a whale shark; part of being a good human is making sure marine animals aren't trapped in swimming-pool-sized cages.

RIP YOUR MUSCLES A NEW ONE IN DALAT (VIETNAM)

Pumping that iron in a sweat-stained building (aka the gym) is not the optimal way to work out, especially in Dalat, a small city sometimes referred to as the Paris of Vietnam (because it was originally built as a colonial-era French resort). Dalat is known for its cooler weather year round (compared to its sweltering neighbors) and for canyoning—a sport that feels like leg day, every day. Visiting the area gives you the chance to fly through the jungle, bounce off walls, jump from waterfalls—and love every muscle-ripping minute of it.

What Goes Up . . .

You will need to buy a tour package with a local company that will provide you with transportation into the forest, lunch and snacks, and safety gear—which will be key to your survival. You can book group trips through hostels, and guides will come along for the wild ride to make sure you're all right. Once you get to a spot where the guides can demonstrate safe rappelling techniques, you'll be let loose. You may feel like you've only learned to crawl, but the school of hard knocks (like, literally banging your knees into rocks) will teach you to fly.

OTP Tip

If you happen to be one of those people that own ugly sportin' sandals, now is the time to use them as there will be lots of water, and sneakers will get dank AF. Wear waterproof sunscreen while you're at it.

. . . Must Come Down

So this is the deal: you will be really high up and know that you need to get down. The only issue is that you have no idea what's down there. It's not a stairway or just one rock face. Your only tools are that rappelling rope, your legs, and pure courage. This area of Dalat is home to a number of fast-rushing waterfalls—some up to eighty feet tall—that majorly swell during the rainy season. Here, rugged rock walls will challenge your athletic abilities, and towering cliffs will force you to overcome your fight-or-flight response (that overwhelming feeling you got as a kid standing on the high-diving board at the community pool). But somehow, you will find the courage to tumble down slippery rocks, tackle gushing water, and plunge into pools from heights that'll make your heart sink. In the end, you'll be telling the jungle, "Come at me, bro."

Chill the F*ck Out

After all the outdoorsy madness, you will want to plop somewhere and maybe not move for a while. Lucky for you, the hostels here are affordable (as low as $5 a bed). There is another option, however, if you're brave enough to let your mind wander to weird places; it's pricier (starting at $35 per night) but a lot more fun. Enter the "Crazy House," or what locals call Hang Nga Guesthouse—an absolute wonder of architecture that's equal parts Gaudi, Dali, and Escher. Designed by local artist Hang Nga, the entire thing is a trippy, cavernous sculpture where every room is a different kind of weird, with themes that mimic the jungle you spent all day conquering.

Art, Culture, and Design

ONE ADJECTIVE THAT WILL NEVER BE USED TO DESCRIBE THE ART AND CULTURE of Southeast Asia is *drab*. Entire cities here are decorated with religiously significant sculptures created with meticulous detail, towering stories in the air, reclining across entire city blocks, and replicated in thousands of reliefs atop temples in bright hues. And art is not limited to ancient sculptures; it also takes the form of healing massage, meditation techniques, fashion, nature, and technology. Take in the fantastic Supertrees of Singapore, pay a visit to Hoi An's famous tailors, learn the art of chilling out in Chiang Mai, then stop by Cambodia's bustling night markets to revel in artisan crafts and open-air market culture. The visual elements of Southeast Asia are guaranteed to inject vibrant color into your humdrum life, and the region's cultural practices will expand your perspective beyond the scope of the Western world.

RUB ONE OUT
(THAILAND)

When your old travelin' bones (all of them) need to be pulled into place, massage parlors—a cultural mainstay in Thailand—will get you in tip-top shape. The massages here are intense, and they won't leave you hanging like that one time your roommate rubbed your shoulders for exactly five minutes before stopping for no reason. Nothing is more relaxing than a professional massage, in which your muscles and joints are attended to after being crammed under your backpack straps for weeks. Leave all that stress behind and get ready to rub (and tug?) one out in Thailand.

Sensual Healing

We know your mind is already in the gutter, but let's first focus on *actual* massages, of the healing kind. Said to be developed by monks about twenty-five hundred years ago, the Thai massage style is less rubbing and more pulling. The idea is to tap into your body's energy lines with a sequence of compressions, during which your masseur will guide your body parts into yoga-like positions and apply pressure. Often called the "lazy man's massage," Thai massage requires nothing of you other than to relax and submit to the motions, which lead to benefits such as joint alignment, tension release, and increased flexibility.

On the Streets

Bangkok, and many other cities in Thailand, are littered with neon signs, printed Microsoft Word flyers, and hecklers advertising massages. Street-side places range from kinda dingy (where the smell of incense will burn your nostrils) to partially decorated dens with mats on the floor. Sometimes you will find endless rows of mats sprawled in public places (such as malls). But if you're fancy, you can book a private or double room at a parlor for a quarter of the price you'd pay in the States. You might be surprised to know that

Thai massage—as opposed to Swedish—is traditionally performed on your fully clothed body, and you will get a pair of massive pants to put on once you're ready to roll. Also, this may not be what you want to hear, but the best masseurs are older women—they are freakishly strong and extra experienced. You can get a spa-like experience at a hotel, but we'd suggest doing that back home. Massage oils are sometimes listed on the menu, along with other, less PG-13, things.

OTP Tip

More of a giver? You can pop into Wat Pho—a gorgeous temple and home to one of the country's best and oldest massage schools—for a few lessons on how to pull people into place. You can also get a student massage for about 10 bucks after touring the temple.

In the Sheets

Thailand is known for many things, and (as you may have guessed, you clever devil) happy-ending massages are absolutely one of them. In Bangkok's red-light district, it's fairly easy to distinguish places that offer nonsexual services like foot massages from those that go for the ol' rub-and-tug. Some spots don't advertise their services as sexy, and finding them is, shall we say, on a "first come, first served" (or something like that) basis. There are also places that expressly do not offer sex services and will report you if you ask. To find the G-spot, look for signage that is obviously sex-related (e.g., featuring exotic or erotic massage, photos of women in bunny ears and lingerie . . . you get the drift). What's on the menu, you ask? Well, you can get a hand job, testicle massage, prostate poke, costumed play, BDSM kinky shit, four-hand massage (two masseurs with two hands each), and more. Women are welcome to play at many places and can sometimes choose between female and male masseurs—the latter can be requested and booked for the next day if the parlor doesn't have one on hand. Full sex may also be on offer with or without the massage, the latter of which actually isn't very good in places that offer sex services. Expect to pay between $15 and $30 for a hand job in addition to the massage, with other services tacked on top. Choose a place that has air-conditioning. Trust us.

OTP Tip

Sex work is work, and it's great when both parties are consenting adults. However, as with any industry that is prone to sex trafficking, be mindful of your surroundings. Don't be afraid to take action if your masseuse or masseur seems uncomfortable, young, or hurt, or if you just get a feeling that things are shadier than they should be. The Thai government has recently cracked down on these violations of human rights, and you can report anything that looks fishy by contacting +66 99 130 1300 via call or text.

MASSAGES! GET YOUR MASSAGES!

In Southeast Asia, there is more than one way to get your massage on. Whatever your kinks, getting massaged from Bangkok to Siem Reap will leave you feeling loose. Generally speaking, here's what you can expect from the various massage styles found in Southeast Asia.

THE SLEEPER (CAMBODIA)

Khmer massages are gentler than massages practiced in other places in Southeast Asia. They can often result in a snooze-fest. Get yourself an extended ninety-minute session, sink into the mat, and wake up when the nice lady smacks you on the back.

MORE THE MERRIER (THAILAND)

Although a happy-ending version exists, a nonsexual four-hand massage is also twice as nice for actual relaxation purposes. These are hit-or-miss, as the four hands in question are not always skilled at working in harmony. But if you've ever seen the face of a cat after you and a friend have both petted it, you will know that having four hands rub you down is always better than two.

BLIND TOUCH (SIEM REAP)

Siem Reap presents one of the few places where you will be rubbed down by a man—and a blind one at that. Differently abled people don't have a welfare system to rely on here. As such, blind men often turn to supporting themselves through massage—

an industry they are uniquely suited for. You've heard how when people lose one sense, another is much more developed, right? The members of the Seeing Hands organization will work their strong-hand magic on you, without ever needing to see your contorting mug.

SLIP AND SLIDE (THAILAND)

Traditional Thai massages are more about pushing and pulling, and less about slipping and sliding. However, massages that employ the help of oils are widely available as well. And while oil massages can be sensual, that slippery goo is actually a great way to get your muscles to unwind. You will need to get naked for this one and battle with a tiny towel to keep your bits hidden.

SQUEEZE ONE OUT (BALI)

Pijat-style Balinese massage is great for those of us that crouch over a computer all day. This style focuses on kneading and squeezing motions that help get you from humpback to upright in no time. A bonus? In Ubud, you can get rubbed down right on the beach.

THE PRETTIEST MUSEUM OF ALL
(MALAYSIA)

The Museum of Enduring Beauty sounds like it may be filled with old makeup brushes and your mom's seventies glitter platforms, but it's not at all as tame as the name may suggest. This place—located on the third floor of the People's Museum in Malacca, Malaysia—is way more intriguing than the hair rollers you may have expected. It is dedicated to the type of beauty that we Westerners find ugly (or, at the very least, frightening because it's different).

Beauty Is Pain

The entry fee is about 50 cents and gives you access to the entire People's Museum—which has sections that focus on the history of the region, exhibits with paintings and other visual art, and a whole thing about traditional kite making. But you're here for the third floor, where it gets pretty weird and awfully hot. The museum is a Ripley's Believe It or Not of sorts, where all kinds of gruesome body modifications thought to be beautiful in cultures across the world are displayed. Below are just a few of the painful beauty practices you will learn about here.

HEAD SHAPING

Many cultures around the world, particularly in the Pacific Islands, bound the pliable skulls of newborns between boards of wood or with cloth for six months in order to shape their heads into an oval, which was thought of as more aesthetically pleasing. Now you know the inspiration for the SNL skit turned nineties cult classic *Coneheads*.

TOOTH FILING

In Western culture, we don't give much thought to our canine teeth—unless we're arguing with a vegetarian. However, in Bali, those particular toofers are seen as problematic because they are the fangs that connect man to beast, which the Balinese see as a bad thing. As such, a rite-of-passage ceremony is performed to file those beastie boys down—a process we imagine feels like the scratch of a thousand nails down a chalkboard.

SCARIFICATION

This one has seen some crossover into the West now that tattoos have lost their shock value. Several cultures—particularly those whose members have dark skin on which tattoos are less visible—use scarification (or the manipulation of skin through trauma to cause scarring) as a way to form social

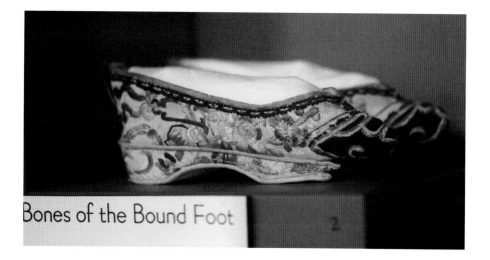

Bones of the Bound Foot

groups. Certain patterns are applied to the body to represent lifelong bonds formed between members bearing the same scars.

FOOT BINDING

The ancient Chinese believed that women with tiny feet were the prettiest, so they tightly bound little girls' footsies to change their shape. Foot binding may have gone the way of the fax machine, but limiting the mobility of women, which today is done with stilettos, seems to persist as a theme of beautification.

WTF IS ETHNO-TOURISM?

Well, it's a double-edged sword that involves cultural exploration—and arguably deeper human understanding and compassion—while at the same time eroding the cultures that find themselves being explored. A relevant example can be found at the Museum of Enduring Beauty in the form of neck rings worn by members of cultures such as the Padaung tribe of northern Thailand and Myanmar to create the illusion of an elongated neck. Young girls are fitted with metallic neck rings, the number of which is increased as they age, that slowly deform their clavicle and push down their ribs, causing the neck muscles to degenerate over time. Removing them can be fatal because the head often collapses onto the shoulders, crushing the trachea and leading to suffocation. The Thai government stepped in to regulate the practice to protect young children (mostly girls) from getting their necks broken for the sake of beauty, with some level of success. However, tourists began flocking to the region in the nineties, seeking out the "freak show" and sparking a revival of the practice, but this time with less cultural significance and a more circus-like flare. Ethno-tourism can be ugly, even in light of painful beauty standards.

OBSCURE MUSEUMS
AROUND SOUTHEAST ASIA

If you're like us, you find weird shit fascinating—but you'd never want to hoard it yourself. Lucky for you, Southeast Asia is filled with museums dedicated to the most obscure (and strangely specific) topics. Losing yourself for an hour in a cat-themed museum or staring at a collection of human bones is totally doable here. Put on your foil hat and get ready to be weirded the fuck out.

KUCHING CAT MUSEUM (MALAYSIA)

Be it the human-mind-controlling parasites they are rumored to carry or the fact that they make you work for their affection like you're some sort of kitty-cult follower, cats are pretty much at the top of the animal kingdom—above humans for sure. This spot, which is dedicated to all things feline, contains more than four thousand artifacts (or "catifacts"?). It will make you miss your kitties back home.

MUSEUM OF DEATH (THAILAND)

Officially called Siriraj Medical Museum, this attraction is a collection of five medical-themed museums with a whole bunch of bones and mummified bodies inside—including one that belongs to serial killer Si Quey, a cannibal that preyed on children in the fifties, for all you true-crime obsessives. Here, you'll see bodies ridden with cancer, long-ass flatworms preserved in jars, and other creepy shit that will keep you up at night.

UPSIDE DOWN MUSEUM (PHILIPPINES)

Stranger Things fans, we regret to inform you that this place will not help you figure out what the hell is wrong with Will. No Demogorgons here, but you'll have a good time nonetheless in this super Instagram-worthy museum where furniture is flipped, scenes are turned on their heads, and you get to pretend you're hanging from the ceiling while selfie-ing from the floor.

BUDDHA TOOTH RELIC TEMPLE AND MUSEUM (SINGAPORE)

There may or may not be a tooth from the Buddha—which critics say is of animal origin but believers claim comes from the enlight-ened one—here, but this $62 million temple is impressive regardless. Come here to meditate and ponder the greater meaning of dental work.

HO CHI MINH MAUSOLEUM (VIETNAM)

This obscure spectacle houses the body of communist leader Ho Chi Minh in a glass casket tricked out with mood lighting. Visitors are quickly moved through the mausoleum in a line that never stops—maybe to keep the intrigue alive, maybe because old Ho Chi Minh's body could very well have decomposed to hell since his death in 1969.

SUIT UP IN HOI AN (VIETNAM)

Dapper and *backpacker* aren't usually terms used together, especially since your method of doing laundry probably consists of washing underwear in a sink and leaving it to dry on your hostel bed's post. However, Hoi An—where the city's two hundred tailor shops outnumber other businesses two to one—is the capital of getting prim and proper, and for a price your broke ass can afford. Hoi An sits squarely on Asia's ancient Silk Road trading route, and the place is bar none when it comes to making you look your best. For about 200 bucks, you can have that lady-boss or baller custom-made suit you've always dreamed of.

To the Nines

The process is pretty simple: you pick your tailor, describe your idea, choose your fabric, get fitted, wait, and pick up your fancy threads. You may want to get that GQ-cover look, with slim pants and a just-so fitted jacket with however many lapels you think will complement your bodacious backpacker bod. Or you can opt for a ruffled-sleeve number, complete with a churchgoing hat and heels that kill. Perhaps you want to re-create Janelle Monáe's transparent rose-appliqué-studded jeans for a fraction of their $600 price tag? The key is to form a relationship with your tailor (many of whom speak great English) and brainstorm together. All of the shops will offer a wide selection of fabric (so much silk!) and patterns, and your tailor can recommend what's best for your buck and style. You will have to be patient during the process as the tailor will take your measurements before stitching up the first fit of your frock—which they generally make on the bigger side to give them room to whittle it down once you come in for your next fitting. It may take up to three fittings (which can amount to several days) to get it right, but having something made exactly to your body will ruin ready-to-wear mall shopping for you forever.

OTP Tip

Pricing varies by shop, but on average expect to pay $15–35 for a men's shirt, $100–220 for a suit, and $40–70 for a dress.

Dress to Impress

Tailoring to tourists is a big business, and not every shop in Hoi An does it with your satisfaction in mind. Many have partnered with hotels and tour companies to siphon customers in, and those spots tend to do the bare minimum—such as send your "custom" order out to a sweatshop to complete the job—or charge you an astronomical amount for subpar work. Stay away from places that are swarmed with tourists, or those that are recommended by other tourist-centric businesses, and make sure you always see tailors working on-site. Canvass the town on foot (note that you will be accosted by people looking to make you a cheap jacket that falls apart in the pits), and pop into a shop that catches your eye. Navigating a sea of fabric might be hard, so here are several well-regarded places to start.

MODERN TAKE

BeBe Tailor is a fairly new family-owned shop that has expanded to three large locations. Tailors here are trustworthy, will listen to all your wild ideas, and can produce a one-of-a-kind gown that you could proudly wear to the next Met Gala—pending your invitation, of course.

FANCY PANTS

Going to Paris for Fashion Week and need a little number to impress all those celebs you'll be hobnobbing with? We know the answer is a solid "no," but if you want a super-high-quality piece that you'll wear to every single one of your friends' weddings for the next ten years, Yaly Couture is the place to get it made. The fabrics here are premium, as is the service.

TIME-TESTED TAILORING

Kimmy Custom Tailor has operated in town for more than fifteen years and is one of the largest shops in the country. The detail-oriented tailors here will not let you leave until your garment is perfect. The flagship shop is in the center of Hoi An, while the second location boasts an upstairs bar that will get you good and liquored while you wait.

BOND, JANE BOND

If you're looking for the button-up shirt of your dreams (i.e., one that won't choke you), Vanda Tailors, which specializes in menswear, will whip one up, complete with custom cuffs and beautiful buttons. For people looking to fit a suit to a more feminine frame, you can get all of your curves and edges taken care of here.

FIVE FASHION TIPS FOR TRAVEL
IN SOUTHEAST ASIA

We get it: backpacker fashion sense can be limited to "whatever doesn't smell moldy." Here is how to stay on-trend (and not piss anybody off) in Southeast Asia.

MIND THE MODESTY

Unfortunately, something that is true in many places of the world (including parts of the United States) is that showing too much of a woman's body is seen as inappropriate and disrespectful. This is particularly the case if you plan to go to temples in Southeast Asia where your shoulders and knees must be covered. Make sure to bring a long skirt and a shawl if you plan to enter Buddhist countries.

EXPLORE COLOR

You may be a black-on-black New Yorker in the States, but while you're in SE Asia let the colorful landscape inspire your wardrobe. Give bright patterns a try, and stop shunning yellow and purple—they're your friends here.

BEAT THE HEAT

This region will give you the swampiest of swamp ass if you're not prepared. Make sure you bring loose, breathable fabrics such as cotton and linen to keep yourself spic and span. A sarong is essential to take you from beach to bar. Leave the zip-off cargo-pants-to-shorts number at home (or in the nineties).

FOOTWEAR WITH FLARE

You already know that a pair of flip-flops is essential to stave off hostel-shower foot fungus. But here, locals sport them 24/7—except at nicer parties and bars, where you'll need to put on more structured sandals, as lack of proper footwear will result in a no-go.

SHOP LOCAL

Clothing shops in this region sell garments in styles, fabrics, and patterns you've never seen in the States. Pack only the essentials, and fill your backpack with regional finds that are both functional and stylish. You will need a hat for sun protection; buy one, don't bring one.

CHILL OUT IN CHIANG MAI (THAILAND)

While sister tourist city Bangkok can be hectic at times, chilled-out Chiang Mai—the largest city in northern Thailand—is a good place to mentally unwind. All those happy, smiling faces in Thailand don't just come from thin air. They are the product of a nation that values spiritual connectivity. People here are big on taking breaks from the hustle to look inward and find their true spiritual beings. Below is a rough course in meditation—a practice that's as old a dirt and as rejuvenating as a cold beer on a sweltering summer day.

Basics of Just Being

In the Buddhist culture, meditation is considered a way to tap into the interconnectedness between yourself and your world. The hard thing is that you can't force it. You can study mathematics and learn how to create a pie chart. You can learn about the scientific method and eventually conduct and experiment with controlled variables that yield a scientific conclusion. But you cannot just study the tenets of meditation and gain enlightenment. The practice originated as far back as 500 BCE, when Siddhartha Gautama (known professionally as "the Buddha") sat under a bodhi tree and gained divine insight. By just. Sitting. There. Modern-day meditation is a mixture of the teachings of the Buddha, breathing techniques to help you chill the fuck out, and sounds (like om) that focus your mind so you can let go of all the bullshit that follows you around all day.

Chilling the Chiang Way

In Chiang Mai, as in most parts of Southeast Asia, taking the time to meditate is a cultural norm. Whereas in the States our imperative is to do the most we can with our days, a big part of Thai culture is to revert to a simple way of being, even if only for a few minutes per day. The city, which takes spirituality very seriously, has many retreats that you can visit to facilitate the environment for finding your inner peace. The Pa Pae Meditation Center is about an hour out of town, smack-dab in jungle surroundings, and offers guided meditation to help you journey to a new out-of-body place. Accommodations are purposefully quaint, meals are intentionally light, and the monks that guide the practice are well seasoned in the art of helping you let go of all the obstacles between you and enlightenment.

Finding Your Zen

Visiting a meditation retreat is a cool way to strategize your spiritual journey, but it is not necessary for finding your Zen. Chiang Mai—with its temperate weather and incredible sights—is a great place to try out self-guided meditation. Really, the whole practice is about mindfulness, and this slow city is an excellent place to practice it. We advise finding a comforting, comfortable spot—the bank of the Pang River, an inspiring statue, or the foot of the jungle—and choosing one (or a combination) of the following meditation practices to get to the core of yourself.

CONCENTRATION

The center of all meditation is establishing *samadhi*, or a laser-like focus on the issues at hand. It is a practice in which you focus on one topic, and one topic only, by aiming your attention at a focal point. Practice the technique by involving a physical object in your meditation—a rock, a key chain, a coin—and focus on only that item. Eventually, you will feel worries and anxious thoughts of other things melt away, leaving you better able to discern whatever confusing shit life throws at you by reverting to that moment of singular focus.

MINDFULNESS

This practice is about isolating single experiences and allowing them to affect you. It might be appreciating a beautiful sunset for the unique natural event it really is, or a moment of loss examined at its very simple level. With a little work, mindfulness becomes a part of your life that helps navigate through confusing and complex times.

CREATIVE MEDITATION

So, we've all daydreamed of being rich and flying our jets to exotic places with beautiful people on board and champagne in hand, right? Well, creative meditation is just that. The idea is to nurture your imagination with far-fetched ideas, or those that you hope will one day materialize in your life. Give yourself creative license (and time) to envision your ideal relationship, career, or world. By allowing yourself to dream your dreams, you set yourself on the path of making them reality.

HEART CENTEREDNESS

This one is about simplicity. Focus on the beat of your heart, and once you are breathing with that rhythm, think about the anatomical existence of yourself. Your heart, your lungs, and your brain create who you are in space, and tuning into that phenomenon is a powerful practice.

Outside your body, imagine the existence of other beings—living, breathing, and thinking much like yourself. Pretty heady shit, eh?

REFLECTION
Choose only one topic, and sit in a comfortable pose. *Why must I have coffee every morning? How will I tell my boyfriend that I'm pregnant with some other dude's kid (yikes!)?* Now, ponder that shit. Do not let your mind wander away from the topic until you have fully explored its implications. Once you are done, get out of your pose and get a drink. You'll need one.

MUST-SEE STATUES AND STRUCTURES

So your meditation game is on point but you need a little inspiration? Well, Southeast Asia is littered with the kind of statues that will make you rethink your meager existence and pray to the gods that be. Here's a sampling of just a few breathtaking structures you should post up in front of during your physical and spiritual journey across the region.

WAT SUWAN KHUHA (THAILAND)

That famous reclining Buddha might be hanging out in the center of Bangkok, but this cave variation is a great place to find a little underground peace. Warning: the monkeys out front are a little aggressive and will steal your shit if you're not stealth.

CEBU TAOIST TEMPLE (PHILIPPINES)

You will enter this temple through a replica of the Great Wall of China and come face-to-face with the Taoist ideals of the ancient philosopher Laozi, a Chinese scholar who promoted a lot of fairy-tale-like philosophies. Worship what you wish, or just relish the qualities of this temple that resemble an amusement park as you venture through its dragon-decorated grounds.

BAYON TEMPLE (CAMBODIA)

All the tourists might be at Angkor Wat, but another nearby temple is the perfect place for you to settle for a while. Exactly 216 sculptured rock faces (thought to symbolize

the Bodhisattva) will stare at you at Bayon Temple, and you will gaze back at them with meditative calm.

PRAMBANAN AND BOROBUDUR (INDONESIA)

A double feature: Prambanan is the largest Hindu temple in Southeast Asia, and Borobudur is the largest Buddhist temple in the world (with 504 statues of Buddha). A trip here is perfect for those overachievers that want to reach nirvana in double time.

KEK LOK SI (MALAYSIA)

The largest Buddhist temple in Malaysia—which means you can contemplate it for days—this structure is best experienced at night during the Chinese New Year, when everything is lit up and lined with shops and stalls. It's not the most meditative of experiences, but it's a wonder to behold.

STUNNING SCULPTURES (SINGAPORE)

Singapore has some of the strictest drug laws on earth—you can get the death penalty for carrying more than five hundred grams of cannabis—which makes it ironic that the country also has some of the trippiest sculptures—the kind that would be great to look at stoned. Scrape all the resin from the pockets of your backpack, and pack it with snacks (but not poppy seed bagels, because those might get you an opium drug charge) before hopping around the country for a sober look at Singapore's most stunning sculptures.

The Merlion

This aquatic lion—whose name translates to "sea lion" but which is nothing like those cuddly dogs of the ocean—is a wondrous sight with its all-white, maned head sitting atop a scaly fish body, spewing a vigorous fountain from its mouth into the Marina Bay at the base of the Fullerton Hotel. The *Merlion* isn't mere decoration, though. The statue is the official symbol of the Singaporean people: it's a tribute to the country's fishing heritage, and the head is a nod to its former name, Singapura (or "lion city"). This guy is the biggest, but five other versions—including a miniature baby merlion—are located throughout the country.

Fun Fact

This special statue used to stand at the mouth of the Singapore River until its view was obstructed by the erection of the Esplanade Bridge in 1997. The move to its current location cost $7.5 million (and you thought you broke the bank on that U-Haul!).

First Generation

Lucky that you're stark sober, because at first pass, this piece—which features five naked kids in various stages of falling into the Singapore River—looks more like an emergency situation than art. Local artist Chong Fah Cheong unveiled *First Generation* in 2000 to remind passersby of the waterfront's history, when children of different immigrant populations carelessly swam in the river back when it was a toxic dump.

Homage to Newton

Salvador Dalí was a wicked genius. His tribute to Sir Isaac Newton, executed in his surrealist drippy style, is the body of a man done up in the finest bronze. Dalí created this work to represent Newton's theory of gravity, a symbolism that is seen in the balls that hang inside the figure's open torso cavity and from its hand. The man stands at the UOB Plaza, in the center of Singapore, where twin modernist skyscrapers cluster together to form an important section of the country's famous skyline.

Singapura Cats

We know you watch a lot of cat videos on YouTube and will love this sculpture as a result. The Singapura (. . . *purrra*) cat, the smallest domestic feline breed in the world, has big adorable eyes, a tiny head, and stupid-cute pointy ears. The Singaporean government placed fifteen statues of these cats (sometimes known as Kucinta, or "love cats") along the river and, for reasons unknown, only three remain—a mom cat and two kittens. If you're lucky, a real Singapura street cat will lounge in the sun near the sculptures, making for a YouTube video you can add to your collection.

Planet

This porcelain-white, seven-ton baby seemingly floats in midair, held up by and balancing only on its tiny infant arm. Erected in 2008, the man baby (his gender is clear, because of his to-scale, but still too large for comfort, penis) measures about thirty feet long and ten feet high, making for what we can imagine was a painful delivery. British artist Marc Quinn created the statue in the likeness of his own infant son to contrast strength and vulnerability, and his giant baby now forever levitates in Singapore's Gardens by the Bay.

Dragonfly Riders

Another Gardens by the Bay gem is a pair of dragonflies that jet out of the lake like the mechanical beasts of your worst nightmares—or that one episode of *Black Mirror* where the metal bees ruin fucking everything. Designed by Shanghai-born sculptor Elsie Chen Chee Yu, the statue's name refers to the two tiny children sitting atop the big bugs, riding them gleefully. The wings and eyes of each dragonfly, one accentuated with blue and the other with red, are made with hand-blown glass and gold flakes that shimmer at night.

Bird of Peace

If you've ever seen a work by Colombian artist Fernando Botero, you will be able to recognize this statue as his creation from a mile away. Botero is a fan of all that's fat, and this plump—nay, obese—bird is a beefy bronze beauty he sculpted in 1990. Double-breasted and with absurdly large clawless feet, Botero's bird isn't inspired by any one specific avian species. Rather, the artist wanted to create something lighthearted and that represents peace and joy, despite its placement in the frenetic UOB Plaza.

Jelly Baby Family

If you were stoned (and we hope you're not—remember the death penalty), this piece would instantly make you crave gummy bears . . . giant, delicious gummy bears. Italian pop-artist Mauro Perucchetti created this family of sweet-looking rotund humans from see-through fiberglass and urethane resin pigmented with bright colors. The whole scene seems so pleasant

and wholesome, until you look closer and find that the artist's message—a commentary on cloning humans—is displayed all over their sinister jelly faces.

Tall Girl

Inside the Orchard Central Shopping Mall stands a cartoonish, thinly stretched lady that is four stories (more than sixty-five feet) high, welcoming shoppers and seemingly judging them at the same time. Her big-ass red-heeled boots alone are hard to view without feeling a bit of vertigo. Berlin artist collective Inges Idee created the piece to ring in the 2009 opening of the mall—the country's first vertical shopping center.

Sphinx Fortuna

Not at all like the Egyptian version of the sphinx, this one is another sculpture from big-baby maker Marc Quinn. It's a white replica of Kate Moss (yeah, the supermodel) doing that one yoga pose where her lady parts are all up in the air and her legs are hanging out right by her face.

Quinn created this extra-weird sculpture on the premise that Moss, who famously refuses to sit for interviews, is an enigma who lacks a depth of character. Accordingly, as you stroll past, Calvin Klein's leading lady stares into your soul with an unaffected gaze that will creep you out endlessly.

COOL FACTS ABOUT SINGAPORE'S SUPERTREES

Part nature, part art, the Supertrees of Singapore are like nothing you've ever seen. Hovering high above the Gardens by the Bay park, the Supertrees have a few tricks up their trunks.

- These trees are tall! The superest of the Supertrees is 164 feet tall, or about the height of a sixteen-story building.
- Twelve of the eighteen trees form the Supertree Grove, and two are connected by a walkable skyway that's suspended seventy feet in the air. Don't look down.
- A total of 162,900 plants—two hundred species that are suitable for the climate but rare in Singapore—are strewn throughout the tree trunks to create a colorful living display.
- Shaped like inverted umbrellas, the canopies that crown the trees were placed at the top using a hydraulic jack system.

- The canopies of eleven of the Supertrees were made with environmental functions. Some feature solar-energy receptors (to help light up the trees at night); others clean the air with exhaust receptacles.
- You can eat in one of the trees: it houses a sky-high bistro where your meal comes with a panoramic view.
- For an hour starting at 7:45 p.m. each night, the trees come alive with Garden Rhapsody—a free trippy light and sound show.
- Admission is free, and they close at 2:00 a.m. Sounds like a party to us.

TRISHAW AROUND MALACCA (MALAYSIA)

Malaysia prides itself on being the epicenter of a blend of cultures, and the city of Malacca (also spelled Melaka) is where the country's Portuguese, Chinese, Indian, Dutch, and distinctly Malay influences cross paths. The best way to get the full spectrum of local flavor is by taking a tour on a trishaw—a tricked-out pedicab that's two parts fun and one part terrifying.

Why Trishaw?

For a couple of bucks, you can board a sweaty bus from Kuala Lumpur to Malacca. Although walking around the historic city would do just fine, putting in the extra effort to trishaw through town really adds that extra flare. This mode of transport—the bicycle version of a motorized rickshaw common in other parts of Asia, particularly India—comes from Japan. The most romantic theory of how it was invented surmises that an American expat cobbled together the man-drawn vehicle to pull his disabled wife around town. In Malaysia, trishaw operators are most always men, and their wives decorate the vehicles (presumably as a nod to that dude who lugged his lady around town) with colorful flowers, sparkly garlands, and lights—which are best seen at night.

Scenic Sights

Once aboard the pedaling party bike—which you can pick up at various locales, including in front of Christ Church—the sights are spectacular. If you're an architecture nerd, you'll love the Dutch colonial villas strewn about town. The hour-long trishaw journey comes with commentary into the town's history, and you'll cruise past attractions such as the A Famosa, a Portuguese fortress—the oldest surviving piece of European architecture in Asia—and Stadthuys, a Dutch structure from the 1600s complete with an adorable green square and a red clock tower.

Nights on Fire

Your final trishaw destination should be the Jonker Night Market, Malacca's most eclectic attraction—even though it has become somewhat pooh-poohed since the city gained its UNESCO World Heritage status in 2008, attracting swarms of tourists. The street food is primo, with options such as corn covered in a variety of spices and sauces, curry-stuffed buns, barbecued quail eggs, sticky rice treats, and puffy ice cream sandwiches. Beyond the simplistic (but fun) act of stuffing your face, the market is brimming with cool trinkets you can bring home to the fam as easy gifts, as well as a steady waft of karaoke singing that ranges from pro to please-stop. It gets fully poppin' on weekends, so plan accordingly.

OTP Tip

Get a fishy pedicure. It may seem strange (and maybe even a little cruel if your feet are especially raunchy from traveling) to stick your feet into an aquarium full of tiny fish, but fish pedicures are actually a very symbiotic arrangement: your feet are cleaned of all your travel grime and left smooth, while the fish nosh on the dead skin on your tootsies.

WELCOME TO WATER WORLD (BRUNEI)

No, this isn't another failed Kevin Costner film. Kampong Ayer, which translates to "water village," is a thriving community that exists—wait for it—entirely on water. Often referred to as the Venice of the East, Kampong Ayer is the largest collection of water villages in the world. It supports four thousand structures like schools, houses, post offices, business buildings, clinics, and all the other stuff that makes up a city ... but on stilts. The thirty thousand–plus population mostly comprises professional fishermen given its location right on the Brunei River. Get your sea legs ready, and hop into a place where water is king (and where land lovers should pack Dramamine).

Liquid History

A national treasure, Kampong Ayer has been floating around for about a thousand years. Why build on water? From the fifteenth to the seventeenth centuries, the settlement was the epicenter of trading for Borneo's sultanate empire, which

didn't want to limit its access to goods available by land alone and therefore built a post that floated at the mouth of the river. Tucked a little closer inland are the villages' houses, hinged together by little bridges. The entirety of the forty-two-village setup is connected by a twenty-three-mile boardwalk.

Splash Around Town

Aside from Instagramable photos of dusty blue, pink, and yellow houses that float majestically on the river, Kampong Ayer offers a few activities in which to partake. One of the obvious attractions is a giant mosque—Sultan Omar Ali Saifuddin Mosque—which, although it looks like it may have survived centuries, is only as old as your granddad. Constructed in 1958, the structure's tallest minaret at 170 feet serves as a vantage point from which you can observe the entire floating city. Dig deep into the culture by visiting the Kampong Ayer Cultural and Tourism Gallery, where you can find artifacts like crowns and swords once owned by people who helped keep this city afloat, and artisan goods created

by those who help it thrive today. You can also take guided tours for fairly cheap, or walk the boardwalk and elevated platforms to explore on your own.

OTP Tip

Too lazy to walk? Water taxis serve as buses in Kampong Ayer. Hop on one to discover the entire place when your feet just won't move any longer.

Modern Comforts

You can pop into Kampong Ayer for just a day, but if you've ever wondered how it would be to live like SpongeBob Square Pants in Aqualand, book a homestay or hostel right in the village. Some families open their homes to visitors, but Airbnb is a good choice if you want something private. The views at night are serene, and the locals are super slow-paced, meaning you will have a relaxed night even if you fear that the river sharks (no such thing) will eat your toes.

OTP Tip
Brunei is booze free, so enjoy the clarity of waking up sans hangover and with the vivid long- and short-term memories of your visit intact.

NIGHT (MARKET) MOVES (CAMBODIA)

You may be used to hunting for souvenirs during the day in other parts of the world, but for a cooler experience (literally, since it's not as hot when the sun isn't beating in your face) check out Cambodia's abundant night markets—where street food and artisan goods mingle in perfect twilight harmony. In Siem Reap, you will find a lot of markets that aim to serve the millions of tourists who come to the region to explore Angkor Wat. However, groovy night markets abound in just about every corner of Cambodia. Here are five worth exploring once the sweltering sun goes down.

Angkor Night Market (Siem Reap)

Visit the most famous market in Cambodia after you have exhausted all the temple-hopping options at Angkor Wat. Start with a foot massage at Baray Spa, which offers traditional Khmer treatments that utilize herbs and cold compresses to bring relief to your swollen appendages. When you're ready to walk upright again, you will find more than two hundred bamboo huts selling goods ranging from the requisite bric-a-brac typical of markets all over Southeast Asia to unique handmade Khmer items (shadow puppets, anyone?) that you'll be proud to bring back home. For your eco-conscious friends, you can pick up recycled accessories at the Angkor Recycled hut. Visit the market's Island Bar, where you can chill with a drink for a pit stop between shops.

OTP Tip
Haggling is expected at most markets in Southeast Asia, because inflating prices for tourists is totally a thing. However, keep in mind that people here live in conditions that are miles beneath your idea of "broke." Get the bargain, for sure, just don't undervalue the hard work that goes into crafting that tiny elephant statue. All negotiations should be performed with respect and a smile.

Noon Night Market (Siem Reap)

Open from noon to midnight, this traditional bazaar is near Angkor Night Market and offers a similar selection of goods, but with one key difference: 10 percent of its profits are donated to a local orphanage. A great place to go to support the local community, Noon Night Market offers fair-trade souvenirs, ornamental jewelry, ice cream, and some damn good Cambodian food at Khmer Bistro Restaurant. If you're brave (or drunk), get a tattoo at the market's Skin Art Shop, or a foot massage that features hundreds of skin-sucking cleaner fish instead of human hands. The on-site Lunar Bar will help you drink away the memory of any bad purchase decisions—or help you make some new ones.

Jet's Container Night Market (Phnom Penh)

Open until three a.m., Jet's Container Night Market is a departure from your typical Cambodian market in that it is built out of recycled shipping containers— a type of construction that's becoming more common for social spaces from San Francisco to London. The market features more than three hundred steel stalls set atop each other in two-story arrangements, and young Cambodians come here to eat, drink, and party into the night. If you're sensitive to sound, this market will fuck you up royally (and also, we can't be friends): all the shipping-container stalls like to play their own tunes, which means that standing outside at any given point will thrash your ears with at least ten competing songs.

Kandal Market (Phnom Penh)

The bazaar in Phnom Penh most recommended by guidebooks (simply called Night Market) is a manicured, tourist-centric shopping and eating experience— or at least it has become more of a sanitized spectacle in recent years. We're not going to tell you about that one. Instead, walk

down the street to Kandal Market to get off the tourist trail for a bit. You will notice that this place is a much more pungent expression of Khmer life. You will probably feel uncomfortable with the way animals are treated here, but remember that you're walking into the guts of a culture that you may not fully understand. This will be a transparent look at where your food comes from—loud, cramped chickens stuffed in cages, and live fish writhing for air among piles of the already dead—which is strikingly different from the closed-to-the-public, heavily policed factory farms back home. This is where Cambodians shop, and while it may be a bit shocking at first, the experience will make you seek out other places that offer unabashed glimpses into cultures that are different from your own—you know, the real reason you're backpacking in the first place?

Crab Market (Kep)

The sleepy town of Kep was founded during colonial times as a retreat for the filthy-rich French. The beachside village is a nice getaway if you're into seafood, sunsets, and butterflies—an abundance of which can be found at the city's national park. Near a more traditional "wet" fish market—one that gets hosed down regularly to wash away the guts and grime—Kep's Crab Market is a group of shoddy wooden

shacks that sell nothing but seafood, mostly (as you may have guessed) crab. Vendors here prepare crab in more than twenty ways, most with a good dose of *kampot* pepper—a revered spice that comes in red, green, and black varieties from local plantations. Don't expect to buy any souvenirs here, as the market only offers a mind-blowing selection of seafood (besides crab, look for squid, prawns, and varieties of fish). It operates until ten p.m., which gives you time to scrub out all the crab shells from underneath your fingernails before bed.

LITTLE INDIA
(SINGAPORE)

You may have blown your humble budget eating six meals per day in Thailand, adventuring around the Philippines, and partying it up until sunrise in Bali, but that doesn't mean you can't pop into India for a minute—without ever having to leave Southeast Asia. Little India is a charming part of Singapore (nestled next to and sometimes overlapping its Chinatown) that you can explore in a day without having to plan a whole separate trip. You should still visit *actual* India another time, as Little India's smells and sights are Singapore's more sterile version of the real deal. Nonetheless, here is how to get a sneak peak of the Indian subcontinent without leaving Southeast Asia.

Wait, India in Singapore?

Singapore's Little India is home to a dense Indian population that brings with it a vibrant culture that both mixes with and greatly differs from that of Singapore. As with many enclaves that are culturally distinct from the country in which they exist, this one had a tumultuous beginning. The English colonized the region in the 1800s and decked the place out in old-English style, complete with racetracks and luxe private residences. Labor was needed to build it, and India sent convicts to toil away making brick kilns. In the process, the workers also infused the area with Indian culture. Today, Indians from many regions come to Singapore to work, and a large population has settled in and around what is now known as Little India—a moniker coined in the seventies to attract tourists. These days, walking down Little India's shop-dotted main thoroughfare, Serangoon Road, you'll get a faceful of incense, an earful of Bollywood jams, and an eyeful of women shuffling around in colorful saris.

Make It to Market

At Tekka Market, a wet market, you'll find buckets of crabs, various animal carcasses, food stalls, housewares, and religious figurines. This is a great spot to browse for a bit, but if you're planning to do some heavy-duty shopping, head to Little India Arcade—where you won't find *Street Fighter 2* machines but you will find everything else. The market's narrow streets have been overflowing with rainbow-hued garlands and textiles since the 1920s, and you can come away with souvenirs that you could easily say you got from India if you are a decent liar.

OTP Tip

Need a phone charger? On the weekends, the Thieves Market operates as a flea market that used to be exactly what it sounds like, but now it sells *not*-stolen stuff at prices that are still a steal.

Lunch Break

Be sure to leave a *dosa*-sized hole in your stomach before heading to Little India, saving room for food from its flavor-forward Indian restaurants. At Banana Leaf Apolo, dishes—such as its famed fish-head curry—are served on banana leaves, while family-run Komala Vilas is where you go to get a mega masala *dosa*. For dessert, treat yourself to a little something from Moghul Sweets, a shop that'll spike your blood sugar like nothing else in town. Get that insulin shot prepped, and down a few *gulab jamun*—a syrupy Indian doughnut that's best paired with a napkin.

Temple Tantrum

The temples of Little India are pretty easy to spot, as they're heavily decorated with carvings of various deities. The Sri Veera-makaliamman Temple (named after the evil-destroying goddess Kali), built in the nineteenth century by Indian immigrants, is the oldest Hindu temple in town. The Sri Srinivasa Perumal is all about Lord Vishnu, who is known for his universe-saving powers and whose image is carved all over the five tiers of the temple's blue-hued entrance. A must-see for temple fiends is the Temple of the Thousand Lights (or Sakya Muni Buddha Gaya), where a three-hundred-ton Buddha statue sits surrounded by lights in a monastery constructed with influences from Thailand, China, and India.

OTP Tip

Don't be fooled by the House of Tan Teng Niah's brightly colored exterior, which looks like it could be an Indian temple. It's literally a house—the only remaining Chinese villa in this Indian area—that was built by a businessman in the 1990s for his wife. You only wish your house could be confused for a temple.

Fest with the Best

The best time to hit Little India (and India India) is during Deepavali (or Diwali, as some Westerners know it). The Hindu Festival of Lights goes down every year in October or November and celebrates the triumph of good over evil. Practitioners get all dolled up in new clothes and decorate their homes with candles and garlands, and vendors take to the neon-lit streets to set up temporary shops.

SOUTHEAST ASIA'S VIBRANT CHINATOWNS

While some Chinatowns are known worldwide—such as those in San Francisco, Los Angeles, and New York City—others fly under the radar. Nonetheless, outside of China, just about every major city has a unique Chinatown, often adorned with a traditional Chinese gate. Visit any of the following during Chinese New Year to really get the full experience.

THAILAND

Bangkok's Chinatown, the oldest in the world, was inadvertently established in the 1700s when King Rama I decided he needed to build his palace along the bank of the Chao Phraya River, an area where many Chinese immigrants lived. The palace forced the Chinese population to shift to Soi Sampeng street, in the process forming the city's modern-day Chinatown, a place that's not hyper tourist-focused, which means it has many traditional Chinese food shops and heritage centers.

MALAYSIA

Here, you have a choice between three well-developed Chinatowns. Kuala Lumpur's version is expansive and *the* place to go for Chinese pastries, counterfeit bags, DVDs, and watches. Named a UNESCO World Heritage Site, the Penang Chinatown is home to the region's most revered temple, Kuan Yin Teng, which was originally dedicated to the sea goddess Mazu, who is credited with keeping Chinese immigrants safe on their journey to Malaysia. The three-street-wide Malacca Chinatown, home to people who migrated here during the Qing Dynasty, explodes in traditional red lanterns and dragons when the New Year comes around.

SINGAPORE

The "official" Chinatown (the Cantonese sector, the best-known among a series of Chinatowns that are divided into various origin-based segments) is nestled right up to Singapore's Little India. Although Chinatown still has its colorful flare, this region of the country has undergone a similar transformation to that of the rest

of Singapore: high-rises have become a status symbol and have taken over the more ornate architecture of yore. Need more Chinatown? Another totally separate one is in Geylang, which is home to immigrants that thought Singapore's official Chinatown was too touristy for their liking.

VIETNAM
The country's main Chinatown, Cholon, located in Ho Chi Minh City, grew out of the colonization of Vietnam as French Indochina in the late 1800s. Strolling through this historic district puts you in earshot of Mandarin music and everything one may need to perform traditional puppet dances (dragon heads galore!). In Vientiane's Chinatown, older generations of mainland immigrants live tensely alongside post-communist dwellers. However, when night falls, the street-food scene seems to be a good grounds to quash any squabbles with bao, noodles, dim sum, and dumplings for all.

PHILIPPINES
Founded in 1594, Manila's Chinatown is a very distinct region of the Philippines for several reasons. On their mission to wipe out everything native to the islands, Spanish colonizers established Chinatown as a way to separate converted Catholic Chinese from the not-yet-converted Buddhists, Taoists, and other non–Jesus worshippers. As such, this Chinatown features many Christian establishments alongside those from religions more widely practiced in China. In addition to all the requisite street food, Manila's Chinatown has its own volunteer fire brigade that cruises around, saving the day, in its purple fire engines.

Food and Drink

IN SOUTHEAST ASIA, IF YOU CAN'T STAND THE HEAT, YOU NEED TO spend more time in the kitchen (or the street). In this region, food with complex flavors is produced with the help of fresh seafood, tropical fruit, and native herbs and spices, combined with hundreds of years of know-how and hot woks, spits, and grills. Then it's served street-side at a price that won't make you think twice about eating out every meal of the day. Cuisine here is centered around rice (sourced from verdant paddies across Southeast Asia) but takes a lot of its carb influence from China (hence the prevalence of noodles) and India (flatbreads), and everyone has their go-to spicy condiment, often spiked with fermented fish parts. You can (and should) eat soup for breakfast in Vietnam, wolf down extra-spicy food in hundred-degree heat in Laos, and pick scorpion legs from your molars in Thailand . . . and savor every minute of it.

BUGGIN' OUT: DINING ON INSECTS (THAILAND)

Edible bugs are what some people's nightmares are made of. However, chomping on this protein-packed food animal is no stranger than eating shrimp—arguably the cockroach of the sea. Thais serve 150 varieties of bugs, fried, boiled, covered in gravy, and on sticks—all crunchy and oozing with flavor. The country is crawling with vendors (usually people on motorbikes with bug parties in their backpacks), packaged buggy goods, and restaurants all making food out of your backyard inhabitants.

Bamboo Worms

The gateway bugs, bamboo worms are fairly neutral in taste and pack a lot of protein. The larvae of bamboo-eating moths, these 'sects are typically deep-fried and served by the platter. The worms are an addicting snack, much like popcorn—crunchy, salty, and satisfying. Planning a horror-movie night with the hostel mates just got a lot more fun.

OTP Tip

Do not confuse bamboo worms with silkworms, which are also served deep-fried, but the silkworms are a completely different, nuttier, and gooier experience.

Giant Water Bugs

This crawler is perfect for black-licorice lovers, as the huge, cockroach-like bug has a squishy bottom filled with anise flavor. Usually prepared simply by boiling and salting, the best way to consume these juicy giants (known as *maeng da*) is to pull off the inedible wings, rip the head from the body, and suck out all that crab-like meat. Return to the head to suck out one more morsel of meat before moving on to the next victim.

Scorpions on Sticks

These fighting bugs are a rare street find but quite a spectacle to behold. Drawn up like a scarecrow on a skewer, scorpions are roasted until their outer shells are crisp and blackened, leaving a pungent meat lurking underneath. Their stingers are removed, so the only danger of eating scorpions is gagging on their mildly rotten-cheese flavor.

Crickets

In Thailand, Jiminy Cricket is not famous for playing his tiny violin. Instead, he is one of the most popular street insects, and his entire body can be eaten whole. Crickets—available in a range of sizes from run-of-the-mill lawn variety to a much larger Hulk-esque bug—are the most "buggy" when it comes to flavor. Their innards often ooze out upon your first bite, and their legs are often, quite literally, hard to swallow.

Mixed Bag

So you like a little variety? Well luckily, you can purchase a mixed bug bag by weight. All you do is point to critters you want, and vendors will bag up the bunch, spritz them with a bit of soy, sprinkle on a little pepper, and you'll be on your way to tasty town. Make sure you get a good selection of worms, crickets, and water bugs—and grab a frosty beer to wash down all those legs.

FIVE BUGS YOU SHOULDN'T EAT

While there are more than fourteen hundred species of edible bugs in the world (and many of them are totally tasty), here are five bugs in Thailand that are more likely to eat *you*.

MOSQUITOES
It's no secret that mosquitoes are the world's deadliest bugs (carrying all sorts of fatal diseases), and in Thailand, where the climate is tropical and humidity makes you feel like taking six showers per day, the little buggers feel right at home. Don't let any of them near your mouth.

ASIAN GIANT HORNET
You've heard of bees, and you may be familiar with hornets, but this variety is like that guy at the gym who's so big he's cartoonish . . . only these bugs also have a big, painful sting. Fucking with hornets' nests is a straight no-no.

GIANT CENTIPEDE
Growing up to fifteen inches long (that's about the size of your forearm), these critters are known for their venomous bites that can get disgustingly infected if left untreated.

HUNTSMAN SPIDERS
Crabs are tasty, spiders are scary, and crab-sized spiders that hide in kitchen cabinets are fucking terrifying. These are big and sometimes hairy, so carry a hammer.

STINGING NETTLE CATERPILLAR
Unless you want to know what it feels like to have thousands of fiberglass shards embedded in your fingers, stay away from petting these adorable bugs.

BANH MI PHO YOU (VIETNAM)

Vietnamese food has fully engulfed the States, but the cuisine's true spirit can only be found in the country itself—where sitting on a low plastic stool in an alley and eating soup for breakfast is the thing to do. You've probably had a tangy banh mi sandwich, but there is so much more to the cuisine of Vietnam.

Banh Mi

Vietnam gained its independence from France in 1954, and its colonial history is best wrapped up in one sandwich: the banh mi. A crunchy-on-the-outside but doughy-in-the-center baguette gets a generous slather of unctuous pâté (another French remnant) before being stuffed with slow-roasted pork, more pork (in the form of cold cuts), and a crunchy heap of pickled daikon, carrots, jalapeño, and cilantro. Aside from inspiring a couple of structural elements, the French had nothing to do with the invention of the mother of all sandwiches. It originated in Hoi An, and you should get yours at the famed Madam Phuong, Madam Khanh (known as the Banh Mi Queen), or Hoa Ma (the unconfirmed originator of the sandwich).

Pho

The oft-mispronounced pho (it's kind of like saying *fun* but with an *h* at the end instead of an *n*), first created in northern Vietnam, makes for a great hangover cure because it's not uncommon to consume it for breakfast. Vermicelli noodles serve as the base, and they're layered with rare-cooked beef, scallions, herbs, and chilies, then doused in a heavily reduced broth (some cooks start simmering their daily batch at two a.m.), which gets its umami flavor from fermented fish sauce (nuoc cham). A dash of hoisin, hot sauce, and a squeeze of lime make this the kind of soup that'll wake up your salivary glands and put your hangover to bed.

OTP Tip

While pho has been popularized in the States, another soup can be found on many a street corner in Vietnam. Bun rieu shares pho's vermicelli noodles and herb condiments, but veers into a different territory with the addition of coagulated blood cubes, fried tofu, crab cakes, tomatoes, and pork bits, as well as a hot broth made with salty crab paste.

Com Tam

This is a comforting dish that, in its simplest form, features meat (either grilled chicken or pork), "broken" rice, and pickled vegetables, served with a little bowl of fish sauce to add moisture. Complex versions of the dish may include fried eggs, shredded pork skin, shrimp cake, and more. The resourcefulness of this Southeast Asian country is encapsulated in each cracked grain of rice—broken rice is nutritionally equivalent to its whole-grain counterpart but is slightly less desirable (and often

not served directly to consumers in other countries) only because it's gotten a little damaged during milling.

Balut

While eating fetal duck eggs isn't everyone's idea of fun, in Vietnam you must at least try one. The rancid little egg—which contains the semi-developed body, bones and all, of a baby duck—comes with muoi tieu chanh (a mix of salt, pepper, and citrus juice) that helps to temper the pungent flavor of the rotten snack. Quail versions are also available, and although smaller, they will churn your stomach all the same.

OTP Tip

Up the adventure factor and try a cotton worm—a plump worm pulled from the Mekong Delta and served in spicy chili sauce while it wriggles. Make sure you pull its pinchy mandible off with your fingers, or prepare for a bloody (as in, your lip will bleed) bite.

Bun Cha

The secret to this filling dish is fat, and lots of it. A popular dish in Hanoi, bun cha is a make-your-own adventure that starts with a heaping plate of white rice noodles, fresh green herbs (including mint), and slices of fruit, all of which take a dip in a fatty grilled-pork broth. Bun Cha Huong Lien is the most touristy place to try the dish: Barack Obama and Anthony Bourdain (RIP) visited the restaurant together, prompting the owner to capitalize on the spot's newfound fame by putting the "Obama Combo"—bun cha served with a deep-fried eggroll and beer—on the menu. However, we challenge you to find our friend (pictured on this page), the kind of little old lady you want making this food.

Snails

Across the country, and particularly in Saigon, there are entire restaurants (called *quan oc*) dedicated to the national pastime of eating snails. A number of snail species come from Vietnam's rice paddies, rivers, and other water sources, and ordering them at these restaurants will require three decisions: type of snail, sauce, and cooking method. The "sucking snail" is usually prepared in a thick coconut-milk-based broth. To extract the morsel of meat inside, you pop the whole critter into your mouth and suck like hell on the shell. A giant snail called oc toi tastes similar to squid. Slurpin' snails is Vietnam's version of happy hour, so chasing whatever snails you get with beer is a must.

WTF IS A HAWKER CENTER? (SINGAPORE)

It may sound like a place to sell your old furniture, but a hawker center is something so much tastier. Think of it as a food court at the mall, but instead of Panda Express and Subway you have a mind-blowing selection of Singapore's diverse, delicious food options. From curry to satay to all the flavorful Hainanese chicken rice you can stomach, if you're hungry for it, these stalls are hawking it.

Hawk History

Cleanliness is ingrained in Singaporean culture, and hawker centers were built in the 1950s to make street food more hygienic. The structures are open-air markets scattered throughout city centers and major transit hubs. All the centers are government regulated, and they're so damn clean that two stalls—Hong Kong Soya Sauce Chicken Rice and Noodle, and Hill Street Tai Hwa Pork Noodle—were each awarded a coveted Michelin star in 2016.

Seas of Stalls

The island is brimming with hawker centers, and the food options—which are internationally inspired—can be overwhelming: smaller centers might have about twenty stalls, while larger ones may have up to a hundred. However, focusing on several staple dishes will give you a good taste of what Singapore is all about. The national treasure is Hainanese chicken rice, which, although it looks as bland as Elmer's glue, carries a lot of flavor due in part to the rice being cooked in chicken fat. Pork-rib tea is a flavorful stewed pork dish of Chinese origin that usually comes with a side of fritters and pork knuckles. Chili crabs are a favorite among locals, and (hygiene be damned) you crack these spiced, hard-shell delights with a mallet before getting elbow-deep in succulent crab meat and sucking the sauce off whatever remains. Satay—chicken, mutton, or beef on sticks—is always a good snack and comes with flavorful peanut dipping sauce. No hawker-center trip is complete without a dose of Singaporean noodle dishes; char kway teow is a fried variety that features flat rice noodles, eggs, and intriguing seafood such as cockles. Oh yeah, there's also fish-head stew for those brave enough to look a fish straight in the eye before eating him.

Hawker Etiquette

While the customs we all know from American-mall food courts do transfer to hawker centers, others are uniquely Singaporean. Seating is sprawled out just like in 'Merica, but there's a recognized system for calling dibs on a seating spot by using a napkin. The system even has an official name: *chope*. You can *chope* a table or a chair or, if you're not traveling solo, have a friend plop down while you order. At the end of the meal, you can either clean up after yourself or just (gasp) leave your shit on the table. Contrary to what this pristine country might lead you to think, leaving your dirty plates on the table is just fine, as attendants will come by and scoop them up.

NATIONAL DISHES
OF SOUTHEAST ASIA

The most popular dishes in each Southeast Asian country share some crossover ingredients and culinary techniques, but each is unique. Listed here are the special dishes that are the pride of every country in this part of the world.

THAILAND: TOM YUM GOONG

Take that pad thai elsewhere. This spicy shrimp soup is the national dish in Thailand. The tasty herbal broth relies on the classic Thai flavor profile of kaffir lime leaves, galangal, chili, lemongrass, shallots, and fish sauce, which is accented by plump prawns and straw mushrooms.

CAMBODIA: AMOK

A white-fish curry made with thick coconut milk, kaffir lime leaves, and lemongrass that is presented in a banana-leaf bowl, this dish can be eaten on its own or over rice. Banana leaves are often used as a wrap in which the fish is steamed.

INDONESIA: NASI GORENG

Who doesn't love fried rice? In Indonesia, it is *everything*. Soft, cooked rice gets a new life when it's fried in sesame oil with meat, veggies, tamarind, shrimp paste, kecap manis (sweet soy sauce), and eggs.

VIETNAM: PHO

Not surprisingly, this hearty soup—traditionally eaten for breakfast—is a staple of Vietnamese cuisine. Featuring quintessential ingredients such as vermicelli noodles, rare-cooked beef strips, scallions, fish sauce, herbs, bean sprouts, and chilies swimming in a flavorful beef broth, pho is best enjoyed street-side while perched atop a red stool.

SINGAPORE: CHICKEN RICE

"Chicken rice" sounds simple enough, and many cultures have something comforting like it—looking at you, Cuba, with your arroz con pollo. You will find a rendition of this dish (formally known as Hainanese chicken rice) on every corner. The trick to making it memorable is cooking the rice in chicken fat and then serving it with slowly simmered chicken and chili sauce on top.

LAOS: LARB

A meat salad might not sound like the best thing in the world, but Laos's rendition kicks sad leafy greens up a spicy notch with its chili-marinated minced (and sometimes raw) meat that has a heavy kick of lime, mint, and padaek—a thicker fish sauce than that found in some parts of Southeast Asia.

BRUNEI: AMBUYAT

A tasty paste that is made from sago palm (which has a texture similar to that of bland tapioca starch), ambuyat is traditionally eaten by slathering it onto a bamboo fork (or *chandas*) and dipping it into flavorful sauces.

MYANMAR: MOHINGA

This soup offers a delightful balance of textures, featuring a broth made from fish, toasted rice, and shallots, along with rice noodles and condiments such as crunchy onions.

EAST TIMOR: PEPES IKAN

Spiced fish steamed in a banana leaf over a grill: simple but flavorful.

PHILIPPINES: ADOBO

A simply spiced dish of meat, vegetables, and/or seafood that has been marinated in vinegar, soy sauce, garlic, and black peppercorns, then browned in oil and simmered in the marinade for maximum flavor and fall-off-the-bone texture.

MALAYSIA: NASI LEMAK

A mound of rice (cooked with coconut milk and fragrant pandan leaves) is the centerpiece here with flavorful accompaniments including ikan bilis (fried anchovies), hard-boiled eggs, sliced cucumbers, toasted peanuts, and spicy sambal.

FINDING VEGAN PARADISE (THAILAND)

Thailand, even with all of its fish-sauce-spiked vegetable salads, is actually vegan paradise. Floating along open-air, water-bound markets, you will encounter fresh fruit vendors and learn that many local dishes can be made without animal products. From Bangkok to Phuket, veg-adventures await in the Land of Smiles.

Talk the Talk

The issue with ordering vegan Thai food in the States is that pesky fish sauce. Although many places in Thailand do traditionally add nam pla to most dishes, the cuisine is based around vegetables, and ordering know-how in restaurants is all you need to get a vegan meal. The only thing you really need to know is the word *jay*, which is tied to Buddhist spiritual beliefs (but also happens to be the way you indicate that you don't eat anything with a mother). Look for little "jay" labels on foods, or muster up the linguistic strength to say "pom gin jay" (if you're a man) or "chay gin jay" (if you're a woman)—the language is gendered.

Walk the Wok

If you've mastered the leftovers stir-fry and maybe figured out how to get your tofu crispy after many soggy dinners, it's time to up your culinary game in a place where cooking is a religious experience. Cooking classes are as common as massages in Thailand and can be booked through hotels or traditional cooking schools, or arranged during a homestay. Almost all group classes will take you through the local market to shop for fresh ingredients before showing you basic cooking and seasoning techniques. With locations in both Chiang Mai and Bangkok, May Kaidee Cooking School and Restaurant is known for its superfun classes where you can learn to make tofu, chili paste, soy-milk-based desserts, raw foods, and traditional Thai dishes such as Massaman curry, tom kha soup, and pad thai. This place even offers fruit-carving classes so that you can fulfill your dream of turning an apple into a swan.

OTP Tip
A traditional demonstration in Thai cooking classes is the production of coconut sugar—a vital ingredient in many of the country's sweeter dishes. It's like a cooking class for the completely inept: most of the time you will be watching how the insides of a coconut flower are turned into sugary syrup with the help of giant bowls and lots of stirring. Will you ever make it at home? Absolutely not. But it's fun to watch.

Eat the Street

Bangkok's Chinatown is a great place to pop into for a quick street snack, but Maeklong Railway Market, about an hour and a half away, is something of a legend. The vendors here are set up right on the train tracks, and although the arrangement may seem like a death wish when a train comes through, the whole thing has been thriving this way for a while. At the market, you'll find an array of veg-friendly dishes such as fried tofu spring rolls, khanom khrok (sweet coconut-rice pancakes), and taro-stuffed grilled sticky rice. If a sit-down place is what you're after, there are many dedicated vegan spots in every city. Bangkok offers its share of vegan fare with familiar spots such as the international chain Loving Hutand Broccoli Revolution, which offers American fare like veggie burgers in addition to a Thai menu. In

Chiang Mai, Khunchurn serves a buffet for about $6 where you can load up on veggies, beans, and prepared dishes such as vegan nam prik (traditionally made with fish sauce but in this case prepared with just-as-flavorful fermented beans). Pure Vegan Heaven in Phuket follows the city's general rule of hiking up prices for tourists, but the food is refreshing, even if the crowds piss you off.

Veg in the Village

Even though Buddhism—which cruxes on kindness to all—is one of Thailand's major religions, Thai people are pretty into eating meat. However, Nakhon Pathom is a village in central Thailand that adheres to the strict teachings of the Buddha. For you, that means animal-free food will not be hard to find. The now more metropolitan city was once known for its fruit orchards, so dishes heavily feature pomelos and jackfruit. The town is also home to the Wat Phra Pathom Chedi (one of the largest *stupas*, or Buddhist shrines, in the world) and the floating Don Wai Market, which is rumored to be home to Thailand's best khao lahm—sticky rice and coconut steamed and served in a long bamboo chute.

GUIDE TO THE WEIRD-ASS FRUIT
OF SOUTHEAST ASIA

In addition to your regular ol' apples and melons, Southeast Asia offers a selection of fruit that in some cases resembles sea creatures and in others smells like old socks. Sure, you can get your run-of-the-mill grapes and watermelons here, but why would you want to when spiky demon fruit is on the menu?

DURIAN

Let's just get this one out of the way. It's big, it's wobbly, and it smells like absolute putrid death farts. Cutting it open both releases the funk and reveals the innards, a fleshy goop that will test your gag reflexes. However, in Southeast Asia, you will have to eat durian, because if you don't you're not allowed to ever come back (not true, but we'll tell everyone that you betrayed the culture by being intimidated by a fruit). The taste? Some people liken it to putrid custardy banana with pineapple and garlic undertones. On the upside, durian is believed to have aphrodisiac qualities, so your genitals would really love you if you could temporarily suspend your sense of smell. You can get durian in the West, but the funk is lost in transport.

SUGAR-APPLE

So you've eaten your wretched bite of durian and think you're in the clear with something that sounds familiar. Wrong. For one, it looks more like a dinosaur than anything, and there's really nothing apple-like about it. Although it's not native to the region, the fruit (also known as soursop) is popular around Southeast Asia. It has a custardy consistency and is loaded with slippery black seeds that you will need to spit out unless you're a fan of asphyxiation. This one doesn't stink like butt.

RAMBUTAN

We once sat in front of a pile of rambutan for an hour waiting for it to move. These things look like angry sea urchins, but once you rip off the exterior hairy shell—best done by scoring it with a pocketknife, but if you're a savage, teeth work fine—to reveal a moist white egg inside. Taste-wise, they are supersweet with a floral tinge and a little crunch.

SNAKE FRUIT

If we were a fruit, just hanging there ripe for the picking by whatever predator decided to stroll by, we'd definitely develop some defense mechanisms. The snake fruit is named after its reptilian skin, which would deter most from eating it. But you shall be brave and tackle a cluster of these scaly (but scrumptious!) beasts. Inside, you will find a butt—a mound of delicious, ass-shaped, sweet-and-sour pineapple-like flesh with two black seeds. Don't eat too many; snake fruit notoriously leads to constipation.

MANGOSTEEN

This purplish fruit has a shell that's almost as hard as a coconut when it's overripe. The round little bottom of a mangosteen contains an adorable flower that tells you how many lobes of fruit are inside by the number of petals it has. If you're a rebel that doesn't follow instructions, just tear into the thing and find out. We hope you're a fan of slime because the texture is pretty damn mucus-y, while the flavor is tangy and floral with just a hint of sweetness.

JAVA JITTERS IN JAKARTA (INDONESIA)

Coffee snobbery has exploded in the United States in recent years. First-wave Starbucks paved the way with its made-up Italian-sounding drink sizes, and second-wave shops—like Four Barrel, Blue Bottle, and other two-word hipster magnets—have turned the humble coffee bean into a full-blown caffeine craze in which sourcing, flavor profiles, and surgical terminology have gained utmost importance in the post-Starbucks era. And while you can get a cup of Java-grown joe in the States, when you're on the ground in Indonesia—one of the main producers of coffee in the world—you will want to wake up to the smell of the real deal.

Coffee's Colonial Roots

Back in the days of the Dutch East India Company, farmers in the region produced rice for food. Europeans, who had developed a taste for stimulants such as coffee, forced the locals to divert their subsistence skills into producing the raw material for their cups of java. Now most farmers work smaller areas of land to grow their beans, of which there are a hundred different species but only two (sweeter arabica and more bitter robusta) that are extensively cultivated.

Cups from the Source

A cup of Indonesian coffee has a distinct flavor profile that is derived from not only the region where the beans were grown, but also the way the coffee cherries are prepared and transported. Of course, regional variations impart different flavors, but the process in which beans are separated from hulls is equally important. A classic cup of Indonesian coffee will have a well-rounded body, because the beans are hulled while wet and are transported in a mucus-covered state, gaining a bluish hue and deeper flavors from the moisture they retain in transit. Capital city Jakarta is *the* place to taste every regional variety of coffee grown around the archipelago.

Kiss your Blue Bottle mornings goodbye and try a cup of that good shit at these cafes instead.

KEDAI LOCALE
Come to one of two outlets of the modern coffee shop Kedai and order a pour-over, which is expertly prepared with single-origin beans the shop rotates monthly. In addition to world-class coffee, the place serves a menu of hearty Indonesian dishes and a wide selection of traditional desserts—such as a sweet roti, indulgent cakes, and toast smothered in Nutella and condensed milk.

BAKOEL KOFFIE
If you're a fan of historical establishments, count this one as the granddaddy of coffee in Jakarta. Established in the 1870s, it lacks the sterile modernity of newer shops. What you will get is a cup with four generations of experience, roasted and blended at a still that has been around since before coffee was cool.

TRAFIQUE
Closer to the kind of shop you're used to, the open space serves as a co-office ("coffee office") for most customers, and baristas are knowledgeable about their beans' backstories. This place serves mostly Toraja arabica beans grown in high elevations on the island of Sulawesi. Order a Lestretto (coffee plus sparkling water) to get out of your Frappuccino comfort zone.

Turd's the Word
You may have heard of bat shit crazy. Well, this here is cat shit coffee—or coffee beans that are processed through the digestive systems of catlike Asian palm civets then spewed out the other end for you to enjoy with steamed milk and sugar. Called kopi luwak, this shit ain't cheap—nor is it abundant—and its rarity contributes to the novelty of downing sewage. Tourists have made this formerly rare (and ethically pooper-scooped) varietal a phenomenon, which has led to really inhumane methods of farming civets. Know that ordering a cuppa comes with the possibility of contributing to an increasingly cruel industry. If you do choose to imbibe, Anomali Coffee sells the shit at four locations in Jakarta, all of which offer fast Wi-Fi so you can tell the whole world about your feces-filled adventures.

THE WORLD'S SMELLIEST FLOWER

The aroma of coffee in the morning is not the only thing wafting from Indonesia. Sumatra is home to the world's smelliest flower, the *Titan arum*—also known as "the corpse flower," an apt name since it literally smells like death. The flower, one of the largest in the plant kingdom, can grow up to eight feet tall with leaves that can span up to thirteen feet. The huge, stinky thing is actually a very useful plant for the diverse and tropical land on which it grows. It smells like murder due to a number of chemicals that make up a combination of odors, including cooked onions, garlic, rotting fish, mothballs, sweaty socks, Chloraseptic throat spray, and a touch of jasmine. You see, by pretending to be a rotting body, the plant geniusly attracts pollinators that want to feast on the corpse. The creatures are instead tricked into moving pollen around to help sustain the island's diverse plant species and the animals that like to chow down on them. If you happen on a corpse flower during your journey, you'll know that it's not your deodorantless pits. It's the plant.

HOLY STREET SNACKS, BATMAN! (PHILIPPINES)

Welcome to the Philippines, where feeling hangry will never be a thing due to the abundance of snacky snacks you'll find on every street corner. Served on sticks and paper plates, in bags and bowls, the street snacks found in the Philippines aren't of your typical Cheez-It variety. From chicken balls (and intestines!) on sticks to partially developed duck embryos (feet and all) to ice cream dotted with cheese bits, snacking in the Philippines is quite an adventure. You can find all these snacks across the country, but if you want to eat everything in one go, head to Quiapo market in Manila—where friendly folks hawk flavorful foods from hundreds of street stalls—and bring a monster appetite. Happy snacking!

Balut, Filipino Style

Balut is the most popular of Filipino street snacks, if only for the "yuck" factor. You eat the partially developed duck (or chicken) embryo, nestled inside its comfy little egg house, by tapping out a hole at the top of the shell, sucking out the goopy bird broth, then crunching on the innards (which tend to be yolky and contain plenty of cartilage) with a sprinkling of salt and vinegar.

Fried Baby Chicks

A day-old chick fried whole to a crisp is actually a resourceful snack, because the egg industry usually discards male chicks by grinding them alive. This baby bird might be hard to swallow, but it's a good fit if you're into the nose-to-tail (beak-to-feathers, in this case) philosophy. Dip it in vinegar, eat the head first, then proceed to the body, where you will find some chewy organs, before finishing with the legs. Have water handy.

Buko

For something refreshing after munching down on gnarly birds, get yourself some buko (young coconut). Find a pushcart loaded with these green-and-yellow orbs, and ask the vendor to hack it open for you with a machete. Inside, you will find sweet coconut water—the kind you've been drinking to cure hangovers—and a silky helping of young coconut meat.

Helmets and Adidas

No, you're not going shopping for leisure-wear. What we have here, friends, is chicken heads ("helmets") and feet ("adidas"), fried whole over charcoal and served on a stick.

Isaw

While it looks innocent enough—just some meat on a stick served in a cup of fluid—isaw, you see, is not what it seems. That tiny kebab is actually a coil of either chicken or pig intestines, grilled over a charcoal flame and strung onto a skewer. Let the intestines soak in their cup of vinegar (usually accented by chilies and onions) before working your way through the spiral.

Lumpia

A popular eggroll-like snack, you'll find these little handheld, golden-fried snacks—which feature a bit of minced meat and veg enveloped in a crepelike, paper-thin wrapper—by the tray-full outdoors and as an appetizer at any social gathering. The lumpia wrapper is used in a number of street-food snacks, including turon—a sweet treat that features a banana and jackfruit chunk surrounded by the delicate dough then fried into a crispy indulgence with a gooey fruit center.

Kwek Kwek

It sounds like "quack, quack," but what you'll get are the eggs of a quail—a bird we're pretty sure does zero quacking. At any rate, its eggs are hard-boiled, coated in a thick batter, and deep-fried until they are crispy spheres that look more like bright orange ping-pong balls than snacks. Dip them in the accompanying vinegar or fish-ball sauce, and keep an eye out for their chicken-egg cousins, tokneneng.

OTP Tip

Obsessed with fried balls? You're in luck! Fish, squid, and chicken balls—heavily coated in flour and fried—are abundant here.

Dried Squid

Best enjoyed with a beer in hand, dried squid is another popular snack in this island nation surrounded by squid-packed waters. Fishermen pull squid fresh from the ocean, flatten them, and dehydrate them in the sweltering sun before grilling and topping them with aromatics such as onions and chilies. This is a chewy one that will take your entire jaw to devour.

Green Mango (with a Twist)

Ready to move on to dessert? If you take your sweets with a smattering of shellfish, then this snack is right up your alley. Green mangoes (an unripened variety of sweet-and-sour, crunchy Indian mangoes) are sliced and served with bagoong, a pinkish paste made from fermented shrimp and krill. The combo might not be something you're used to, but it strikes that balance of sweet and salty that makes Filipino school-children salivate.

Halo-Halo

Now for the real dessert. Halo-halo is the most popular frozen treat on the streets. On sweltering days, nothing feels better than a bowl of shaved ice. But this isn't just sucking on ice cubes. At the heart of halo-halo is shaved ice soaked in super-sweet condensed milk, then doused with toppings that complement its cooling frozen-water component. You will find this dessert crowned by jelly bits, chopped fruit, tapioca pearls, sweet beans, coconut flakes, toasted rice, and a scoop of ube halaya—an ice cream made from ube, a purple yam commonly used in Filipino desserts. The Philippines is also home to a variety of ice cream options, the most popular of which is keso—a treat that features bits of cheese suspended in frozen cream (and whose name derives from the Spanish word for cheese).

PUT ON YOUR FANCY PANTS: UPSCALE RESTAURANTS
IN SOUTHEAST ASIA

Your wallet will likely feel pretty full while traveling around super-affordable Southeast Asia, so we recommend splurging on the fine-dining champs of the region—meals like these would cost you your firstborn in New York or Los Angeles. Put on your big-boy bib and shell out a few bucks for the following highly acclaimed Asian eateries.

GAGGAN (BANGKOK, THAILAND)

The ultradramatic Netflix series *Chef's Table* highlighted Gaggan, and for good reason. Rags-to-riches Indian chef Gaggan Anand re-creates flavorful Indian cuisine in ways you never see coming. You won't find big servings of curry or dal here, but this place is worth the price point—even though it's as far from Thai cuisine as you can get in Bangkok. Expect "progressive Indian cuisine" with dishes that look too good to eat, inspired by the chef's memories of his homeland.

'NAMO TUSCAN GRILL (SAIGON, VIETNAM)

We know that you didn't travel the world to go to just another steakhouse, but hear us out: Italian chef Ivan Barone has a passion for sharing regional cuisine from da boot with Vietnamese natives. For you, that means complex Tuscan flavors buried deep into dishes such as grilled sausage, lemon-infused salmon, and a selection of mouth-watering steaks.

GALLERY VASK (MANILA, PHILIPPINES)

Helmed by Spanish chef José Luis "Chele" González with surroundings curated by Juan Carlo Calma, this establishment is more than a gastronomic experience: it blends art with food for the ultimate fine-dining adventure. Tasting menus, which can span sixteen courses, include ingredients caught fresh by Philippine fishermen and tapas-like preparations of regional produce. The full "Alamat" menu is designed to be a journey; for those preferring a day trip, the shortened "Lakbay" menu means you can be in bed before sundown.

LOCAVORE (UBUD, BALI, INDONESIA)

Each tasting menu—with an available vegetarian option—is all about sampling the bounty of Bali, from the ingredients down to the serviceware on which they arrive, which are sourced from local artisans. Dishes change often, but the constant is that the origin of every ingredient on the menu—from short ribs to kohlrabi—is traced back to a local farm.

A WORLD OF HURT: THE SPICIEST DISHES IN THAILAND

If you spent your teens bingeing on Flamin' Hot Cheetos and your adult years trying to one-up your friends in spicy-wings challenges, then Thailand is the place to put your ability to withstand heat to the test. You'd think that in a locale that's sweltering hot for most of the year, food choices would be on the cooling side—and you'd be wrong. Because in Thailand, you beat the heat with more heat, and when you're sweating to get through a meal, the outside temps don't seem as bad as the inside of your mouth. Get ready to bite into some face-burning, mouth-singeing, heart-palpitating spice with these ten Thai dishes (in order from hot to hot-damnedest) that promise to have no mercy on your heat-loving soul.

Papaya Salad (Som Tam)

You've had this; you know this. It's just shredded green papaya and some tangy sauce, right? Oh so wrong. In Thailand, they don't placate your sugary-sweet American palate; instead, they load this sweet-and-sour dish with a shitload of Thai bird's-eye chilies. A few bites will leave you gasping for air and reaching for more.

Neua Pad Prik

The name of this meaty dish translates to "Thai pepper steak," and while it may stoke thoughts of peppery beef jerky, this thing is way more devious. A savory mixture of thinly sliced meat and vegetables arrives at your table, begging to be munched down in a few bites. Slow your roll, though, because the dish is loaded with chilies and will impart what will feel like third-degree burns on your tongue if you're not careful.

Khao Phat Nam Prik Narok

The name translates to "fried rice with chili paste from hell," and the dish features a concoction of garlic, palm sugar, chili paste, rice, and fish chunks, which all deliver on the combo's devilish promise. It's both tangy and spicy, and is great for a first-course introduction to what heat-forward Thai food is all about. You will find it a struggle to get through the entire mound, but it's worth every bite.

Pad Ka Prao

This dish comes smothered in holy basil—known as Thai basil or tulsi, an herb with Indian origins—a welcome sanctuary in a dish that is packed with chilies and, most often, chicken. Sometimes, pad ka prao comes topped with a sunny-side-up egg, whose runny yolk helps to balance the spice. This one has become popular among the backpacker crowd. As such, places with high tourist traffic have adjusted the dish to be a little on the bleh side.

OTP Tip

Ordering Thai food stateside—even if you exclaim that you can hang with spice—will result in spice levels that servers believe you can handle (read: bland). In Thailand, cooks are more liberal with spice but will still need a little proof that you can take the heat. Before ordering your dish "authentically spicy," tell them you have a "Thai tongue." Say, "Ped bab cone Thai ka" (or "kup" if the speaker is male). Then, prepare for some mouth-damaging eats.

Larb

A well-made larb (or spiced-meat salad) will set your mouth on fire. While it may resemble a safe-ish dish, this meat-and-heat bomb is not for those that color inside the lines. The chicken or pork traditionally used as the dish's foundation is pounded and mashed with chilies, creating a deceptive pâté-like presentation with a cobra bite.

Tom Yum Goong

If you are feeling a little congested in Thailand, a bit of tom yum (the unofficial national food of Thailand) will completely knock the snot out of you. A soup that gets a tangy undertone from a hefty dose of lemongrass, tom yum is decidedly spicy from a blend of fried chili paste and whole chilies that you will find floating ominously on top. Spoon with caution, friends.

Tom Laeng

Falling-off-the-bone pork pieces are the only reprieve to the punishing spice conspicuously hiding in this soupy dish. Green chilies punch up the brownish broth, and every spoonful will make you wish that a bowl of ice were at your disposal during the entire meal. Don't let the green herbs fool you—this meaty soup can set off fire alarms.

Gaeng Tai Pla

This is the kind of dish that people watch you eat, expecting you to crawl under the table to rock back and forth like a wee baby. A stew that was arguably created by the devil himself, gaeng tai pla is made with fermented fish innards to give you a little side of salty with your spicy. If you finish the whole menacing bowl, you will earn the (invisible) medal of backpacker spice lord.

Gaeng Som

Thai curry comes in three colors: green, orange, and red. If you're thinking that these colors are a handy, stoplight-like guide to their spiciness levels, you are wrong: each has its own distinct spice. Gaeng som—an orange variety that will punch you in the nose hairs—is a runny curry made with seafood and tamarind. Do not pour your curry over all the rice that it comes with. You will be left with soup—of the ass-kicking variety.

OTP Tip

Thai iced tea is not just a morning alternative to coffee. It serves as a cooling beverage—made in different ways but most popularly with cold black tea and condensed milk—that helps you survive the herculean task of putting pure dragon fire into your body with every bite.

Gaeng Kua Kling

Dishes from southern Thailand are spicier than those from the north, and gaeng kua kling is one example that takes things up a notch. A dry curry made by tossing meat in a pan filled with lemongrass, chilies, kaffir leaves, galangal, turmeric, garlic, and shrimp paste, this dish is always made full-blast spicy and will force you to cry tears of fiery joy.

OTP Tip

Ordering a cooling cucumber salad, sprinkled with chopped peanuts and not much spice, can be a nice little vacation from the hell hole that is your mouth after going hard on Thailand's hottest dishes.

ORDERING ORGANS . . . AND OTHER WAYS TO FEED YOURSELF IN CAMBODIA

Whereas Thai and Vietnamese foods have made their way onto American plates, Cambodian cuisine has yet to fully cross the pond. Some similarities exist between

Khmer dishes and traditional foods of surrounding countries, but Cambodia has got a distinct culinary culture of its own. Here, you'll find an array of traditional bites—from Khmer sandwiches made with soft French baguettes, to lungs, livers, and pig's ears served on a stick with a side of fried tarantulas. The following are ten Cambodian dishes that paint a picture of the country's vastly diverse culinary landscape.

Lort Cha

The word *lort* in this classic noodle dish refers to the fat little rice noodles that make up its base. The noodles are fried and topped with Chinese broccoli, bean sprouts, and chives before being doused in a thick sweet-and-spicy chili sauce, loaded with succulent beef, and finished off with a fried egg. Lort cha will put your hangovers into a chokehold.

Fish Amok

A curry dish that is traditionally served in the banana-leaf bowl in which it's cooked, fish amok is composed of flaky catfish (or other white-fleshed fish) that has been steamed into a custard consistency, its delicate flavor balanced with citrusy aromatics such as kaffir lime and lemongrass. The dish is served in high-end restaurants, but street varieties are just as good or better because they don't break the bank. Also, catfish is not the only protein in town—amok can be made with chicken or sometimes snails.

Chive Cakes

Y'all like pancakes? These are not them. Popular savory street snacks hawked from bikes, these little Chinese-influenced patties (called nom ga chai) are made from a glutinous rice flour that gives them a bit of a chew. The light cakes are stuffed with chives, fried in a shallow pan for a browned exterior, and served with fish sauce. They are best hot off the pan, but they can burn you if you're too eager.

Organs . . . on a Stick

This is the food equivalent of conquering a kingdom and skewering your enemy's innards on your sword. Skewered pig intestines, stomach pieces, hearts, livers, ears, and mystery balls are available for 25 cents a pop with a side of sauce. They all taste about the same—like the sinewy organ meat that they are—but the texture is what matters most. Lungs are chewy but soft, and ears proffer a bit of a welcome crunch. Finding them among other kebabed foods is easy. Look for the signature lackluster gray color of offal in stalls that are frequented only by locals.

Snails

Snails are abundant in Cambodian waters and, as such, are plentiful in the streets, where vendors precook the slimy suckers before letting them dry in the sun on their carts. You'll find these more frequently in Phnom Penh than in Siem Reap, and they are sold by the cup or the bucket. Coated in garlic and salt, or chili, snails are meant to be sucked out of their shells, so don't be shy. Sometimes they are cooked up with aromatics and then doused in good ol' Coca-Cola as a finishing touch.

Sausage

Bright red pork sausages line the tops of street carts, strewn together in what look like those chili-pepper garlands that line your favorite Mexican restaurant in the States. These tubes are half meat and

half fat with a touch of palm sugar, and the experience of eating them is juicy and satisfying. Get them on a skewer, sliced, or in the form of sausage balls.

Giant Squid

You've had calamari, shrimp, and lobster, but this experience is not one you can find at any seafood restaurant. Squid in Cambodia are the size of cats and are skewered whole for an impressive presentation. Go to Central Market in Phnom Penh later in the afternoon for this meal-sized animal. The squid is expertly grilled until its edges are caramelized and near crispy before being chopped and topped with chives. It's next-level calamari with a barbecue bang.

Cha Houy Teuk

A rainbow-hued dessert that's got just about everything you can ask for in one dish. The base is agar-agar jelly (which is usually available in an array of colors); then it becomes a DIY dessert adventure waiting for you to add starchy sago and taro, coconut ice cream, sweet red beans, jackfruit, and a bit of ice for extra refreshment. If you don't think beans belong in dessert, getdafuckoutta heah!

Coconut Water

Why is this postparty staple special here? Well, unlike the aseptic containers you are used to seeing it in, in Cambodia it comes fresh from the source. Sold as an accompaniment to many a street food, a fresh coconut is cracked in front of you with a cleaver before being served whole. The inside flesh is soft and slippery, while the liquid is refreshing and full of potassium and other minerals—meaning you may be ready to hit the Cambodian street-food scene for a part deux, if the first time around sent you to the shitter more times than you could count.

Fried Tarantulas

The caviar of Cambodia, these little buggers, which sell for about $1 each, are much more expensive than most street-food snacks. Although they're regarded as a delicacy now, back during the bloody Khmer Rouge regime, starving Cambodians resorted to eating whatever crawled around the region. The tarantulas are first dipped in seasoned milky water before being wok-fried to perfection. The hairy experience—which you can think of as eating land crabs, if that makes you feel better—is best paired with a cold beer or any other alcoholic beverage that can make you forget you're eating horror.

TASTE ALL OF ASIA IN MALAYSIA

In Malaysia, you can taste a bit of everything Southeast and mainland Asia have to offer. The country is a delicious mash-up of authentic (and decidedly inauthentic) Chinese, Indian, and wholly Malaysian cuisine, with variants and influences strewn throughout. Plus, the Malay people eat almost competitively: six meals per day is not uncommon. Breakfast, lunch, and dinner (the main meal) are supplemented by noodle breaks throughout the day and "elevenses"—an eleven a.m. second breakfast that is real and not something limited to the hobbits. Plenty of street-food vendors will heed your need to eat, and the selection of dishes will lure you into eating the Malay way.

Breakfast

If you've ever had Indian food, you know that roti is a staple for every meal of the day. Malaysia's version, roti canai, made with a stretchy dough and served with curry or lentil dal, is best enjoyed early morning. Nasi lemak is a breakfast must-have that comes to you on the pandan leaf in which it was prepared. A variety of flavors and textures mingle on said leaf, including flavorful meat curry, crunchy peanuts and anchovies, perfumed coconut-milk-infused rice, a sliced hard-boiled egg (or sometimes an omelet), cooling cucumber, and spicy sambal— a holy sauce in Malaysia made with a blend of chilies, calamansi lime, and shrimp paste. Get it with fried chicken to really seal the leaf deal. For a sweeter start, kaya toast features creamy coconut-custard jam (kaya)

sandwiched between two griddled pieces of buttered bread. Avocado toast who?

OTP Tip
Didn't get to eat all of these at breakfast? No worries, elevenses is just around the corner. Tuck into whatever you missed—may we also suggest an oyster omelet served with a side of sambal?—to get your stomach nice and stretchy for lunch.

Lunch

Start with popiah, spring rolls made of a thin rice crepe that is stuffed with veggies, tofu, and egg before being fried to perfection. Then move on to a lunchtime classic, Hainanese chicken rice, Malaysia's signature dish even though its origins are from the island of Hainan in China. The dish involves boiled chicken with equally boring-sounding white rice prepared in chicken stock—which meld to compose a surprisingly succulent dish served with a ginger and garlic dipping sauce spiked with a touch of chili. Laksa is an iconic Malaysian curry that varies across the country and in Penang often comes topped with congealed pig blood. For those times when you just can't figure out what the hell it is you're craving, pasembur—a smorgasbord of whatever is on hand

(maybe squid, or prawns, or sometimes octopus, all doused in a peanut-based sauce), fried and piled on top of rice—will answer the call for a little of everything.

Noodle Break

Oh the horror! It's been an hour and you have not chewed anything. Sounds like it's time for some heavy-duty snacking—and you will be in good company because Malay people ferociously get down with some midday noodles. Find a street hawker with the most charcoal on their grill and order mee goreng, a wok-fried yellow noodle dish dotted with shallots, made salty with soy and belacan (shrimp paste), and fragrant with garlic and the surrounding smoke of the grill. Sold mostly by Muslim Indian vendors, mee rebus is a brothy noodle-break favorite that features rempah—a spice blend that's a combo of fruits and roots and that makes up the hearty backbone of Malaysian cooking. And the noodle break need not be just about carbo-loading. Satay—which you may be familiar with if you've been to Thailand—is marinated meat on a stick, grilled to order, and served with a distinctly Malaysian spicy peanut sauce. Full? It's time for dinner.

Dinner

Pork, it's what's for dinner—at least it is if you order wonton mee (or wantan mee). It's a noodle combo dish that's reminiscent of sweet-and-sour pork (which makes sense since it's of Cantonese origin) that is both fried in pork lard and topped with pieces of saucy pork, all served with a side of brothy wonton soup that features another little touch of pork to drive the point home. Need more pork in your face? Try bak kut the, a rich, nearly gelatinous pork soup that is packed with slow-cooked ribs spiced with a bit of cinnamon. Finish off your pork feast with some warm tea to help your stomach fight the impeding pork coma. Beef is not forgotten during dinnertime, and rendang is the best example of how Malays do the popular protein. The dish is slow-cooked throughout the day until it turns fiery red due to its heavy chili content and develops a pungent, rich taste imparted by asam keping (a sun-dried sour fruit that's native to the region). If dinner is a sit-down event, there will be plenty of crab—the popularity of which is shared with bordering Singapore—cooked shell-on in a tomato-based sauce with a tinge of tamarind. Malays don't do bibs, so learn how to crack into crab without causing a total disaster.

OTP Tip

If hunger strikes again at midnight, the best thing you can do is go out for some char kuey teow, a noodle dish loaded with seafood (such as cockles, prawns, or both), fried over a smoky charcoal grill, and lubed in lard for a fatty finish. Now go to bed.

YOU DOWN WITH MSG?
(YEAH, YOU KNOW ME!)

Do you remember how all of a sudden everyone thought they had celiac disease (a rare illness that affects a mere 1 percent of the American population) and put a moratorium on gluten for no goddamn reason? MSG fell victim to the same fate. Americans have shunned monosodium glutamate for decades because of an unmerited stigma that stems from our futile attempts to remove foreign ingredients from our foods. However, in Southeast Asia, this shit is in everything—and rightfully so as it imparts a salty umami flavor to all food it touches. Like Parmesan in Italy, MSG (which looks like a crystal-y salt) is added to dishes by the spoonful to enhance flavor. If you're *actually* allergic to this deliciously savory seasoning, you can always ask vendors in Malaysia to hold the flavoring by saying, "Tolong tidak pakai micin, saya mempunyai alergi." However, because MSG is in soy sauce, bouillon cubes, and other prepared ingredients, chances are you'll still be eating it even when you think you're not. We hate to break it to you but you've probably been eating MSG in the States as well, because it occurs naturally in fermented foods and is often labeled as a different compound that's commonly present in packaged soups, meals, and energy bars.

Festivals and Music

BURNING MAN AND COACHELLA HAVE NOTHING ON THE festivals in Southeast Asia. Your comfort zone will be repeatedly pierced during Malaysia's Thaipusam celebration, where spiritually driven body mutilation is on display in the streets. For more bloody face holes, check out Phuket's Vegetarian Festival. Although the food lacks animal flesh, humans make themselves into meaty shish kebabs by skewering their cheeks, climbing towers dotted with razors, and singeing their feet in pits of fire. Get an earload at the annual (homemade) fireworks festival in Laos, and watch monkeys chow down on eight thousand pounds of chef-prepared food at a Khmer temple in Lopburi. Music festivals are common, too, as are live, intimate musical performances in bars and DJ sets in clubs. Perhaps the best way to fest in Southeast Asia is by engaging in a healthy mix of music and madness.

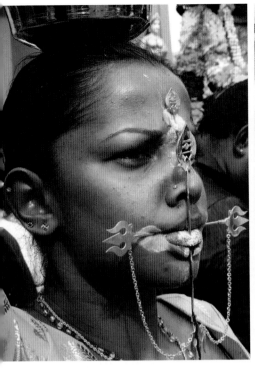
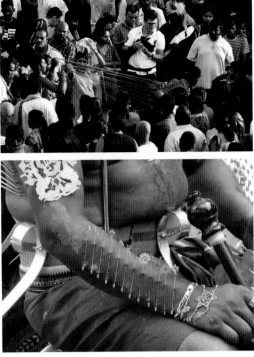

BODY-PIERCING EXTREME:
THAIPUSAM (MALAYSIA)

Did you pierce your septum in college because you thought you were hot shit? Or let your friend talk you into stabbing a needle through your nipple to just see what happened? Well, during the religious Thaipusam festival, all that is child's play. Devotees stab their cheeks, tongues, and mouths; some carry chambers filled with spikes that stab their entire bodies as they walk. We'd say that beats your nip ring, big time.

First Blood

All this hurt is not for nothing. The Tamil festival, which originates in India, is related to giving praise to the Hindu god of war, Lord Murugan, who, throughout time, has allowed the people to persevere by supplying them with weapons and strength. Every year, when the full moon rises during the Tamil month of Thai—in either January or February—practitioners take to the streets to honor Murugan with self-mutilation. The purpose is to commemorate Murugan's *vel* (spear), and the more sharp objects, the merrier.

To the Batcave!

Thaipusam is observed all over the world, but for added intrigue, go see it down at the Batu Caves in Kuala Lumpur, where a golden 140-foot statue of the lord himself stands frozen in time. Not only will you be in a place where bats fly around like pigeons, but you will be privy to the wildest of Thaipusam festivities, which include particularly dedicated participants carrying a *kavadi*—a traditional harness worn by people who have been celibate for forty-eight days (!) that is equipped with multiple spears that poke the wearer's exposed body from every angle. This is done to symbolize the expulsion of burden, which also takes the form of people shoving hooks in their skin and pulling wagons through the pain. Other forms of bloody holes include those in the face, particularly in the mouth area, which are meant to silence the devotee to bring awareness to the gift of speech. This awesome/gruesome fest draws more than five hundred thousand revelers, so know that accommodations will be scarce and transportation will be packed.

OTP Tip

This is not the time to pretend you are Logan Paul. Although the festival is quite horrifying (and revelers are adorned in Instagram-worthy orange and yellow hues), the religious element of sacrifice is very important to participants, and gathering "can you fucking believe this guy?" content for social media is super douchey. Stay out of the way, and respect the powers that be.

Dang, Penang

Malaysia's expat-loaded island of Penang is a little less crowded during Thaipusam, which means you won't feel as anxious about bumping into a dude who's already having a hard time being skewered in the kidneys by his materialized burdens. Here, you'll get a front seat to the festival, where people carry milk jugs on their heads and chant and drum in hypnotizing harmony for three full days. Murugan makes his appearance as a statue hauled along Penang Street on a chariot drawn by oxen. In addition to breaking skin, another fun ritual during Thaipusam is the coconut smash. Demolishing coconuts is a symbol of destroying the ego to reveal the pure white goodness inside. The nuts are scored prior to the event for an easier smash, and every coconut thrown onto the street is cleared by a motorized vehicle to allow the procession to continue. Roadside coconuts are then set on fire, which will make you want to get a flaming coconut cocktail to commemorate the great Lord Murugan.

FLOATING BASKETS AND FLYING LANTERNS: ABSOLUTION FESTS (THAILAND)

Many religions and cultures champion the idea of absolution. Whether it's Catholics confessing their sins to a priest inside a confessional or Jews observing Shemittah, in which creditors and debtors are absolved of their obligations every seven years, the idea of seeking forgiveness and closure from a higher power is not uncommon. In Thailand, the practice is symbolized by two distinct (but related) rituals. Both are mesmerizing to watch, and if you have some sins to confess, they are super relieving to participate in.

Loi Krathong

A festival dedicated to the appreciation of water and, in some cases, the absolution of whatever messed-up shit you might have done throughout the year, Loi Krathong involves sending a banana-leaf float down a body of water (usually the Chao Phraya River) in November (the twelfth lunar month) to cast off the bad and welcome good intentions for the year to come. Some people load their floats (or *krathong*) with hair, nails, and coins, which they discard in hopes of a better year. The celebration is bolstered by fireworks, performances, food, and a beauty-queen pageant—the latter of which is a patriarchal symbol we can do without.

Yee Peng (Yi Peng)

This tradition—which happens at about the same time as Loi Krathong—is more about gratitude than absolution. Lighting a paper lantern and releasing it into the air is all about letting go of whatever was bothering you that year, practicing a Buddhist principle of living with no regrets. Aesthetically speaking, the fest, which takes place during the full moon, will blow your mind. Imagine hundreds of man-made fireflies soaring overhead. Yee Peng is also all about parades and decorations, which means wherever you are things will be damn pretty. The tradition is so widespread that airports in Chiang Mai ground planes during Yee Peng to make sure that no aircraft activity is obstructed by the floating lanterns.

The Takeaway

Festivals that urge you to reflect on the way you have lived your life in small measurements are helpful in allowing you to evaluate your values and goals—a privilege that should be afforded to all. In 2010, trans people were finally allowed to participate in these commemorations. When you visit, float (or fly) a message of inclusivity into the water (or air) to celebrate the idea that people who were once ostracized from events unrelated to gender identity now have official recognition. Perhaps your gesture will stick with the gods—or better yet, with the people currently living on earth.

MONKEY BUFFET FESTIVAL (THAILAND)

Every year, the monkeys of Lopburi, Thailand, are treated to a Thanksgiving-style feast on the last Sunday of November. It began in 1989, and the city's three thousand monkeys have been convening for their banquet in front of old Khmer temple Prang Sam Yot ever since. Organizer Yongyuth Kitwattananusont has been known to parachute into the event wearing a monkey suit just to up the ridiculous factor even more. Prepare to watch thousands of people watch thousands of monkeys eat thousands of pounds of food.

Monkey Business

Chefs spend hours preparing more than four tons of food—ranging from fresh fruits and vegetables carved into decorative shapes to Thai desserts and sticky rice—which is laid out buffet-style on a platform near the temple. It's pretty much like a birthday party for a Saudi Arabian prince, complete with ice sculptures, except the only invited guests are thousands of long-tailed macaques (which are said to bring good fortune). Invitations attached to cashews are handed out to monkey guests prior to the event—presumably so they have time to put on their best party attire. An equal number of tourists will come to watch the hungry monkeys—who sometimes steal glasses, jewelry, and whatever else they think resembles food. Unfortunately, American culture has influenced this festival in a crappy way: monkeys are also given cans of Coca-Cola and other sugary beverages that we know are better for cleaning car engines than ingesting. Outside the celebration, the monkeys are fed by the local government three times per day to keep them satiated (and to make sure they don't harass tourists too much).

Fun Fact

The city is rumored to have been founded by a heroic monkey that saved a young bride from a ten-headed demon. The monkeys that live there now are said to be direct descendants of the heroic fellow.

Getting to the Action

You will need wheels to get to the monkey madness, which is located about a hundred miles north of Bangkok. There are sixteen daily train departures from Bangkok to Lopburi. The trip takes a little over two hours, and the train station in Lopburi is right near the monkey temple. Alternatively, buses, which take about three hours, depart every twenty minutes from Bangkok. In town, songthaews—pickup trucks tricked out to be more like (very shaky) buses—run along the city's main road and cost 10 baht (or 32 cents). Or hire a samlor (pedicab) to take you to your monkey-infested destination—or, if you prefer, to the many other ancient ruins in the old town.

OTP Tip

Once you're done mingling with monkeys, head to the city's expansive sunflower fields, which bloom between November and January, blanketing the ground with bright yellow flowers that are about the size of your head.

THE WORLD'S LARGEST WATER FIGHT (THAILAND)

Whereas most places gear up for midnight fireworks to ring in the new year in the dead cold of winter, Thailand celebrates by unleashing the biggest water fight on the planet. The Songkran Festival—Thai New Year—is celebrated when the sun transits Aries, which occurs in mid-April, the hottest time of year in Thailand. Water warriors of all ages equipped with super soakers emerge from every corner of the country and soak their targets head to toe, repeatedly, for three days. It might seem strange (and super refreshing), but there is a method to this madness.

Why the Water?

Songkran, like other New Year's celebrations, is a ritual of cleansing that symbolizes people's wish to bring prosperity, luck, and health to the coming year. The tamer portion of the holiday involves praying at temples and pouring scented water on monks. People clean their houses prior to the celebration and then flood the streets to pay their respects. In addition to water, a milky, sometimes colored talcum-powder mixture is carried in small buckets by the locals and smeared on people's faces to symbolize the sins of the past year, which they hope are washed away by water. Also, it's stupid hot, and getting wet is the best way to survive. Aside from escaping the heat, unloading a water storm onto your neighbor is a great release of built-up tension that involves good-hearted violence and no real crime. Win-win.

Cocked and Loaded

Ready to get wet and wild? It gets pretty wacky in Bangkok, and Chiang Mai really explodes into a full-on water riot. In fact, just about every place in Thailand gets drenched, so it doesn't really matter where you are; you have to be down to water-battle at the drop of a dime. And for that,

you need gear. A water gun is easy to come by prefest for about $3, and vendors set up stands selling rows of aqua-artillery. If you want to go hard, double up on the guns Rambo-style and put on some snazzy getup that you won't mind tossing afterward. Now hit the streets, where you'll find local restaurant owners armed with ice-water buckets, entire families unloading water artillery, and trucks turned into mobile pools (and splashing weapons). The most unsuspecting passerby will be your mortal water enemy, and you must get them before they get you.

OTP Tip

The unofficial dress code is all about floral prints—as in, those Hawaiian shirts your uncle wears to weddings. Flower wreaths are optional but encouraged (and easily purchased from street vendors). Goggles and earplugs are a nice touch, too.

Nobody Is Safe

It really doesn't matter if you're in a wheelchair or wearing nothing but a white sheet, you will be soaked—often by a little kid hiding around the corner with a super soaker. If you don't look Thai, you will be a juicy target because everyone loves to shoot a foreigner right in his moneymaker. If your stuff matters to you (as in, your phone or a particularly nice handbag that you have no business backpacking with in the first place), raise it above your head and let your body take the beating. You can also buy protective Ziploc bags from vendors who mysteriously appear, fully soaked. The best advice we can give is to just put all that shit away, jump into the middle of the action—not into the street, though, because drunk-driving casualties

are the highest this time of year—and let yourself become that ten-year-old who flew head first down the Slip 'n Slide, again and again.

OTP Tip

If you're not into reveling (you scaredy-cat!), you can hide out inside a local bar and watch the action. However, if you are on the street during Songkran, you are a fair target, and complaining is customarily looked down upon. Will you get a UTI and/or skin rashes? Very likely. But it will all be worth it.

DIY FIREWORKS FEST (LAOS)

Blowin' shit up has been cool since always, but this Buddhist festival takes fireworks to a new level with some of the most dubious explosives you'll ever see. Whereas some people perform a tame dance to welcome rain, Laotians go all out with elaborate parade floats, lots of hard alcohol, and homemade fireworks that'll blow the roof (or your fingers) off the party. The Rocket Festival—in which traditional fertility festivals meet the ninth-century invention of gunpowder—means things are going to be all kinds of explosive.

Boun BANG Fai

The Rocket Festival (officially called Boun Bang Fai) is all about asking the rain god Phaya Thaen for a good season, but a romantic backstory always makes for a much more interesting celebration. The story goes that the most beautiful girl in town, Nang Ai Kham, was given the lead position on a procession float, and her rumored soul mate (Phadaeng), who showered her with gifts, had to have the loudest, most obnoxious rocket in town in order to win her admiration. The fest didn't go as planned, and the girl's male family members won the rocket competition instead, a very incestuous outcome that nobody could get behind. Shit went astray, and the town was flooded until Phadaeng saved the day on a white stallion, sweeping Nang Ai Kham off her feet, literally and figuratively. But the lady friend, tragically, fell off the horse and into the abyss, never to be seen again. What does this have to do with rockets and debauchery? We're not sure, but a long-ass Lao poem tells the tale with a lot of dirty language and what in that day would have been considered dick jokes.

Fire, Away!

It is no coincidence that the celebration starts at the beginning of the wet season (May), and that many fest-goers bring along phallic ornaments—a nod to the event's origins as a fertility festival. Rockets that spew liquids onto revelers (called spitting rockets) are totally normal—and extra sexual. People carrying rockets large and small compete for the attention of the rain gods—and the biggest and best gain the kind of prestige you only wish your Tinder profile projected. Plus, all of them fire with no planned target (sound familiar?). Never thought you'd need to pack a helmet and shield in your backpack, did ya? (We seriously do recommend caution here . . . people have died.)

Lao Whiskey and Cross-Dressing

Foul-mouthed humor is prevalent during the festival—and a lot of it comes from everyone being piss drunk on sura—or Laotian whiskey (also known as Lao-Lao). This staple drink is made from rice, and local women often earn a second income distilling the amber or clear-colored concoction. The stuff is about 40 percent alcohol, costs a buck a bottle, and can be found at just about every store in Laos. How does cross-dressing fit into all of this? Well, it's a last-ditch effort among men already drunk from that damning whiskey to "sin" in front of the rain gods to coax out punishment in the form of rain to relieve the dry season. This last thing might be outdated—and the whole thing is for sure fairly dangerous—but shit, when have you launched a misguided rocket pumped-up on back-alley whiskey? Let 'er rip.

BLOODY GAPING FACE HOLES
(AKA THAILAND'S VEGETARIAN FESTIVAL)

In most places, vegetarian festivals are defined by an ample supply of hummus, a few protesters condemning the consumption of animals, and perhaps a veggie burger or two. Not in Phuket. The vegetarian fest here is all about shoving skewers straight into your cheeks until they come out the other side, running across hot coals, and climbing a tower of razor blades, in praise of the gods that be. This is *not* a party for those that can't stand the sight of blood.

The Horror!

Lore has it that Chinese performers traveled across Phuket in the nineteenth century and got stupid sick with malaria—a disease that had people dropping like flies back then. As a DIY cure, the group adopted a strict vegetarian diet and prayed to the nine emperor gods—which somehow worked. Since then, a celebration has been held in honor of the gods (and the vegetarian diet) that helped them pull through. Now, more than forty shrines around the island partake in the festival for nine full days beginning on the first day of the ninth Chinese lunar month (October).

Why the Bloody Face Holes?

Of course they could just pour a little Hennessy on the ground to thank the gods, but in Phuket that won't do. Self-mutilation is thought to invoke the nine gods, so devotees ream objects through their cheeks—such as skewers, horns, umbrellas, arrows, and rods—that'll make your septum ring look like child's play. Other methods of getting in good with the gods include fire walking, tongue slashing, and climbing a giant tower dotted with razor blades. A third of Phuket's population is Thai Chinese, meaning the celebration has lots of participants, so there will be blood.

Rules of the Game

During the festival, people must abstain from alcohol, sex, and meat. Participants must stay as clean as possible (minus the blood?), and pregnant or menstruating women cannot attend (not the right type of blood, perhaps?). Fireworks are fairly common and not regulated, so onlookers should have their heads on a swivel to avoid losing an eye—though that wouldn't be the goriest thing to happen during the fest.

Worked Up an Appetite?

You will absolutely spend the day wondering how the revelers—with grapefruit-sized holes in their cheeks—can ever eat again. If you get hungry during these thoughts, many great dishes are served at the fest. Stalls around the island offer vegetarian versions of classic dishes—swapping out meat with soy- and wheat-based proteins and other alternatives. Look for little yellow flags with red writing to distinguish the meat from the wheat.

MUSIC VENUES FIVE WAYS IN SAIGON (VIETNAM)

Sitting around the hostel with your trusty guitar and a new group of strangers-turned-jam-buddies is a requisite on any trip abroad, but getting out on the town to listen to some local tunes is an equally good way to bond. From big concert venues to intimate gatherings, Saigon's music scene is worth a listen no matter what you're into.

Metal Heads

The name Rock Fan Club may conjure up images of people playing Guitar Hero in unison, but this spot legit rocks out. Sure, you'll get some pop-rock bands on the stage, and every now and again somebody will do a Tool cover, but most performers here are local rock bands that range in genre from alternative to metal. The venue is your typical concert hall, and the sound system is top-notch. Smoking is still legal

inside, so you'll leave RFC with a second-hand-smoke rasp that'll fare well for your Screamo career.

Jazzy Jonesers

Sax n Art Jazz Club is owned by a Vietnam-ese saxophonist, so you know this shit's gonna be good. A warm-up band hits the indigo-lit stage at nine p.m., before owner Tran Manh Tuan and his band headline the performance with smooth jazz tunes. A $5 cover gets you in for a night of nondebauch-erous fun in the center of Ho Chi Minh.

Soul Seekers

Yoko Cafe—yes, *that* Yoko—features a grab bag of musical genres, great for those days when you just can't figure out what you want. The atmosphere is den-like, with portraits of icons such as James Brown, Jim Morrison, and (of course) John Lennon strewn about. Musicians set up in the dimly lit corner to do their thang nightly, from shortly after nine p.m. until late.

Low-Key Listening

Not-a-Bar is not a bar. Rather, it's a funky two-floor venue where musicians come to jam in a setting that's the type of romantic we backpackers can get behind. Bring that well-worn guitar for Acoustic Open Mic Nights on Tuesdays, sit back with one of Not-a-Bar's thirty beers and watch live music on Wednesdays, and chill to DJ-spun vibes all other days of the week.

OTP Tip

For a weird take on Western, Seventeen Saloon is a quirky mix of country—complete with cowboy regalia adorning the walls—and an in-house Filipino band that plays cover-classics from Ricky Martin, Guns N' Roses, and similar superstars plucked right out of the Wild Wild West.

Karaoke Creeps

Are you the type that feels deep pleasure when other people fail? Then popping into one of the hundreds of karaoke bars across Vietnam with a group of hostel friends will be the time of your life. The songbooks at most of them are fairly outdated, and you will watch people struggle with lyrics they read off a moving screen, likely against the backdrop of scenic photos from different locales in Vietnam. Your ears will hate you, but your fail-loving heart will be full. We wouldn't attempt singing anything unless several rounds of good liquor are involved.

OTP Tip

While many karaoke bars are just for fun, some are run as a business to lure dumbass foreigners. The scenario is usually like this: a bar manager asks your group if you'd like to have a few ladies in your room, and you feel awkward saying no. You order some drinks, then some snacks, and next thing you know, those ladies and the intimidating dudes that showed up seemingly out of nowhere won't let you leave until you've paid your $500 bar tab plus tips. Best way to avoid this is to get a price quote prior to the singsong fest.

Club Kids

The popular club for the backpacking crowd is Apocalypse Now, where the tunes that move you will range from eighties throwbacks to indiscernible house. You can rage there until four a.m. in a sea of "working girls," or move on to Lush for some hip-hop, Republic Club for EDM, or MGM Club—a four-story venue where fist-pumping to techno is of prime impor-tance. You have to promise us one thing,

okay? Do not go to the Hard Rock Cafe at any cost. Sure, you will find a DJ there on weekends, but please, save your visit to Hard Rock for when Aunt Linda drags you to Vegas.

OTP Tip
If you need to keep the dancing going until sunrise, Crazy Buffalo is open twenty-four hours, so you can beat your eardrums until their ringing feels like the new norm.

Water Puppets?

Not a live music show per se, but a culturally important form of entertainment nonetheless. In Vietnam, water-puppet theater has been a staple of the culture as a storytelling technique since the eleventh century. The performance takes place around a pool of water that is set up as a stage with puppeteers in the back controlling thirty-pound carved wooden puppets rooted in the water. The spectacle is accompanied by a classic Vietnamese orchestra featuring cymbals, horns, gongs, and bamboo flutes. The most popular places to get your fill of water puppets are Golden Dragon Water Puppet Theater in Ho Chi Minh City and Thang Long in Hanoi.

RAINFOREST MUSIC FESTIVAL (BORNEO)

The Rainforest Music Festival is not a trippin'-on-acid-in-the-jungle type party. It's more a one-of-a-kind cultural experience. This three-day event, held in either July or August and located right in the thick of the forest, has taken over Sarawak Cultural Village on the island of Borneo for more than twenty years, attracting music-loving travelers from around the world. It won't be anything like Coachella, but we guarantee you'll have a great time anyway.

What to Expect

A three-day pass is about $80 and is well worth it for the amount of entertainment at your fingertips. The performers are carefully curated to include more than a handful from Sarawak, which is a nice way to promote culturally significant music—a percussion-heavy style with a lot of gongs, coconut shells, and bamboo instruments. The balance of musical acts, gathered from across the globe, will include Balkan bands, groups from various parts of Africa, some European artists, and folk performers from the States. The mix of sounds is spread across several stages in and around the village. Some international bands collaborate, producing fusion music like you've never heard (think Chinese/African funk), and after-hours DJs spin into the night when you've absorbed all the cultural jams and are ready to dance.

OTP Tip

Are you an aspiring club promoter? Your parents would be so proud! You can hone your skills here, as the festival requires the efforts of more than a hundred volunteers per year to help organize the event, run traffic control, interact with performers and media, help set up instruments, and other tasks the organizers describe as "schlepping" —which, let's be honest, is a valuable skill to learn if you plan to get any job in the real world.

Getting into the Groove

The festival is all about creating an immersive experience. Musicians conduct various workshops that focus on learning new instruments and traditional dances. The Rainforest World Crafts Bazaar, which takes place in conjunction with the musicaal portion of the programming, features local artisans skilled in traditional weaving techniques, woodcarving, cloth making, and more—all of which you can learn to do yourself. We usually leave festivals missing a few shoes and brain cells. However, you can depart from the Rainforest Music Festival with handmade souvenirs!

The Grounds

When you want to take a break from the beats (re-entry to the festival is all good as long as you don't lose your wristband), the surrounding jungle is a welcome respite. This lush part of Borneo is zigzagged with rivers and home to the kind of animals—clouded leopards, proboscis monkeys, pythons, and giant leatherback sea turtles, to name a few—you only see on *Planet Earth*. Several giant things can only be found in Sarawak: the rafflesia (the world's biggest flower) and the tualang (the world's tallest tropical tree). The region is also known for its giant cockroaches, which we hope don't grace your path as you're dancing the night away.

OTP Tip
There is a campsite within a stone's throw of the fest—right at the foot of Mount Santubong—where two- to three-person tents can be rented for about 18 bucks per night.

MAGIC TATTOO FESTIVAL (THAILAND)

If you thought getting a full sleeve was an out-of-body experience, wait until you've seen an otherwise friendly Thai man lose his shit and become possessed by his own body art. Sak Yant tattoos are in a different class of ink. The monks that stick them into you are said to infuse the tattoos with magic powers—which must be renewed every year at a festival that will make your arm hairs stand. Hold on to your tramp stamps—things are about to get weird.

Possessed at the Fest

Every year, ten thousand people gather at Wat Bang Phra Buddhist temple near Bangkok to witness the Wai Kru festival, the largest of its kind in Thailand. The night prior to the big event, tattoo masters (*ajarns*) and monks apply a thousand tattoos in traditional designs to participants using the stick-and-poke method, which is done with a long, sharpened piece

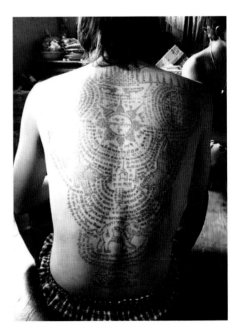

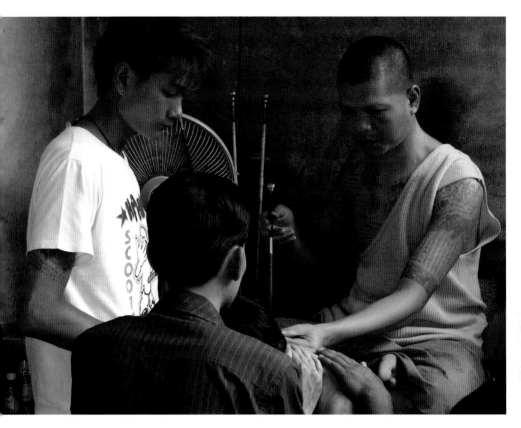

of bamboo and ink made from natural ingredients (like snake venom!). The freshly tattooed revelers descend upon the crowd the next day. Some become overpowered by the magic of their new tattoos and embody the spirit of whatever the tattoos represent—which manifests in men acting like possessed monkeys, tigers, and crocodiles. The zombies rush across the sitting crowd and toward the temple entrance, where security guards rub their ears to bring them back into the now—a method we use on our cats when they get into the nip.

The Devil Is in the Details

Sak Yant tattoos date back to ancient Cambodia, where warriors displayed on their clothing and armor certain symbols meant to guide and protect them in battle.

They eventually got the symbols tattooed onto their bodies, presumably to save money on laundry. Each tattoo pattern—which is sometimes done freehand, although you would never know it by how intricate it appears—has its own special meaning. The three "master yants" are designs reserved for first-time Sak Yant-ers, while those who return for multiple tattoos are given a broader choice that includes tigers and sacred geometry.

Hah Taew

A design that features five vertical lines of text that were composed by a monk in 1296. Each line, from left to right, represents a separate magical spell with specific intentions to prevent unjust punishments, cast off bad fortune, prevent black magic, bring good fortune, and (finally) attract the opposite sex—which would suck if you are gay.

Gao Yord

The basic structure of this revered design represents the nine peaks of Mount Meru (the mountain of the gods) and features the nine Buddhas—which may be represented in ancient-script Khom at the base. The interior of the design is filled with a patchwork of intricate squares, each representing spells that protect you from everything from accidents to violent attacks and grant you the will to fight the good fight.

Paed Tidt

If you're a backpacker (and we know you are), be aware that this design—which consists of eight points—protects those whose body it graces from evil in every direction they travel. The mantras written inside the concentric circles should be recited when embarking on long journeys.

Tattoo, Too

Pretending to be possessed by spirits as a foreigner is likely looked down upon, but you too can get a tattoo. It is quite possible that foreigners have been getting Sak Yant tattoos for decades, but when Angelina Jolie got the Hah Taew on her back in 2003 (followed by a whole bunch of other designs), she opened the floodgates for Westerners looking to tap into some of that holy ink. You have a few options when it comes to getting your own Sak Yant tattoo. The cheapest (but also kind of risky due to unscrupulous needle hygiene—ahem, HIV) is to be found at the Wat Bang Phra temple, where the festival is held. Here, you will purchase offerings at the entrance and give them to the monks inside—who are bustin' out the tats fast to accommodate the long lines of people waiting their turn. Your donation

of time he spends with you. He will ask you about your life, the two of you will decide on the design and placement that works best for your particular journey, and you will walk out with a tattoo that has a deep personal meaning. If you want Angie's guy (Ajarn Noo Kanpai, who did her shoulder piece in fifteen minutes flat!), it'll cost you about $1,000.

(throw a 100 baht in the bucket for good measure) is the price of your tattoo. The monk will pick the design of your tat if you don't speak Thai and put it on your back if you don't specify otherwise. The entire process, even if the monk chooses a larger tattoo, will be lightning fast, be super precise, and hurt like hell. Alternatively, you can find an *ajarn* to ink you up. Bring a translator, as the higher price of getting inked by a master is justified by the length

OTP Tip

You must follow certain rules for twenty-four hours prior to getting a Sak Yant tattoo, some of which prohibit you from consuming gourds of any kind (pumpkin pie pretattoo is out of the question), touching women who are on their periods, ducking under clotheslines, and eating leftovers (the horror!).

Sex and Partying

THROWING A MASSIVE NUMBER OF BACKPACKERS INTO A HOT, sweaty place can only result in one thing (and you will be carrying plenty of condoms so that it doesn't result in the other thing). In other words, Southeast Asia is teeming with opportunities to hook up and party. OG full moon parties are in full effect every month in Thailand, and Cambodia is starting to get in on the action, too. Entire islands (looking at you, Gili T) are dedicated to the art of the party. From midnight beach ragers, to booze-cruisin', to bars, clubs, and festivals, parties here come in every flavor. While good manners (limit that PDA) and morals (sex trafficking is a thing) should be upheld, a party can be had at the drop of a baht.

RED LIGHTS! CAMERA! ACTION! (THAILAND)

Adult entertainment in Bangkok, and other parts of Thailand, is the kind of stuff Vegas can only dream of. Many destinations in Southeast Asia have one (or zero) red light districts, but Thailand is home to a handful, each as fiery red as they come. This isn't Amsterdam's window-shopping experience, either. Thailand's sex scene is bright, in your face, and intoxicating—making you almost forget that prostitution is technically illegal in the country. With this much sex, things do get shady in all sorts of ways. Here is what you need to know to handle the adult action without feeding its dark underbelly of exploitation.

Districts

Prostitution has not always been illegal. Brothels in Bangkok—once a popular trading route—have existed since the 1300s, when men came from far and wide to get their rocks off. During the American War (known to Americans as the Vietnam War; see page 179), "girly" bars popped up to service American soldiers and have remained an important source of income for women in the region ever since (even after an official law banning the practice was put on the books in 1960). Now the city is aglow with a number of red-light districts, some strewn together in the popular city center and others thriving in nearby locales. Soi Cowboy is loaded with more than thirty neon-lit bars where anything goes, and Soi Twilight is a paradise for gay men. Nana Plaza is a one-stop shop where you can watch shows of the naked variety, dance a while, and get laid, all in the comfort of a single three-story complex. Patpong is a remnant of war-era red-light districts near Silom, where things can get as freaky as you want at Barbar Fetish Club or cheap and fun at Thigh Bar. The resort town of Pattaya, about sixty miles from Bangkok, is well known for its sex scene. Sex workers spill out onto the main street, hoping to lure a horny dude into the bar for "lady drinks" and whatever ensues thereafter. Pattaya is known for its ping-pong shows, rather fascinating displays of vaginal acrobatics.

How to Score

Looking for sex workers in the States may send you to the dark corners of the internet, but here, just walking into a bar can put you right in the thick of it. Merely looking at a woman will signal her to approach. It is customary to buy her a drink, chat for a while, and then negotiate the night's activities—which will be either a "short" time (one bang and you're done) or a "long" time (she stays with you the entire night). Prices vary, but budgeting $60-100 for the night should work out fine. The woman is employed by the bar and must pay the *masaman* (not quite a pimp, more of a manager) for the time she is absent from her post. Also, she gets half of what you pay for her drinks, and the number of drinks you buy is a reflection of her ability to bring the bar money.

OTP Tip

If you're planning to take someone home for any duration of time, make sure wherever you're staying allows guests. Otherwise, it's a no go.

Ladyboys

Transwomen—known as *kathoeys* (or "third gender") and often referred to as ladyboys—come to Thailand from other Southeast Asian countries because they are more accepted there (in a sense) and can find work in prostitution, onstage entertainment, and beauty salons. Transmen aren't a tourist attraction in Thailand, but younger generations of transmen have begun living more visibly in recent years. While Americans argue over which bathroom people can use, Thais of all gender identities continue to be the life of the party. Certain bars (particularly those in Nana Plaza and Pattaya) feature ladyboys, some of whom are strictly onstage entertainers, while others are willing to take it offstage. All the same payment and etiquette rules apply.

Don't Be a Dick

The pull of red-light districts is magnetic— we get it. You may not be from a place where sex is so readily available, and the idea of boning someone who's a ten (when you're a woeful five) is exciting. We can tell you until we're blue in the face to be mindful in your pursuits—still, spotting a trafficked woman is not easy. Bangkok's bright lights and exposure to tourists bring the watchful eye of the government, which is currently trying to shake the stereotype that Thailand is only about cheap thrills. However, more remote cities (in Thailand and beyond) remain relatively hidden from public view and protection, which means that if you go looking for sex there, you'll likely find practices we hope you will be too morally outraged to support.

KHAO SAN ROAD:
THE BACKPACKER'S MAIN DRAG

One of the first destinations you will likely visit in Thailand is Bangkok's Khao San Road, where backpackers have swarmed for decades to hang at the dive bars, lively clubs, and tasty food joints. Get the most out of the street by . . .

EATING
Promise us that if it's your first time here, you won't go for the Western options (no pizza for you!). Instead, hit up the street vendors for some spring rolls, bugs, seafood, curries, and things on sticks you won't get in the States. Skip the pad thai—it's watered down with soy sauce for backpackers who can't tell the difference between it and what Thais consider the proper version of the dish.

DRINKING
First lay down some roots at Brick Bar, where the drinks are cheap, the live band is cheerful, and you'll likely pick up a few other people to party with later. Take your new friends to Hippie De Bar, a little hop off the main drag where throwback jams will get you in the mood to dance or just chill on the outdoor patio with cocktail in hand. Need a bucket of booze to really amp up the night? Oxxi's Place has got your back.

PARTYING
When it's time to go to da' club, hit up The Club—a three-story backpacker haunt that features a wide range of DJs, laser light shows, and plenty of room to dance. A fan of hip-hop? Lava Gold Club sits right in the middle of the road—you'll have to go down a few steps to get to its red-lit core.

PARTY ON GILI T (INDONESIA)

The Gili Islands—three distinct land masses with their own personalities—float right near Lombok, and party people flock to Gili Trawangan, affectionately known as "Gili T." Here, the kind of sand and water you're looking for in Bali (and may or may not find) is amplified by thrice-a-week parties, and sometimes enhanced by a good dose of shrooms. Want in? Take a fast ferry from Sanur port to Gili T for the party of a lifetime.

Pre-Party

Gili Beach Bum Hostel is the only one of its kind in the area, and its Lava Bar is pre-party central that you can hit whether or not you're staying at the hostel, which also has a rooftop that's great for more low-key lounging. Here, you can meet like-minded partiers (sometimes in costumes, depending on the night) and hit other local pre-party bars, such as Jiggy Jig, known for its dirt-cheap happy hour,

where a drinking challenge will help you get started. The norm is having drinks near the beach until sunset, then raging into the night.

Party x 3

When a place has a party schedule—with three big-ass shindigs scheduled each week—you know things are going to get wild. Gili T is known for its (technically illegal) shrooms, and getting some is an easy way to add a little vibrancy to the island's poppin' nightlife. Start the week off right with a Monday-night party at Blue Marlin's, where dancing in your swimwear goes late. Wednesdays are all about the Irish bar Tir Na Nog; the local DJ spins

tunes that turn out a massive crowd of partygoers splayed across the open-air bar. On off nights, Tir hosts silent discos to help people chill out. On Fridays, Rudy's rages until three a.m. with packed beach-side parties, and while a little seedy on drinks (some have poisoned partiers with methanol, so maybe pre-party before drinking here), Rudy's can point you to some solid shrooms.

OTP Tip
Cops rarely travel here from the mainland. That fact should make you breathe a little easier if you happen to have consumed a few illegal substances. However, it shouldn't turn you into a law-breaking a-hole who's wielding broken beer bottles or being belligerent—the cops will figure out a way to find you if that becomes the case.

Rinse and Repeat
Aside from its party ethic, one of the best things about Gili T is its lack of motor vehicles—which means your wretched hangover will not be stoked by the sound and smell of a revving engine. The entire island takes calculated rests between parties, and you should, too. If your legs work, hop on a bike; if not, grab a *kalesa* (a horse-drawn carriage) and head to the main drag to procure refreshing fruit, hearty hangover-curing breakfast options, and massages. Then it's back to the beach for a swim and to push the party restart button.

OTP Tip
If you want the full party experience, avoid coming during Ramadan, as the island gets a little less raucous and a lot more religious during that time.

BACKPACKER BEACH PARTY (VIETNAM)

Nightlife in Vietnam technically has a midnight curfew, and although it's rarely enforced, random nights occasionally shut down early. This is the farthest from the truth in beach town Nha Trang, where the revelry goes until you have to beg it to stop. Many backpackers flock here for the party scene, and equally for the three-mile crescent of beach, where a spattering of islands jet out of the water.

Beach Boozin'

Get at least two tanning hours under your belt (maybe with a bucket or two of jungle juice) before hitting the bar-to-beach scene. Head into the Louisiane Brewhouse for a flight of any beer varieties you'd like to sample, then grab a few full-sizers and take them to the beach. Sailing Club is another poppin' spot where partygoers—fueled by DJ sets—spew out onto the beach, booze in hand, drunkenly gathering around a bonfire that burns into the wee hours of the morning.

OTP Tip
Keep a close eye on your bucket (or cocktail if you're classy). Drink spiking is on the up here, and while getting drunk may be your goal of the day, being robbed is likely not.

Booze Cruisin'

Those tiny islands in the water are accessible by boat—and not just any boat, but by vessels running booze cruises that feature seafood-centric meals and live music and will ferry you around the South China Sea until you're good and tipsy. Cheapo tour company Funky Monkey offers an early pickup (8:30 a.m.), a live boy band, snorkeling, a floating bar, and plenty of drinking games—all for about $8 plus the cost of drinks. You'll be back at the hostel by 4:45 p.m. and, after a well-deserved nap, be ready to rinse and repeat that beach-boozin' action. Does the mere thought of

drinking while boating make you seasick? Meet Booze Cruise, a local bar with a formidable happy hour, debaucherous atmosphere, and cheap-as-dirt beers (about 80 cents each).

Postparty

You may be used to chugging coconut water, eating a greasy breakfast, or partaking of hair-of-the-dog remedies to cure that hangover. However, this island's miracle solution to a late night of drinking is a dirty, dirty cleansing mud bath. The town boasts three thermal baths, and for about 10 bucks you can spend an entire day at I-Resort, steaming out those brewsky remnants and playing in the mud to calm your woes.

FAMOUS FULL MOON PARTIES (THAILAND)

The rumored origin of the full moon party was a small gathering on the beach in honor of a hippie traveler's birthday. However the ritual started, a whole bunch of Aussies and backpackers took the reins and made it about puking in the same buckets from which they got drunk. Approximately forty thousand partygoers ferry to the island of Koh Phangan every time the moon is round, and rave all night in various states of fucked-up-ness.

Buckets of Drinks

Whatever Solo cups can do, buckets can do better. Thai booze buckets, which can be purchased from beachside stands (bring lots of small bills), contain a varied magic mixture typically consisting of SangSom rum, Coca-Cola, and Thai Red Bull (which goes by the brand name Krating Daeng and was the inspiration for the Red Bull you live on back home) to keep your heart pumping all night. Bucket-binge wisely, because Krating Daeng packs significantly more punch than the Western version. Purchasing the bulk bucket spares you travel time to

OTP Tip

Now that you're nice and relaxed, you may feel like confessing your sins. While you won't find a Catholic priest anywhere in town to absolve all that morning-after guilt, what you will find is a giant white Buddha behind the Long Son Pagoda temple. You will have to hike up 180 steps to tell that guy all of your wrongs, but we promise he'll do his best to make it right.

and some reports say that undercover cops are among the party crowd—sometimes cracking down, sometimes looking for a bribe to squash the threat of taking you to prison.

Never-Ending Neon

Unless you're a mainstay on the Northern California party circuit, it's not every day you can replace most of your clothes with neon paint. At this party, if you're not covered in neon, you're not doing it right. Bring your neon workout shorts, tights, and bras, find some paint in town, and go full *Rambo* on yourself—get a friend/friendly stranger to do your backside—and accent everything with a few glow sticks (which tend to sell out, so plan accordingly).

To Sleep or Not to Sleep?

the bar; no interruptions means more time for dancing. The party's atmosphere—with its calming ocean waves, white sand, swaying palm trees, and neon bodies gyrating to the beats—seems conducive to trippin' balls. As such, many use the bucket drink as a chaser for Molly and her friends. Local police are not absent,

Getting to the island several nights before the full moon is ideal. Hostels in Haad Rin are fairly cheap (between $10 and $20 per night), but prices begin to creep up (by as much as threefold) closer to party time.

You may or may not be sleeping while you're there, but you sure as hell don't want to lug your backpack onto the beach. Alternatively, you can book accommodations in advance on Airbnb—some of which may have a multiday minimum—to get a few good nights in before the party. Some people choose to stay on neighboring island Koh Tao, accessible by ferry.

OTP Tip
Are your moon cycles out of whack? Worry not! You can hit up a half-moon party or a black-moon party, which take place during different phases of the moon. This island is a party almost any time of the month.

CAMBODIA'S GOT FULL MOONS, TOO

If Koh Phangan is too normie for you, Cambodia's Sihanoukville is an emerging party island where full moon fests are just getting into full swing. Serendipity Beach features tiny bars that will get you pre-party tipsy during daytime; from there, the crowd moves downstream to Ochheuteal Beach, where all-night dance parties are the norm. Sessions is a great bar to get things started, and JJ's Playground urges you to get wasted (its six a.m. closing time ensures that you do).

WHITE PARTY: THE BEST GAY FEST IN ASIA (THAILAND)

The debate about where to spend New Year's Eve always revolves around NYC (where the ball will drop, every year, as it did the last year, and people will piss themselves in the cold waiting for it to happen) and Australia (because they get it first, and it's summer). Both of those destinations take a back seat to Bangkok, however, where the White Party (aka the mother of all gay-stravaganzas) goes down for three days to ring in the new year with a bang or two.

The Sights

Started in 2015, WPBKK attracts more than fourteen thousand partygoers every year. The playgrounds are at Bangkok's big-ass shopping mall, Central World, where stages are set up for different nights, culminating in a rager on New Year's Eve at which most people just sport tighty-whities to participate in the evening's theme. Every year, the organizers come up with a different theme for the pre-parties; festgoers in years past have been inspired to dress up as intergalactic space cowboys or strapping young military lads—which is an impressive feat considering the lack of material, such as shirts and pants, these boys are working with. If you follow any famed Thai hotties on Instagram, you will spot them here. While gay men make up most of the party demographic, people of all sexual orientations and genders are welcome to attend.

The Sounds

The venue is decked out in strobing lights with a ceiling centerpiece that resembles the *Starship Enterprise* (gay me up, Scottie!) with sounds to match. Top DJs from across Asia, and some imports, spin ass-shaking house all night to make sure

you're good and sweaty in the few clothes you'll be wearing. The sound system (and the rest of the party haps) is set up by Cloud 9 Inc., one of the best concert companies in Thailand. Live musicians (also drag queens) will take the stage from time to time to break up the EDM. Plus, the event donates a portion of its proceeds to support the gay-rights and health organization TestBKK's "Suck, F*#k, Test, Repeat" campaign, which advocates for HIV testing in the city, so you can feel good about bumpin' uglies on the dance floor.

OTP Tip
While getting freaky on the party grounds is totally acceptable, keep it to hand-holding while out in the city. Out and proud is the best way to be, but Thailand is still stingy—regardless of sexual orientation—about PDA.

The Hangover
Three days of partying is not going to fix itself overnight. Luckily, Bangkok is home to many gay saunas and massage parlors, where happy endings can be found by the dozens but legit relaxation is also on the menu. Check out the gay saunas in the Silom area to help that hangover along. If you're more committed to spending the whole day in a vegetative state, head out to the acclaimed gay beaches on the island of Koh Samet (about a four-hour drive from Bangkok), where the atmosphere is laid back and the boys are as hot as those at the White Party (if you can remember anything from it, that is).

MALAYSIA: WHERE GAY IS NOT OKAY

Malaysia is a country where religion is law, and the Muslim faith (which a majority of the population practices devoutly) places a high sin tax on being anything but heterosexual and cisgendered. Currently, an antisodomy law is in place in the country, which means that being queer—or even being suspected of it—is punishable by a twenty-year prison sentence. While these types of laws exist around the world (including in more than a handful of US states), most governments do not actively enforce them. However, antigay sentiments in Malaysia are fueled by the media, putting everybody at risk for violence. In 2018, the Malaysian newspaper *Sinar Harian* published the following checklist, translated from Malay, to help its readers identify gay and lesbian people (the translation is reprinted here verbatim):

What Are the Features of LGBT?

The characteristics of gay people (men) include:
- wearing tight clothes to show off six packs
- frequent gyms not to work out, but to admire other men
- love their siblings
- like growing beard and mustache
- like to wear branded clothes
- for gay men in the same position [sic], they like to see handsome men. Their eyes light up when they see handsome men.

For lesbians:
- despise and belittle men
- prefer to be alone
- intense jealousy
- tend to hug each other and hold hands when walking.

Although local activists have fought against the country's outward discrimination against the LGBTQ community, the antigay sentiments published in *Sinar Harian* have devastating implications. Can you wear a V-neck to the gym without raising suspicion? Can a woman hug her sister in public without being penalized? How deep can this rabbit hole go?

BEER HUNTING IN CAMBODIA

When temps are at 105, a cold one feels like a lifesaver. Cambodia is a great place to explore local beers that aren't too watery and carry plenty of bite. Cambodians are proud of their national adult beverages, and a craft-beer scene has been brewing for a few years. Here, taxes and regulations on alcohol are lenient, making the country a prime place for that golden beverage. Take the day off from trying to find your spiritual self in the country's temples and answer to an even higher power. The beer gods await!

Beers for Years

If you thought $2 PBRs were a steal, you'll be pleasantly surprised to learn that drinking the brown water in Cambodia won't cost you more than $0.50 to $1.00 a pop. All Khmer beers are distinctly branded with proud nationalistic logos, with the most popular being Angkor Premium—a

lager named after the famed temples near Siem Reap. This one, widely available on tap, is a popular accompaniment to spicy noodle dishes. Cambodia Lager, another light lager that's available in cans at street-food stalls, pairs well with a lunchtime Khmer ham sandwich. If stouts are more your thing, Cambodia's got your back. Angkor Premium's stout counterpart, found mostly in corner stores, is a thick, chocolaty beverage with enough ABV (8 percent) to give you a good buzz. A well-designed container doesn't always mean a great beer, but Klang—available as either a pale lager or a heftier stout—comes only in cans that sport a badass black-elephant logo, making for an aesthetically pleasing (and tasty) experience. Having a beer with every meal, and taking a few for the road at your local convenience store, is a great way to spend the day, or week, in Cambodia.

OTP Tip

It might strike you as odd, but many Cambodians drink their beer over ice—which they do not to cool it down, but to dilute it. When you're drinking with locals, whenever they propose a toast, they will shout, "Ha-sip pea-roi," or the more dangerous "Moi-roi pea-roi." That means you will have to chug either half your beer or the whole thing, respectively. If you remember what chugging this much beer in college felt like, perhaps it's best that you, too, crack some cubes into your brew.

Breweries, Bro

Drinking Angkor until you can't feel your limbs is fine and dandy—and many a backpacker ends up facedown in the sand after such shenanigans. But if your tastes tend toward the fancier, know that

tracking down craft beers in Southeast Asia is tough but not impossible. For a sit-down beer-garden atmosphere in Phnom Penh, visit American-run, hard-to-find Botanico, where up to ten styles of expertly crafted beer can be enjoyed for $3.50 each in the brewery's expansive yard. For street-side drinking, at Siem Reap Brewpub you can people-watch as you recline on comfy chairs under umbrellas while sipping on a proper IPA—or a beer cocktail if you need a little fruit in your brew. We're big fans of playing dangerous games like darts when we're beer-drunk, and the best place to hit an unsuspecting stranger in the ear with a sharp flying object is Hops Brewery (Phnom Penh), where outdoor couches will cradle your ass after $8 flights of four (very decent) pours bring you to the ground.

OTP Tip

Pub Street is the popular tourist-bar epicenter in Siem Reap. It's fun for a once-over but becomes a little nauseating when it's an every-night affair. No need to ask where Pub Street is; it will find you.

Dance Your Drunk Away

Sauced up on all that Khmer beer and now all you want to do is dance? The two popular clubs in Phnom Penh are Pontoon and Heart of Darkness, which are luckily across the street from each other so you don't have to stumble too far to get double the action. Speaking of which, both are known for their abundance of prostitutes—some on duty and some off. If you prefer shaking your beer-drunk ass to some trance, head to True Face Club, where the locals go to party and the tourists aren't creepin' for sex. Don't forget to hit the convenience store on your way back to the hostel for some brewskies—just for the sake of congruence.

OTP Tip

If you find yourself sloppy and hangry, street carts in Cambodia stay open fairly late (until about one a.m. to three a.m.) and serve everything from tacos to traditional Khmer fare like bobor—a hearty chicken and rice soup that will make you feel like your grandma is holding your hand as you walk back to your hostel.

SUNSETS AND ISLAND COCKTAILS (INDONESIA)

When you're surrounded by lush forests, coral reefs, and the kind of beaches that make you want to quit your day job, guzzling down a six-pack of Natty Ice and waking up near a pile of *maybe* your own clothes just won't do. Cocktails—particularly margaritas—are the right way to roll in Bali and Lombok, where expert mixologists can blend the islands' best fruit into something sassy to sip during that beautiful sunset. Here are five can't-miss beach bars in Bali and Lombok where the sunset is just as much of an attraction as the booze.

La Plancha (Bali)

This spot is not quite beachfront—it is just straight-up on the beach. Grab one of La Plancha's colorful beanbags, nudge it under a mismatched umbrella, and graciously flag down a Hawaiian-shirt-clad staff member to bring you something cold and a few tapas. Melt into the sand as the sun graces the horizon of Seminyak, Bali's most famous beach.

Old Man's (Bali)

We can say with confidence that elderly men and dirty booze definitely mix, particularly at Old Man's—a no-frills lounge and local party spot in Canggu. Head down on a Wednesday when the margaritas are as dirty as the disco and the beer pong is in full swing. The place also serves frozen drinks if you need to knock down your internal temp from blazin' the dance floor.

La Laguna (Bali)

Pounding liquor while on an unstable bridge is usually a no-no, but at La Laguna we recommend breaking that rule. Have a seat, and hang your feet over the edge of the bar's famed bamboo bridge. It extends into the water over Berawa Beach, making this rickety-chic bar the place to hold an island cocktail in one hand and take snapshots with the other hand of yourself doing so—with the pink-and-purple sunset in the background.

Potato Head Beach Club (Bali)

The mixologists here create cocktails from fresh local fruit juices. To make it to sunset, you'll have to move slowly through the menu of signature drinks. The beachfront bar pours into an infinity pool overlooking the Indian Ocean, which explodes in shades of red come dusk. Get here around lunchtime, keep your peepers propped open until sunset, and enjoy the world-class music that often accompanies the club's sultry vibes. There's also a gelato shack to keep your mouth busy between drinks.

Hotel Ombak Sunset (Lombok)

Located in the Gili Islands, this resort is home to a swing set, sitting right in the water, that has been made famous on Instagram. You'll need to make a friend or two to get that from-behind shot that level-one Bali visitors covet. If you're more like us, you'll let the kids have their swing and you'll plop on the beach instead—where the big boys are having their cocktails from 6:30 to 7:30 p.m. nightly.

OTP Tip

Don't forget to cruise along Balangan Beach, hit a *warung* (a small beach shack with snacks), and sip on some cold Bintangs (local beers) to soak up the sun.

DETOX IN NUSA PENIDA

Did you overbooze it in Bali? Good news! You can escape to nearby Nusa Penida, where nightlife is nonexistent and the island's spectacular daytime activities will sober you right up. Nusa Penida boasts some of the most breathtaking views in the region—complete with a land formation that looks as if a tyrannosaurus rex is lying on his (her?) side in the crystalline waters. To get that last bit of liquor out of your pores, Nusa Penida offers an ass-kicking hike down to Seganing Falls on a trail that snakes high into the cliffs. You are only protected from falling into the ocean by a rickety fence. To reward yourself for all that hard work, head to Atuh Beach or Crystal Bay Beach, where the white sand and bright turquoise waters will not disappoint. The island is a great spot for snorkeling, particularly if you'd like to get face-to-face with manta rays, which you can watch swimming from Manta Ray Viewpoint. To cap off the trip, stay in one of the island's three famed treehouses ($40 per night), popularized by Instagrammers for their dynamic views of land, sky, and sea. In the morning, you'll be ready for the next leg of your adventure.

HIGH TIMES IN VANG VIENG (LAOS)

Every backpacker in the mid-aughts heard about Vang Vieng—which was the city equivalent of that one girl in college who couldn't leave her dorm without a puke bucket in lieu of a handbag. Many parts of Southeast Asia are notoriously tough on drugs, but this Laotian city used to let it all hang out. Its main river throughway became a place where backpackers came for a day, stayed for a week, and in a month's time (and thirty days of doing opium later) had transformed into what was known as a "river rat." Vang Vieng is not what it used to be . . . and that's a good thing. You can still get high here in a way that doesn't feel like a never-ending float trip.

Dark History

In the nineties, travelers came to Vang Vieng to get a little high and go tubing down the Nam Song River until the wee hours of the morning. As this laid-back activity became more popular—particularly among Australians, Americans, and Brits—bars sprouted along the river to service the new crowd, which continued to grow in size and collective drug consumption. Things got pretty ugly in Vang Vieng between 2009 and 2011, when backpackers turned the river into a drug-fueled death trap and nearly thirty people partied to their deaths every year. In 2012, the government cracked down on riverside bars—which served as refuel stations for meth and opium—and now allows only four (out of the operational twelve) to be open per day and only until early evening. The famed slide is gone, and the river has a tubing curfew of six p.m. (after which you will pay a small fine for tubing). The place is slowly becoming tamer, but not all that is fun is gone.

Get High

The bars that are still operational—such as Tifalcony Space Bar—serve an entire menu of items: mushroom, opium, and weed shakes, along with bags of weed and joints. At Milan Pizza, you can order from the "happy" menu, which features lightly enhanced shroom shakes, teas, and pizzas; weed-laced omelets, pancakes, soups; and weed-butter-slathered garlic bread. You can also get an opium joint, but we'd stick to that sticky icky.

Lay Low

No matter how sneaky you think you are, do not ever use or buy drugs out in public on the street. You will be busted. The police here operate in a way that has pissed off many a backpacker. They will turn a blind eye when you smoke a joint in a bar (a business that makes money for the local economy). But the moment you step onto the streets and are naive enough to be baited by a kid trying to sell you a joint for $2, you will quickly learn that the kid will make another $2 from the cop he immediately rats you out to when the transaction is complete. Once you're at the police station, that cop will make an additional 600 bucks (the standard fine for *any* amount of weed, or you can take a year-long jail sentence instead) off of you. The government is extra cautious about drug use given how shitty things became when they previously loosened the reins. Just do your drugs at the bar and enjoy the high (quietly) elsewhere.

OTP Tip

When the cottonmouth starts creepin' in, make sure you drink filtered water. The tap will give you the runs once your high wears off—or sooner!

Float Away

Relive the days of pre-shitshow Vang Vieng by taking on the inner tubes. You'll put down a $7 deposit and pay about $6 for renting the tubular tire, then set off on a slightly high adventure down the river—which will take you through the jungle toward some pretty awesome rock formations. If you're not a lazy stoner, hitting the town's majestic limestone caves will be a trippy experience. Each of the three karsts are filled with tunnels, caverns, lagoons, streams, and plenty of spaces to let your feet and imagination run wild.

Managing the Munchies

The eateries in town that aren't connected to Vang Vieng's sordid past actually serve some tasty fare to help keep your munchies at bay. You can grab a quick lunch at Gary's Irish Bar, which opens at nine a.m. and serves a mix of typical greasy Irish food and spicy Lao dishes. For dinner, head to Le Cafe de Paris, where French food—terrines, lots of duck-based dishes, and boeuf bourguignon—will set you back only $13 but will make you feel like the fanciest stoner in town.

PART II

GET YOUR SHIT TOGETHER

Getting from your couch to an unfamiliar airport in Southeast Asia may seem like a daunting task. Just hopping on the nearest flight to Hanoi and letting magic do the rest will leave you sorely underprepared for the bumpy ride to come. In this section, we've laid out how to plan for your adventure, pack efficiently, create a reasonable budget, land the best transportation deals, and get all your docs in order. We also offer a bit more insight into the culture, political climates, health and safety issues, and living arrangements you will encounter in the region so that you can feel fully confident to let go and jump into the wonderful abyss.

Accommodations

IN MOST SOUTHEAST ASIAN COUNTRIES, YOU WILL BE ABLE TO SPLURGE ON SNAZZY digs that would cost you a small fortune per night stateside. However, the old adage "Just because you can doesn't mean you should" is strong when it comes to choosing a place to crash in the region. We know you didn't come here to spa-hop and order room service; you came here to understand a culture that may be different from your own and to meet like-minded travelers who are on a similar journey. Choose a place to lay your head that will also fill it with new experiences.

HOTELS

Your average Ramada-type situation will be less expensive here than back home and will come with all you expect from a cookie-cutter room—a TV, air-conditioning, private bath, and that horrid wall art that doesn't make the room more homey at all, anywhere. You will get the hotel bar, minimal breakfast, an information desk, and, if you're like us, a sense that you have turned into your parents. Hotels are good when cheaper accommodations are booked, or as a "treat yourself" option (in Cambodia, $30 per night almost always guarantees a hotel with a pool), or when you'd like to be antisocial for a day or two, but not as an everyday choice. Note: in many places (Vietnam, for instance), the lines between hotel and hostel (and dump) are very blurry. Check out what you are being offered before making a payment, and know that taxes may not be initially quoted in the price of your room.

GUESTHOUSES

Sometimes a step up from a hostel, sometimes a word that means *hostel*, a guesthouse typically comes with the bare minimum: four walls (one of which may or may not feature a window), a cold-water faucet (you pay extra for hot), and a simple bed. On the fancier end, you may happen upon guesthouses that offer private balconies, less squeaky beds, and a buffet breakfast. Booking online is typically a good idea, but pay ahead for no more than a night or two in case the place is a roach motel upon arrival.

HOSTELS

Like living on campus in college, hostels (which run $5-10 per night in most places) offer dormitory-style accommodations with bunk beds (sometimes crammed together so closely you can smell strangers' morning breath), double rooms (shared with one other person), or private suites (which cost more). Many have communal kitchens and showers, expat staff, and places to play beer pong or passionately discuss politics. This option is great when you're looking for travel buddies, but awful if your main concern in life is personal space—which you should probably reconsider altogether if you're backpacking through Southeast Asia.

HOMESTAYS

Homestays, a whole new adventure in accommodations, are available in larger cities, and are often the only lodging option in remote parts of countries such as Thailand, Cambodia, Laos, and Vietnam. The actual sleeping part will likely be no more than a mattress on the floor in a communal area with a blanket, pillow, and little else. Homestays are a roll of the dice: some places will rent you a spare hammock; others are situated on lush grounds (or islands) where you are welcome to roam and pick fruit. In most every case you will be welcomed as a temp-member of a local family, who will feed you meals (for a little extra cash) that you will rarely find on the tourist trail. Don't be surprised if a squat toilet (you know, a hole in the ground) is the only way to poo, and never forget to take off your shoes when entering the home.

CAMBODIA: RESORTS VS. HOMESTAYS

In Siem Reap (the landing pad for visiting Angkor Wat) and elsewhere throughout Cambodia, high-end resorts and hotels are sprouting up left and right, and you can make one your home for the night for the price of practically peanuts (particularly in the low season, i.e., before November and after March). But note that all these places are owned by foreign investors, which sucks for locals.

First of all, Siem Reap is a poor place, and when you stay in a nice resort located in a poor neighborhood, we guarantee that you will feel like a dick the moment you step outside the hotel and realize how disconnected you are from local culture. Second,

instead of helping the local economy, you're putting profits in the hands of rich foreign investors who couldn't give a shit about hardworking Cambodians.

As a young, broke traveler, staying at a resort that you can actually afford is a great opportunity to feel fancy, so it's understandable to want to experience it for a night or two. But if you want to help the local economy and have a much richer cultural experience, seeking out homestays for most of your trip is key; you'll learn a little Khmer, eat authentic home-cooked meals, and get a chance to connect with a knowledgeable local, not a concierge. Resorts can wait for when you retire in Saint-Tropez.

YOU WILL PAY MORE . . .

- **For air-conditioning.** Just about every part of Southeast Asia, with the exception of hilly northern areas at night, is hot and humid for most of the year. AC is a top commodity, and you'll pay a premium if you can't figure out how to live without it.

- **For a private bath.** We get it, some people like to know for sure that they will not get a fungal foot infection the moment they hop in the shower. Advice? If you don't want to pay more for a private bath, bring some flip-flops and get over it.

- **During festival season.** When everyone is flocking to the same place at the same time for an annual event, the cheapest and closest accommodations book up fast. The worst feeling is planning all your travel only to discover that some wild festival has made it impossible to find an affordable room. Research upcoming events prior to paying for anything.

- **When Australians decide to "go on holiday."** Festivals aren't the only reason every hostel room gets booked at certain times. While it's hard to predict when they will appear, Australians (whom we love dearly) often travel off of their isolated continent in packs of twenty, laying their kangaroo-lovin' heads on every pillow in town. For you, this means upping the price to a single when a shared dormitory is full, or heading to a hotel to steer clear of the "Aussie Aussie Aussie oy oy oy" chant in the middle of the night.

- **In Singapore.** Hostels won't cost you as much as they do in say, London, but this country is more expensive than others in the region, with singles running between $20 and $50 per night.

- **If you don't ask the price first.** Because prices for accommodations fluctuate frequently between low and high seasons, among other reasons, it's hard to know exactly what to expect price-wise any given day—which creates a good opportunity for a tourist trap. Negotiate a firm price first, then settle in.

- **If you book through an agent.** Nobody works for free, and having someone find you a place to sleep is no different. Agents charge a commission, so it's best to book your own spot.

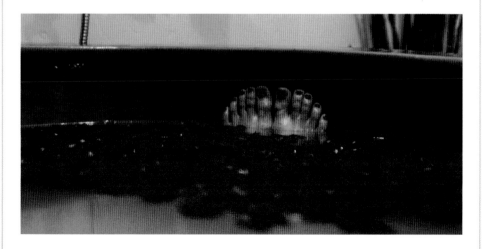

TO B OR NOT TO B?

For the cost of a bunk-bed-packed shared room in NYC, you can get yourself a beachside villa, treehouse, or luxury chateau almost anywhere in Southeast Asia. We almost always advocate staying in hostels or homestays—they're cheap and you meet like-minded travelers—but sometimes you just have to take advantage of the fact that you can finally afford something swankier. Listed here are a few not-so-humble abodes in Southeast Asia that you can Airbnb on the cheap. The prices shown are approximate and fluctuate seasonally.

TREEHOUSE, BALIAN BEACH, INDONESIA ($86 PER NIGHT)

Always wanted a treehouse but the closest you ever got was a pillow fort? Well, you're in luck because you can rent one for a few nights to finally quench your childhood yearnings. Located near Bali's Balian Beach (which is accessible only by a dirt path), this driftwood and bamboo treehouse features two quirky stories, several verandas, a rain-shower room, and a canopy bed. The property has a turquoise-hued pool (which emits a romantic glow at night) and a lush garden with plenty of spots to lounge. The host, Made, constructed the entire thing from the ground up, and he cleans the place with his wife every day. As the cherry on top, you are free to pick whatever fruit you find in the garden, which, depending on the season, can be coconuts, lemons, passion fruit, or papaya.

OTP Tip

When the treehouse is all booked, check out the property's Funky Glass House ($70 per night), which is a gem in its own right. It features arty inlays in the walls, plenty of space to spread out, and an open deck from which a panoramic view of Bali's famous sunsets is a guarantee.

RICE BARN, CHIANG MAI, THAILAND ($62 PER NIGHT)

While a number of rooms (each with a private bath) are available here, the main rice-barn family room is where it's at with wood-paneled walls and rustic finishes like Thai bird sculptures. Windows wrap around the entire sleeping area, which is equipped with a king bed and two bunks and opens onto a balcony overlooking the grounds. There's a pristine swimming pool, a barbecue area, and an expansive indoor/outdoor kitchen. The estate is also home to some nonhumans you can befriend, including dogs, ducks, and sheep. The rice barn is super close to Hang Dong Canyon (known as the *other* Grand Canyon), a cliff-jumping, inner-tube-chilling, beer-drinking getaway where you can spend the whole day.

BEACHSIDE CHALET, SABAH, MALAYSIA ($152 PER NIGHT)

Located at the very tip of Borneo on a cliff where sand meets water, the Hibiscus Villa is the kind of spot you visit to get away from the internet for a bit and replace it with the intense calm of ocean waves. It includes access to a secluded white-sand beach, where you can snorkel while forgetting about the trash-littered tourist spots of weeks past. The spacious sleeping quarters open to a deck that's perched above said beach, the perfect place to finally

start journaling in total isolation about your adventures. This place is run more like a resort than a homestay, but the staff is not all up in your business; they understand the unique chilling opportunity their accommodations provide. People come here to honeymoon; you can come here to be a total sloth, no judgment.

MODERN LUXURY, SIEM REAP, CAMBODIA ($84 PER NIGHT)

The Luxury Gekko Villa is like one of those houses you drool over when looking through architectural magazines. Never thought you could crash at a pad like that? You're wrong. The spacious three-story house is vertically built with a minimalist aesthetic that features two living rooms, four air-conditioned bedrooms, four bathrooms, a sprawling kitchen with a six-person dining table, and an outdoor pool complete with jacuzzi jets! The place accommodates eight people, so share the wealth with friends and you'll only pay, like, $10 bucks per night. On top of everything, the villa is only fifteen minutes away by tuk tuk from the area's famed temple, Angkor Wat.

PRIVATE ISLAND, EL NIDO, PHILIPPINES ($440 PER NIGHT)

Sure, 440 bucks seems pretty steep, but hear us out: you get your own fucking private island that you could split with twelve friends (which, with a base fare, works out to $84 per night). Live like Richard Branson for a week on Brother Island, where (aside from the hosts, who live on the other side) the nearest neighbors are a boat ride away. Although sleeping on the beach hammocks (naked?) is totally acceptable here, indoor accommodations include a two-story house with seven bedrooms and minimal decor. Spend your time playing out "stranded on a desert island" scenarios, snorkeling, getting beach massages from staff, and eating an abundance of home-cooked Filipino food (three meals per day are included, bam!). This is paradise found, and you don't need to be a millionaire to feel like you've really made it (for a week, at least). The best part is that even if the queen of England wanted to book a stay while you were there, her ass would get booted because the island is yours, and only yours, until you leave.

Packing

LESS IS ALWAYS MORE WHEN BACKPACKING TO MULTIPLE DESTINATIONS, ESPECIALLY to places where it's perpetually summer, you can cheaply buy whatever you need, and looking less like a tourist is a big plus. Give your shoulders a stretch and get packin'.

CHOOSING YOUR BACKPACK

In many Southeast Asian countries you will want to look as little like an American tourist as possible. The minute you step foot into a big city such as Bangkok or Phnom Penh, you will be accosted by countless people selling goods and services because Americans are (understandably) seen as wealthy. Not only a touristy red flag, wearing a huge sack on your back is also like pouring salt on the wound—which will become very literal if you choose an uncomfortable backpack that you have to lug around while sweating profusely. Go to a sporting-goods store (even if you end up purchasing on Amazon), where the sales staff will be able to assist you in finding a fit that won't mangle your torso. If you're thinking of shoving as much shit as you can into a bag that is as big as possible, take a step back. You will not need a winter coat, boots, or much of anything else. Go for a smaller pack, and enjoy the freedom of both looking less obnoxious and keeping your vertebrae properly aligned.

WHAT TO PACK

When gearing up for a trip, there are two kinds of people: those who see packing as an exciting step that gets them closer to their dream trip, and those who dread the day they shove their shit into a backpack three hours before their flight. Be the first person, unless you want to be stuck in 120-degree heat with two wool coats and a bunch of random junk. A general rule is to lay out everything you plan to take, pack half of it, and carry a little extra cash to cheaply buy a few things along the way.

Clothing

We could give you a concrete list of how many pairs of shorts, socks, shoes, and shirts you should bring depending on how many days you're planning to spend in each location, but we're not your mom and never want to be. You want to bring two pairs of underwear and one pair of mismatched socks? That's cool. What we can urge you to do is pack really (big emphasis on *really*) light. Because you will spend a lot of time at the beach, two bathing suits is a great idea so that one can dry while you swim in the other—unless you're a fan of UTIs. Hiking is a must in Southeast Asia, and we're sorry to break it to you but those ugly (but breathable!) hiking sandals are golden when the afternoon sun beats down on your already swollen feet. Pack T-shirts you don't mind cutting into tanks when the weather gets unbearable. Rain might start pouring with no warning, and you will bear the sky water without an umbrella—which will not fit in your backpack. Instead, an ultralight waterproof rain jacket will save the day. A scrunchy hat is as great a fashion accessory as it is a sun blocker. Bottom line: pack less, hand-wash more.

Sleep Gear

Keep in mind that your travel probably won't be limited to the round-trip flight from home to your first destination. You did not fly all the damn way to Southeast Asia to just check out one region and bounce. That said, you will find yourself on many buses, ferries, flights, and other rickety forms of transportation, and nothing is more comforting than a good pillow. A standard neck pillow may be too bulky, but an inflatable one is easy to fit into any pack. Earplugs take up a tiny portion of your bag but will save you many sleepless nights.

Bathroom Stuff

One month before you depart, start training yourself to do more with less when it comes to toiletries (aka the bulkiest things to carry). Combo shampoo and conditioners are great space savers, and hair products that serve only one function (like getting rid of flyaways) should just stay home. Invest $10 in a large bottle of Dr. Bronner's, and use it for your hair, body, face, feet,

laundry, and dishes. Wet wipes or baby wipes are versatile little tools you can use to stave off swamp ass and keep your pits feeling fresh.

First Aid

Fill all your prescriptions (ahem, birth control) to last for the duration of the trip, and clearly label each bottle. While drinking filtered water in Southeast Asia is the way to go, you can also pack a few water-purification tablets in case you're in a pinch. You should also bring Band-Aids, allergy meds, and whatever you take to make your hangovers feel a little less brutal.

Safety Gear

Some guidebooks will tell you to bring a money belt, and while they're not wrong, we think you can figure out how to keep your cash and passport safe without looking like a total paranoid weirdo. Do, however, bring a padlock. Some hostels in the region are not very secure, but many provide lockers where you can stash the important stuff, lock it up, and know that you won't be shit out of luck (and money) when you return from a day trip.

Technology

Phone and charger? Check. A set of earbuds is also essential. A GoPro might cost extra, but if you're planning some fast-moving or underwater adventures (which we think you should), it would be nice to have a tool to capture it all. Remember that you may have to go many hours without access to an electrical outlet if you're out in the wild, so bring backup juice. Please, *please*, leave the selfie stick at home.

Forgot something? Night markets—where you can buy anything from a phone charger to a live chicken to a fancy dress—are a thing of beauty in Southeast Asia.

PACKING TIPS AND TRICKS

- Even if you plan to be abroad for a month (or more), stick to a fifty-liter backpack—anything bigger will feel like a burden.
- It may be a little more expensive, but a backpack with padded shoulder and hip straps is the way to go if you don't want everything you own digging into your skin.
- A daypack is your backpack's kangaroo baby, and having one will feel like absolute freedom. Forget purses, totes, and the idea of carrying your big pack to the beach. A daypack is large enough for a day or weekend trip, and small enough to not get in the way of fun.

Daypack! →

Fanny packs might be kind of cool right now, but daypacks are the timeless little black dresses of the traveling world. **Pro tip:** Not all backpacks come equipped with removable daypacks, so be sure to look for one that does.

- Maximize space by using the roll method. Instead of folding everything like you (presumably) do before putting it into your drawers, roll your clothing into cylinders.
- Leave bulky beach towels at home: you will be able to get one wherever you land and save a shit-ton of space inside your pack.
- Bring a waterproof sack for things like electronics and that last dry pair of panties. Southeast Asia is moist, and you don't always want to be.
- Sunscreen gets expensive in Southeast Asia, so BYO. While we hate to add bulk, cancer is a bigger bitch than lugging around twelve ounces of lotion.
- Always bring a pair of shower slippers; this is not negotiable (unless you love foot fungus).
- Modesty may not be your middle name, but if you want to visit any temple, you'll have to cover up your T&A (as well as your shoulders, knees, and sometimes hair) with a sarong or something similar.
- Condoms are important to have, and you'll want to double up for this trip, just in case.
- Headlamp: It might be a little nerdy, but light is essential for illuminating a cave or your path when you need to take a piss without waking up your hostel mates by turning on the thousand-watt lamp on the nightstand.
- Don't forget your toothbrush.

Flights and Transportation

SURPRISINGLY, TRAVEL TO THE MAIN INTERNATIONAL HUBS OF SOUTHEAST ASIA (I.E., Bangkok, Manila, Singapore, and Kuala Lumpur) will cost you much less than a flight that is similar in length to anywhere else—that is, if you play your cards right. Common sense tells you that booking in advance (about two weeks to a month) will get you the best fare. You can sometimes finagle a lower fare by looking for flights to Taipei or Hong Kong on major airlines, then using Asia's many budget airlines to connect you to your Southeast Asian city of choice. Assume you'll spend a full day for travel (if not a bit more) there and back, and allow yourself plenty of time between flights to explore.

ONCE THERE

Welcome to the sweaty fun time that is your life for the next couple of weeks (or months?). Now that you're here, you will have access to all kinds of wheels and wings—and a few floaters—to get you to the cool shit you so desperately want to see, eat, and feel.

Planes

It might go against everything you were ever taught, but domestic airfare in Southeast Asia is sometimes comparable in price to a bus ride—and a hell of a lot faster.

Of course, flying out from some remote region will be tough, if not impossible, but if you're around any country's capital city, you can hop on a plane, cheapo. Air Asia serves a bunch of domestic destinations out of Bangkok, Manila, and Kuala Lumpur, while airlines based in a particular country (e.g., Cebu Pacific Air in the Philippines, Tigerair in Singapore, and Lion Air in Indonesia) are the best ways to get in and out of that country. You will hear a lot of buzz about Jetstar because the airline services many airports and is backpacker-budget friendly.

Buses

Border relations between Southeast Asian countries are primo thanks to the 2015 adoption of the ASEAN Economic Community (AEC)—which is sort of like the EU but without all those pesky Europeans. Your experience with land borders will likely happen on buses, which range from fairly posh (hello, air-conditioning!) to over-crowded and stinky, depending on price. You can grab a sleeper bus for long treks, and many private companies will vie for your dollars. Always bring snacks, and don't expect to use the pooper until a scheduled stop, as on-board toilets are not a thing here. Public-transit buses within cities vary depending on the destination, but three things you will always encounter are overcrowding, frequent stops, and often (in bustling cities) grueling traffic.

Ferries

One thing you'll notice in Southeast Asia if you're from, say, Iowa, is water. *Lots* of water. At times, the only way to get to that set of islands you want to lounge on is via boat. In Indonesia, the islands of Sumatra, Java, Bali, Sulawesi, and Nusa Tenggara are connected by ferries that will get you to where you want to go *eventually*, as they seem to run on their own schedules (as opposed to the ones posted) and tend to be rickety and overcrowded. On the other end of the spectrum, Vietnam's hydrofoil ferries (in comparison to their crappy barges) are pretty snazzy and sometimes feature snack bars and other modern comforts like pixelated television programming. All of this is to say, if you want to go by boat, you'll get a mixed bag.

Trains

You will need to learn to accept that in Southeast Asia, punctuality is up for interpretation. An extensive railway system will take you from Thailand to Malaysia in about twenty-six hours, meandering through everything in between, and running on a schedule that is loose to say the least (and not at all according to a timetable). It's a good option if you want to take your time to see things roll by on the way to your destination. You'll pass through Kanchanaburi, where the Death Railway (officially the Burma Railway) looms as a reminder of a dark past when forced laborers built the connection between Thailand and Myanmar. A pricey option is hopping on the Eastern and Oriental Express, which hosts multiday excursions that will take you back in time with the train's ornate cabins, a "bar car" complete with piano, and miles of moving landscape visible from its curtained windows. It's basically the *Darjeeling Limited* minus Owen Wilson, plus Southeast Asia.

Cars

Renting a car in Southeast Asia is similar in process to doing so in the States and can be accomplished at airport kiosks in major cities, as well as in city centers. You will need to get an International Driving Permit (IDP) at home predeparture, which will be valid for a full year. Insurance is a must, as accidents in Southeast Asia happen often. For that reason, taking photos of your rental car before you leave the agency is smart; they can be used as evidence that you did not cause that massive ding after you drove it off the lot. The density of vehicles on the road is drastically different between urban and rural locations. Uber canceled its service in Bangkok in 2018 because shit got too crazy, which should give you an idea of what city driving will be like.

Motorcycles

The moment you land, you will realize that people here are obsessed with anything that has two wheels and a motor. Motorcycles and scooters are a common way to get around and can be a great way for you to explore the countryside. Renting one in a big city is not hard, but you'll have to have your wits about you to make sure you don't get a rickety deathtrap. When

it comes to being on the road, remember that driving defensively is the way to go in places such as Vietnam, where nobody waits their turn patiently. Road conditions vary by country—from pothole paradise in the Philippines and Indonesia to great, smooth highways in Vietnam. The inclement weather in Southeast Asia often creates mucky challenges in remote areas. If you're ready to take on new terrain, design your own motorcycle adventure with our guide on pages 20–21.

Bicycles

Anyone who chooses bikes as their preferred mode of transportation knows that they're a good option for myriad reasons, including covering more than you would on foot, seeing more than you would by bus, and fitting in some exercise while cheaply moving about. Bicycling in Southeast Asia adds a little adventure element that you might not find in metro areas in the States. Although you can lug your fixie from home (don't), renting a bike is fairly easy in big cities—as is buying one, but you have to know your shit to make sure you don't get a lemon. Bike tours are fairly common as well, and they allow you to experience temple cities on wheels, as well as mountain-bike paths through regions like northern Vietnam. Navigating dizzying city streets on bikes is a different story (the punch line of which is: wear a helmet).

MOTO-MADNESS (VIETNAM)

Ever wonder what it would be like to be swarmed by scooters? Well, if you visit Vietnam, you will experience firsthand being surrounded by their buzz in every which direction. Here, entire families are crammed onto one scooter, and crossing the street is an act of sheer bravery. Standing in one place to observe the moto-madness, while entertaining, will seem as though you're in a fast-moving carousel nightmare that you can never get off of. Traffic laws do exist, but scooter swarms follow their own unspoken rules. And not only are you illiterate in the Vietnamese-language department; you also have no idea how to speak scooter. Unless you decide to jump into the mix yourself by renting one, your encounters with this form of transport will be limited to (1) braving the madness to cross the street amidst a mob of motorbikes, or (2) hopping on a motorbike "taxi." In the first scenario, looking both ways will not suffice as a safety precaution, because cars and scooters won't take heed and let you pass. You will need to buck up and cross with conviction, allowing the drivers to swarm around you. The second option is actually safer. Motorbike divers hang out everywhere and charge half the price of a car taxi. Once you take a seat on the back, remember to relax your body a bit to let the driver balance your weight, and keep your long legs tucked in so the two of you don't bump knees with passersby. Most importantly, trust in the fact that Vietnam has been buzzing with scooters for ages and knows what it's doing—most of the time.

Planning and Research

LOOSE PLANS ARE ALWAYS THE BEST WHEN VISITING MULTIPLE COUNTRIES IN ONE GO, but having no plans will get you in trouble—especially if you're trying to keep to a strict budget. Plotting out exact travel routes that you intend to follow meticulously will leave you in hot shit when a train or ferry is inevitably late or when you learn about a destination not on your radar that you get all FOMO about. We're here to help you strike a balance between planning like a pro and traveling like a robot. Read on, friends!

MAPPING YOUR ROUTE

Many travelers descend upon Southeast Asia from north to south (Bangkok to Bali), with a little backtracking in between. First, plot the countries you want to visit, and allow at least one week to explore each. Adjust what you are able to do against your budget, and trace out the route that makes the most sense mileage-wise within the time period you can reasonably spend abroad. That may mean you start in Manila and move your away up north to Bagan, or you just stick to the cluster of Thailand, Vietnam, Cambodia, and Laos and save the Malay peninsula for a later trip. Remember to leave your plans a little loose for those times when you meet fellow travelers that inspire you to change route, you learn about some new must-see attraction, or a destination draws you in for longer than you planned. You won't want to rush through anything just because the travel itinerary you imagined back home tells you it's time to go.

CLIMATE AND SEASONS

When it comes to seasons, you have two choices: dry or wet, which vary in duration between mainland Southeast Asia and its island components. Arriving right after a wet season will let you experience the lush greenery refreshed by the rain. Generally, tourist season spikes between December and February, with many preferring to travel during the dry season to ensure that they don't encounter monsoon-triggered landslides on their hiking and biking adventures. Shoulder seasons (those that fall right before and right after the high season) are the best in terms of cost and availability, but will be a little less predictable weather-wise. Luckily, Southeast Asia's weather patterns are fairly consistent from year to year, with a few surprises thanks to our dear friend climate change. Nail down the activities you absolutely must do, and visit each country during a good time to accomplish them—for example, know that the wet season floods caves and makes climbing slippery rocks super dangerous, and that once a heavy monsoon clears, underwater visibility is ideal for scuba diving. Choose your weather battles wisely, and be smart once you reach your destination.

POLITICAL CLIMATE

Southeast Asia boasts a total population of more than six hundred million—much of which is concentrated in Indonesia. Tourism is big business in most places: 60 percent of the workforce is in the service industry. For you, this means that each individual nation, regardless of its political tensions, is focused on preserving the stream of tourists. Still, political unrest is brewing in and between countries. Myanmar stepped into democratic(ish) rule in 2015, but its government remains heavily influenced by the military, which staged a genocide against Rohingya Muslims that forced many people to flee for their lives. Thailand continues to battle its image of being the human-trafficking capital of the world. Communist Party-led Vietnam keeps big time tabs on its people—and visitors alike—and is increasingly censoring websites (including blogs) that speak out against its leadership. Cambodia is poor as fuck, Singapore is shooting upward as an economic superpower, and every place is still trying to shake off the remnants of the colonial era. Corruption exists across the spectrum, and while you are not likely to get caught in the crossfire, a good rule is to keep your nose out of situations that your gut tells you may turn violent. Government-sponsored safety resources in the United States will often warn you to stay away from places that are fairly safe to visit. For a broader picture, check travel advisories for Southeast Asian countries through Canadian, UK, and Australian government websites, or check in directly with the region's governments and locals by following relevant Twitter feeds and staying up to date on your world news.

FESTIVALS, HOLIDAYS, AND EVENTS

Southeast Asia is a religiously diverse region—filled with holidays and festivals dedicated to all kinds of deities, ancestors, and moon phases—and travel to each area is affected by whatever might be going on at the time. For instance, during Ramadan (which occurs during the ninth month of the Islamic calendar, starting in either May or June), places like Muslim-heavy Malaysia are less rowdy, and things close early in accordance with the holiday's practices. During the full moon festival on Koh Phangan, accommodations in nearby locales are booked by backpackers in advance to assure that they don't have to sleep on the sludgy postparty beach. Thailand's New Year (in mid-April), which is celebrated with a huge water fight, makes driving around the country an accident waiting to happen. In Myanmar, fourth of January celebrations marking the end

of British rule engulf the whole country. If you intend to visit regions during their most popular fests, increase your travel time and hostel budget accordingly, and prepare to change plans if things are inaccessible or all booked up.

CULTURE SHOCK

Even in dense cities in the US, we are spoiled when it comes to personal space. In Southeast Asia, you'll experience buses crammed to capacity, sidewalks overflowing with feet that seem too close to vehicle tires, and just a shit-ton of people in general. It might be uncomfortable at first to smell what a stranger had for breakfast, but you will get used to it. Speaking of smells, they will be quite different than the relatively squeaky-clean ones back home. In touristy areas, you will find Western-style toilets—because Southeast Asia has literally adapted to our butts—while more rural places will feature that feared squatter pooper (which you will master when the need to shit surpasses your squeamishness). If you're an animal lover, you will have to brace yourself at marketplaces, where animals are openly slaughtered after being stacked in cages far too small for comfort—which, as shocking as it may seem, also happens behind closed doors in the States. Refrain from dismissing something as too weird for you, and abstain from hiding in corners of comfort, like your hostel, where English speakers abound. Stick your neck out to experience the cultural variations of Southeast Asia; learning about them is the reason you came here.

THERE'S AN APP FOR THAT

Jumping straight into Southeast Asia with no little-helper tools is a brave way to go, but there are a number of great travel apps to help you find the cheapest transport, plan the most efficient in-country and multicountry itineraries, keep track of your budget, and communicate with locals to lift a little of that language-barrier anxiety. Download these before departure to stay in the know in unfamiliar territory.

MAPS.ME

Similar to Google Maps but with better offline functionality, MAPS.Me allows you to download map data for any specific region and reference it when you're out and without Wi-Fi. A great tool to help you avoid walking in circles through winding and confusing streets.

GOOGLE TRANSLATE

Knowing a few key phrases when you visit any place is always recommended, but for times when you just can't get your point across with hand gestures and limited language knowledge (particularly in Vietnam, as Khmer is a tough language to master quickly), trusty Google Translate will help turn your gibberish into a productive conversation.

XE CURRENCY CONVERTER

Traveling to multiple countries means you will be handling various forms of currency whose values fluctuate frequently. Combine that with a tendency for some locals to try to screw tourists out of their dollars, and you'll need an up-to-date way to understand what your money is worth. XE Currency, which works offline, converts all forms of currency into something you can understand. It will help you keep more change in your pockets.

HOSTELWORLD

There's only so much lodging you can (or should) arrange predeparture. For all your hostel-booking needs on the road, Hostelworld is the best-organized and easiest way to find available bunks wherever you are, complete with reviews that discern the rip-offs from the right-ons.

SKYSCANNER

An aptly named app, Skyscanner surveys the skies to find you the best rates on international flights. If you don't have solid travel plans between destinations, you can use the app to guide you to the cheapest flight and then book it on the fly.

TRAIL WALLET

This app was created for backpackers by backpackers to help you keep track of your expenses. Trail Wallet lets you hop back and forth between currencies, your budgets, and trip plans, and motivates you to stay within your means even when you're living on the road, eating six meals per day, and drinking your liquid weight in beer.

LINE

Line is a popular communication tool (similar to WhatsApp) that is used by many humans and businesses across Southeast Asia.

EVERNOTE

This is a great little app for organizing your research about the various destinations you plan to visit. You can take notes, make lists, clip portions of things you find online, save screenshots, and store scanned docs (like your passport, don't forget!) for a streamlined resource you can reference on the road.

LAZY BONUS

Foodpanda is the Seamless/Eat24/Grubhub of Southeast Asia. Now, we know you're better than ordering food to be delivered to your lodgings while traveling, but sometimes unforeseen circumstances may mean you're bound to your hostel bed or its friend, the hostel toilet. For those times, this app will hook you up with delivered meals if you're in Brunei, Thailand, Singapore, Philippines, or Malaysia.

TRAVEL STYLE

Traveling solo is the best way to go if you plan to hit multiple countries. While taking your best bud (or SO) for a two-week trip to Spain sounds nice, hauling that person along to a place where it's mucky and sometimes uncomfortable will absolutely strain your relationship—and may mess with your adventure. We can assure you that even if you think you know and love someone when you're in your comfort zone back home, once on the road (particularly in places that are as hot as balls) that person could turn into some unfamiliar monster that needs to sleep, shit, and eat on a schedule that does not mesh with yours. If you must travel in a group of two or more, here are three tiny tips to help you stay sane:

- People here do everything they can to avoid fighting in public, and losing your temper is highly frowned upon. Prior to departure, have a sit-down with your group, and agree to save your arguments (preexisting or otherwise) for when you return from your trip. Agree that when shit hits the fan, each of you will walk away, wipe the shit off, and come back to it later if it still smells.
- One, if not all, of you will get sick. If you accept this as a fact, you will be better able to help your friends when they turn into whiny babies. Between you and your fellow travelers, bring plenty of meds, and try to only be obnoxious when you are actually dying.
- Carve out alone time. You will need to defect from the group to eat that pile of fried stuff your friend said he couldn't choke down, find peace at temples where you needed to shush your group the day prior, and take in local culture through your own lens.

RESEARCH TOOLS

We created this guidebook as a jump-off point for you to get the wheels turning, knowing damn well that the age of lugging heavy books around the world died when lighter digital resources became available. Set aside some time to browse the interwebs for both inspo and concrete travel advice. Instagram is a great place to start your research, but keep in mind that what flashpackers choose to showcase may be skewed by the kickbacks they got from a hotel or tourist board that wanted them to tout the destination in exchange for a free stay. Travel blogs are omnipresent, but they also serve as great research tools. Treat them the same way you do Yelp: one-star reviews are sometimes influenced by factors you couldn't give a shit about (like ambiance). Well-established blogs like Indie Travelers or those created by expats living in-country or locals covering their native countries are good places to start.

TOUR PACKAGES

We're not big fans of buying planned-out experiences in places we'd like to hands-on explore, and we plan to save tour-package deals through travel agencies for when we're at an age where comfort supersedes everything else (maybe around age seventy?). That said, Intrepid Travel does offer a few package deals in Southeast Asia that might stoke your interest, as does STA Travel, an agency that is geared toward the twenty-something crowd.

Money and Budgeting

COMPARED TO JUST ABOUT ANYWHERE IN THE WORLD, TRAVELING TO AND AROUND
Southeast Asia is cheap, but it's still not free. You will need to budget your trip to account for a number of things, or risk getting miserably stuck in paradise.

BEFORE YOU GO

Backpack
$150-300

If you don't already have a good-fitting sack for all your junk, you'll need to get one for this trip. A trip to Southeast Asia means you'll be hopping from place to place often, so invest in a pack that can handle the hustle. Pick one that evenly distributes weight across your back, and spend a little more on one that has a detachable daypack—you'll use it often on shorter and off-track trips. Invest in a $10 padlock, or pay the price of leaving your shit wide open for the taking. We got your back with all the pack deets on page 155.

Vaccinations
$150-350

The required yellow fever vaccine will cost you a minimum of $149 if you find a great travel clinic, which charges an initial consultation fee and the price of the shot, typically $110. The higher end of the range listed above represents what it would cost at your local doc's office. The lesson here is to team up with a travel clinic to cut costs, and the doctor there can advise you of other shots to consider based on your itinerary. Err on the more cautious side with vaccines, and lay down a little dough prior to departure to ensure that you feel 100 percent during your trip.

Transportation

$1,000

Getting over to the region on a superlong flight will obviously be your biggest expense. You can cut costs a few hundo by booking several weeks in advance, choosing a major coastal airport (LAX or JFK) for your departure stateside, flying to Southeast Asia through a big travel hub like Bangkok, or visiting during the low tourist season (which will come with comfort costs as it will either be superhot or extra rainy). For example, a round-trip flight to Bangkok from LAX is $800-900 in April, and goes up to a whopping $1,200-1,500 during high season (December and January). You can trick the system a bit by flying into mainland China or Taiwan, then catching a cheap local flight into an international hub in Southeast Asia. Booking through a travel agent (which comes with a fee) is nonsense nowadays.

Travel Supplies

$30-40

Leave your froufrou shampoo and perfumes at home. Everybody will be sweaty, and your $160 bottle of Dior will not help you. Face masks and foot scrubs, teeth-whitening apparatuses, and fancy shaving creams all need to stay as well. Instead, you should spend your tiny budget on a multipurpose soap, a good sunscreen, some antidiarrheals, and cut yourself off there. Everything else you might need will be available for cheap once you land.

Passport/Visas

$0-30 per country

Make sure your passport is valid for at least a year beyond your departure date, which may mean dropping $145 for a renewal. Several countries will let you stay for thirty days for nada, while others will cost around $30 bucks per visa (and about $50

for an extension)—head to pages 188-190 for details on specific countries' visa rules. Decide where you want to go, and bring enough exact change to pay for entry. Or go the cheap route, and stick to zero-cost entry into Brunei, Malaysia, the Philippines, Singapore, and Thailand. You may get slightly scammed by border officials, who charge you made-up "administrative fees" that they'll pocket, so budget a few bribe dollars ($20 or so). If you overstay, you will pay upward of $20 per day.

Travel Insurance

$0–250

We spent most of our twenties without any kind of medical insurance, and nothing major happened. It is tempting to skip this expense and just hope for the best, but a few circumstances particular to Southeast Asia require a little extra protection. Traffic accidents are rampant in Vietnam and Thailand, where scooters outnumber people and slick rain makes the already buzzy roads super slippery. Petty theft is a thing, too, and having a little coverage will ensure that you can sleep soundly underneath your mosquito net.

ON THE ROAD

You didn't endure that daylong flight—and the consequential jet lag—to just dip your toe into Bangkok and head home. Budget-wise, that means you will be juggling a number of costs that fluctuate from country to country. Each place has its own currency, but carrying USD will always pay the way. You'll have access to ATMs in big cities. However, if you plan on hitting country roads and hillside villages, keep some cash on hand. You can scrape by on about $20 to $25 per day, and live like royalty on just a little bit more.

Accommodations

$4–40 daily, plus $100 per week for funsies
Staying at hostels, guesthouses, home-stays, and beach hammocks will be cheaper than they would for your average Euro trip, which means you should budget at least a few resort splurges. You can score a hostel bed in Cambodia or Malaysia for as little as $4; hostels in more touristy areas (ahem, Bangkok) will cost a bit more. A homestay will often include food (score!), so its higher cost is justified. In some pricier places (looking at you, Singapore), you'll want to strictly go for hostel dorms or cheap guest rooms. Do play around with more expensive stays if you can. For instance, in the Philippines you can get your own private island through Airbnb for a pretty reasonable price (peep page 151).

Eating and Drinking

$6–20 per day, plus $50 for a blowout meal. That $10 avocado toast will become a distant memory the moment you hit the streets of Southeast Asia. Grabbing some organs on a stick in the Philippines, guzzling a bowl of pho in Vietnam, scarfing down noodles from a hawker stall in Singapore, munching on chive cakes in Cambodia, or going hard on the sticky rice in Thailand will each cost you less than a McDonald's happy meal. A buck will get you copious street snacks in most places—or a bag of bugs in Thailand if that's what you're after. Sitting down to a shared meal will never run you more than 10 to 15 bucks, and going out to one or two of the most expensive affairs (check our fancy-pants restaurants on page 93) is an attainable treat.

Transport

$100 per week
You can cheaply hop around Southeast Asia on budget airlines, buses, and ferries by planning ahead. However, you will find that your plans might change last minute. In that case, you will shell out a little more for a fast ferry, bus, or spur-of-the-moment flight. Taxi drivers and tour operators will always try to rip you off just a little because you're foreign. Here, your wits and bargaining powers will determine your daily transportation costs. Traveling during high season impacts the prices of everything, transportation included.

Activities

$10–90 per day

A lot of what you do for fun in Southeast Asia—hiking, beaching, some museum-going, and the like—will be free. However, organized tours and trips to remote places and through jungles will require a little cash. Some temples are upkept by donation only, while bigger sites, such as Angkor Wat, will run you as much as $37 for a day pass. You will find yourself in many places that are surrounded by water, diving into which might become your number-one priority. Snorkeling shouldn't cost you all that much anywhere in Southeast Asia, but if you want to scuba (and you do), you'll have to budget a few bucks. In Indonesia, you'll spend about $90 on a two-tank dive, while an aquatic-wonderland trip in the Philippines will run you half that price. Pick a daily itinerary that includes a little of the free and some of the fee, and we promise you'll have a great time without breaking the bank.

Partying

$2–15 daily

Once you land in Southeast Asia, gone will be the days that you stand in line for an hour to pay a $20 cover charge for a club. Pregaming at the hostel (or the hostel bar) is always a good idea, as is hitting a local watering hole in the early evening, where beers will be considerably cheaper than you're used to. This region boasts entire islands dedicated to partying for cheap, booze cruises that'll run a fraction of the price of a night out in NYC, and festivals where the name of the game is pure partying. Sometimes the kind of party you want is nothing more than a bucket of beer on the beach—which can be yours for pennies.

BILLS FOR BEERS

Your US dollars will do, but knowing each country's currency is key. Here's a breakdown of the currency used in every part of Southeast Asia in order from best to worst exchange rates, weighed against how much cheap beer (aka the most essential backpacker expense) you can buy for the equivalent of $5. You will get the most for your buck in Cambodia and Vietnam and scrounge for change in Singapore and Timor-Leste.

Vietnam, *dong*
$5 = 114,458d = 15 beers

Cambodia, *riel*
$5 = 20,148r = 10 beers

Indonesia, *rupiah*
$5 = 72,455Rp = 5 beers

Myanmar, *kyat*
$5 = 7,195K = 5 beers

Philippines, *piso* (or *peso*)
$5 = P266 = 5 beers

Laos, *kip*
$5 = 41,850K = 5 beers

Malaysia, *ringgit*
$5 = 20RM = 2–3 beers

Thailand, *baht*
$5 = 166B = 2 beers

Singapore, Singapore dollar
$5 = S$6.81 = 1 beer

Timor-Leste, US dollar
$5 = $5 = 1 beer

Note: You may have noticed that Brunei is not on this list. That's because the sale and consumption of alcohol is illegal there. The country is about as expensive as Singapore and uses the same currency.

Souvenirs

$5–30

Thank the gods that be for night markets, where you can find an array of artisan goods (alongside counterfeit Louis Vuittons and live animals being sold for slaughter) to take back home to your less-travel-fortunate friends. Some villages are known for their particular crafts, such as woven fabrics, carved wooden figurines, spiritual ornaments, and one-of-a-kind musical instruments. Know that haggling is expected, but engage with a conscience: remember that some people subsist on less than $2 per day and spend their time and energy making that trinket your mom will put on some obscure bookshelf in the dining room. Play fair, and never lose your temper. Save your shopping for the tail end of your stay in any given place, or commit to having to haul your souvenir bounty on your back throughout your visit.

Random Shit

$10–20 per week

This is what we call our "under-the-mattress stash" or just-in-case funds. Saw a completely useless knick-knack at the night market that you *must* have? Your night of karaoke suddenly turned into a $100 bar tab (which would be quite impressive)? Keep falling victim to tourist pricing? Need just one night of air-conditioning to give that heat rash a rest? All of these are situations in which having a few extra bucks can really help.

History, Culture, and Politics

IF YOU'VE NEVER BEEN OUTSIDE THE BUBBLE OF THE UNITED STATES, SOUTHEAST ASIA might come as a culture shock. Things in metropolitan areas move at unrelenting speeds before dissolving into slow-paced island life. People are generally incredibly nice, but there is a little air of suspicion, especially in places like Vietnam and Laos, where the government keeps a close eye on its residents and tourists. Buddhism, Islam, and ancient animist practices all mingle here, sometimes peacefully, and the effects of colonialism remain even after a country's respective colonizer no longer holds the reins. As a traveler, you're both considered an outsider and welcomed as part of the family. Leave your preconceptions about this culturally rich area at the door, and let Southeast Asia bend your Western perceptions of the world.

The region has some shared history, but as a whole Southeast Asia is a collection of individual cultures with past conflicts that resulted in varied political climates. We're not here to give you a deep history lesson—you should have paid attention in school to get that—rather a rough understanding of the factors that shaped the background and contribute to everyday life in this diverse region. To fully understand the whole of Southeast Asia, you need to have a grasp of its individual parts.

THAILAND

Compared to the rest of Southeast Asia, Thailand falls in the middle of the poverty scale. Tourism presents a big opportunity for moneymaking, and the foreigners (sometimes creepy pedophiles) it brings fuel the (technically illegal) sex industry it is well known for. People from all over Southeast Asia come to work in Thailand's tourist industry, which pays more than it does in their home countries. Thais are all about Theravada Buddhism, and every male is required to serve as a monk for a period of time—kind of like mandatory military servitude but with fewer guns and more robes and bowls.

Politically, the country is a struggling democracy (with a long history of military rule and public opposition to it), and one where the monarchy is still highly respected—despite the fact that the royals have little actual power. The country's constitution, which has been in limbo for more than a decade, was written in 1997 with promising language that served the public but then was rewritten in ways that supported corruption and military control. Business tycoon Thaksin Shinawatra—who now lives in self-exile in Dubai on a cushy $2 billion net worth—was elected as prime minister in 2001 before selling his family's business and his country's soul (in a $1.88 billion, tax-free deal) to Singapore. Old Thaksin's sister Yingluck took over (as the country's first female prime minister), and she also screwed up royally by making hefty promises to eliminate poverty by raising the minimum wage and creating a rice-subsidy scheme that would supposedly benefit farmers—which she eventually abandoned. A protest orchestrated by the People's Democratic Reform Committee to combat corruption ousted Shinawatra from power in 2014, and she was replaced by a military junta. The current prime minister is Thai Royal Army general Prayut Chan-o-cha, who is a big fan of censoring the media.

Despite all this, Thailand is known as the "Land of Smiles." Thai people are definitely friendly as fuck and live for fun—quite literally, as one of the central tenets of Thai society is *sanuk*, which translates to, you guessed it, "fun." People operate on the principle of saving face, and would rather smile and move on from conflict than become angry in public. You should do the same.

CAMBODIA

Cambodia's heart is one that has been broken by poverty, warfare, and slavery, yet its people—96 percent of whom are ethnic Khmers, making for the most homogenous society in Southeast Asia—maintain an air of hope. The generational divide here is palpable. A large portion of the population, about 40 percent, is under the age of sixteen and engages in all the shit that young people do (you know, partying and playing around on Facebook). Standing in stark contrast to the young 'uns is the older generation, which still remembers the horrors of the Khmer Rouge. The regime's policies created a deep poverty in the late 1970s that still plagues Cambodia today (minimum wage hovers around an astounding $170 per month).

As evidenced by its impressive temples, Cambodia was once a place of much wealth and virtue, especially during the flourishing Khmer empire prior to the thirteenth century. It has since been enthralled in a tug of war between neighboring Vietnam, Thailand, and looming giant China. The French stepped in to protect the fledgling country in the 1800s and, while properly colonizing it, delivered on their promise by keeping the country safe from demise until 1953, when Cambodia declared its independence. However, the situation did not stay very peachy: during the American War (see page 179), the Viet Cong and American forces used Cambodia's land and people to carry out their military schemes, leaving the country devastated. Things got real bad when the war ended in 1975 and a new sort of war began under dictator Saloth Sar (popularly known as Pol Pot). As head of the Khmer Rouge, Sar adopted the goal of wiping Cambodia's history clean and starting anew as an advanced agrarian society. This resulted in slave-labor camps, the execution of intellectuals, mass starvation, and disease, leading to the deaths of some two million people. The genocidal regime continued to remotely wage civil war upon the devastated country, despite UN intervention, until 1998. Current prime minister Hun Sen was installed in 1985 by the Vietnamese. A member of the Cambodian People's Party, Sen has 9.6 million followers on Facebook, which may suggest that he is a progressive leader. On the contrary, his thirty-plus-year rule has been characterized by eliminating opposing political parties, prosecuting those whose views don't align with his on the grounds of treason, and generally suppressing dissent.

Buddhism (which was wiped out during the Khmer Rouge by the murder of a lot of monks) and family are two unifying factors that Cambodians credit for staying grounded in times of violence and uncertainty. As such, barangs (that's you!) bond with locals here over a family meal paired with more than several rounds of beer.

VIETNAM

Perhaps what is best known to Americans about the culture of Vietnam, and for good reason, is the wretched war that tore through the country for decades. The national identity of Vietnam can be characterized as one of resistance, however divided the country may be, to opposing forces. After its culture was scrambled by early Chinese rule, Vietnam came up on France's radar as the place it wanted to colonize on its efforts to gain a leg up on Britain (which it hoped to do by controlling the trade along the Mekong Delta and gaining access to lucrative regions in China). Following years of French colonialist rule, communist revolutionary and world traveler Ho Chi Minh wasn't having it any longer. He organized the League for the Independence of Vietnam (a nationalist party known as Viet Minh). After World War II, France was weakened by its fight with Germany, and the Japanese moved in to occupy Vietnam. In 1945, Japan loosened its hold, as it had bigger fish to fry once the Americans dropped a bomb on Hiroshima. Seizing the opportunity, Ho stepped in and established the Republic of Vietnam in less than a month's time. This precipitated an eight-year war with the French and ultimately created a dividing line—officially designated the Seventeenth Parallel during the Geneva Conference—demarcating North and South Vietnam. The guerilla forces of the National Liberation Front, called Viet Cong, operated from the jungles below this line to help instate Ho's communist ideals.

What you know as the Vietnam War was an American intervention—under the guise of preventing the spread of the idea of communism throughout Vietnam—in what many deemed a war that was not ours to fight. The US unleashed devastation on the region in many forms, including routinely using toxic chemicals such as Agent Orange. In Operation Rolling Thunder, begun in 1965, the US indiscriminately dropped eight hundred bombs per day on Vietnam for three and a half years.

Bombings continued as an American strategy through 1975. Vietnam was reunified and currently operates as a one-party Communist state (officially called the Socialist Republic of Vietnam).

After all this shit, you'd think that the Vietnamese people would hate our guts—and we wouldn't blame them. However, relations between the US and Vietnam

have improved in recent years, as trade between the two is thriving. Westerners are seen as walking cash cows, so if you're a traveler (particularly if you're white), locals will very aggressively approach you to sell you merchandise and services. The proper response is to be jovial and conversational, which the Vietnamese will return.

When it comes to the freedom of its press, out of 180 countries, Vietnam is rated number 175—meaning that the voices of its journalists are more oppressed than in any other country in Southeast Asia, even more than in censorship-loving Laos, which comes in at number 170. All media in Vietnam is controlled by the ruling Communist Party, and the only independent journalists are bloggers, whom the state persecutes under an antigovernment-propaganda legal code that results in exile or long jail sentences, as evidenced by the plight of citizen-bloggers Tranh Thi Nga and Me Nam, who received nine- and ten-year terms, respectively, in 2017. Puts your "Fuck Trump" tweet in perspective, doesn't it?

THE AMERICAN WAR

The American War (known as the Vietnam War to Americans) is something the Vietnamese people are still very much recovering from. Here are a few incredible facts about Vietnam that remain after the carnage officially ended in 1975:

- Ten percent of the population is still terribly affected by Agent Orange, an extremely toxic chemical the United States dropped all over the country.
- So much Agent Orange was dropped that it will continue to impact soil and agriculture for the next three hundred years.
- The Vietnamese population has more than doubled since 1975—growing from forty million to ninety million.
- The current average age in Vietnam is thirty, making it a country filled with young energy.

- The Vietnamese are on a path of healing and reconciliation. They've been colonized for so many years and have been through so much war that they prefer keeping things peaceful. They welcome foreign investment and tourism, which allow the country to flourish.

OTP Tip
The War Remnants Museum in Ho Chi Minh City is a *must* experience for travelers. The museum's shocking photos and artifacts will put the terrors of war into perspective.

HOW TO NOT BE A JERK

In Southeast Asia—where tipping is not customary but often appreciated—you will notice that some behaviors you're very much used to back home are considered faux pas. Take these tips to heart to avoid being a total jackass.

COVER UP

Due to the unbearable heat, we know it might be tempting to go from beach to temple without putting on pants and a shirt. However, this region's religious respect runs deep, and you should follow suit by covering bare skin when entering places of worship. Also, women, keep your top on at the beach—this isn't Europe.

TOUCHY TOUCHY

Don't ever touch monks; they are considered sacred, which means you shouldn't paw at them unsolicited. Women (sorry) are not allowed to sit next to monks, even on public transportation. Touching people on top of the head (the most spiritual part of the body) is a big no-no in general. When it comes to touching objects, avoid climbing on religious statues, and pose with them in respectful ways.

BOW DOWN

In place of handshakes, people bow at each other all the time. Each gesture and bow is determined by class and seniority. You don't have to try to understand your place in the world to give a respectful bow. The best approach is to put your hands together as if in prayer, with your pointers near your nose, and do a little bow.

PORK AND BOOZE

Sounds like a great combo, right? Well, for Muslims, these two are taboo. Know dietary restrictions when striking up a conversation or ordering food (e.g., if you're in Malaysia and want to discuss your love of beer and pork rinds, do it with hostel mates, not locals).

PHOTOS

Capturing people's images is a tricky thing. Some find it completely disrespectful (particularly if you don't ask for permission first) as they believe that photographs trap an individual's spirit, while others will take photos with you all day. Just be mindful of whom you capture when that selfie stick rears its ugly head.

DO I SHOE?

It is customary to take off your shoes when you enter homes, temples, and other buildings. If you see shoes by the door, take the hint and throw yours into the pile. Also, whether your feet are bare or shoe-d, do not prop them on chairs when sitting; it's considered rude to put your feet (the lowest and dirtiest part of the body) where somebody else might sit. Avoid pointing your feet at Buddha statues or people at all costs.

PDA

Many places in Southeast Asia, particularly Indonesia and Singapore, are not cool with people tickling tongues in public. The no-PDA rule particularly applies in Buddhist temples—romantic places where you should refrain from hand-holding or any other PG-13 physical contact. Get a room and reserve your groping to dimly lit places.

BARGAINING POWER

Haggling is a cultural norm, but you have to take a few things into consideration when trying to get that trinket for dirt cheap. People selling their wares—which may have required a lot of time and energy to make by hand—earn about as much per day as you earn per minute. Pay them a fair price; you'll still get a bargain.

DISPLAYS OF ANGER

Outward expressions of anger, like raising your voice or throwing a toddler-style temper tantrum, are never okay. Here, people convey their feelings calmly and smile often, even when things aren't great. Keep your cool, and walk away instead of making a scene.

CHOPSTICKS OF DEATH

What you do with your chopsticks is important in most parts of Asia. Don't ever stab

them vertically into a bowl of rice as that imagery is associated with the way incense is placed during death rituals. Instead, lay them across your bowl when you are done or on the table next to the bowl when you're just taking a break.

THE KING IS KING

In Thailand, there is no separation between royalty and state. You will hear the king's anthem played many times while you're in the country—and you will need to stand still during it.

LAOS

Laotians are laid back to a point that makes you forget that the government is notorious for causing social progressives to disappear. Surrounded by oft-invading forces from all sides, the Lan Xang (Land of a) Million Elephants existed under French colonial rule until it gained sovereignty in 1953. Laos's geographical location has always made it the fighting, and training, grounds for wars that had nothing to do with its own residents, including the American War—the long-lasting consequences of which (lots of unexploded land mines) the nation still suffers today. While the US bombed the shit out of the country between 1964 and 1973, communist forces (Pathet Lao) united and created the Lao People's Revolutionary Party, led by Kaysone Phomvihane.

Democratic ideals are hard to come by in Laos to this day, and the land-locked country, led by Bounnhang Vorachith (who studied socialism in Vietnam), is one of the world's few remaining true communist states. Interestingly enough, whereas Theravada Buddhism, Laos's dominant religion, was actively suppressed from 1975 until 1992, monks now are coming out of the woodwork to openly practice the nonviolent belief system, and old animist traditions, which remain officially illegal, linger and manifest in figurines (to ward off bad spirits), ceremonial practices, and a general sense that spiritual guardians and demons are running the show.

MALAYSIA

Malaysia's landmass is separated by 660 miles of South China Sea, and its people have historically been just as divided when it comes to racial and religious politics. The prosperous empire of Melaka attracted the glimmering, greedy eyes of many European imperialists, including British dude James Brooke, who straight up appointed himself as raja (king) of a part of Sarawak—one of Malaysia's thirteen states on the Borneo side of things—and created a dynasty that lasted a hundred years. When the Brits couldn't deal with their colonies while trying to keep up with the costs of WWII, the Brooke dynasty imported Chinese and Indian laborers to keep building Malaysia, setting up a racial shit storm of tensions and protests, notably the violent interracial riots of 1969, for years to come.

After gaining independence from British rule in 1957, the country was run by Prime Minister Najib Razak of the Barisan Nasional (BN) coalition and its major party, United Malays National Organisation (often accused of corruption and cronyism). Over the years, Razak drifted closer and closer to Sharia law, as almost all Malaysians are Muslim and Islam is the national religion. Despite what may sound like an unwelcoming place for people of different faiths (or none at all), Malaysians are friendly to foreigners.

In May 2018, after sixty years at the top, the BN was ousted by an opposition alliance led by former Malaysian prime minister Mahathir Mohamad, who left retirement to become the world's oldest elected official at age ninety-two. Considering that the last person who tried to run against the BN party was imprisoned for five years on (likely false) sodomy charges, Mohamad's win was a big one.

PHILIPPINES

A collection of more than seven thousand islands, the Philippines is a prime example of how colonialism is a muthafucka. This might break your heart, but remember the explorer Ferdinand Magellan? Think he was a pretty cool guy? Well, he happened upon the island nation—where people happily did their own thing—and claimed it for Spain before forcing everyone to become Christian, resulting in the violent deaths of those who did not. After Spain was done with the Philippines, America stepped in to see how much they could squeeze out of the region. During WWII, the Japanese unleashed a violent

and differs from Trump in that he publicly supports the LGBTQ community and thinks number 45 is a bigot.

INDONESIA

The most populous country in Southeast Asia—and the fourth most populous in the world—Indonesia until recently has had a hard time maintaining harmony among its 257 million citizens (who collectively speak more than three hundred languages). With its diverse, conservative-leaning population—combined with the forces of Mother Nature that constantly pound the country and man-made environmental disasters created by its destructive palm oil and logging industries—Indonesia has a lot of shit to deal with.

military regime on the then-American colony before losing the Battle of Manila in 1945. Throughout their colonial history, Filipinos were always ready to take back what was rightfully theirs—as was made evident during the Philippine Revolution, when revolutionaries avenged the 1896 murder of national hero José Rizal by driving the Spanish out. Nearly one century later, the Filipino spirit remained strong when the People Power revolution ousted dictator Ferdinand Marcos in 1986 after he had presided over fourteen years of devastating military rule.

The independent nation enjoyed prosperity after 2010 under the leadership of Liberal Party member Benigno Aquino III, who helped cleanse the country's "sick man of Asia" reputation by bringing economic development and political stability to the region. The Filipino people continue to endure hardships and success with a zeal that can be observed in the way they talk, laugh, cook, and dance.

The highly anticipated 2016 election resulted in a shocking win. Former boxer Rodrigo Duterte, known professionally as "The Punisher," now runs the country

The archipelago was dominated by Hinduism during the grand Majapahit Empire of the thirteenth through fifteenth centuries, until Islam took over most of the country, relegating Hindu beliefs to areas such as Bali. European superpowers fought over Indonesia's riches before the Dutch gained control through the Dutch East India Company's spice trade and, after a brief stint of British rule, again after the Napoleonic wars. The nation's first president/dictator, Kusno Sosrodihardjo (known as Sukarno), declared independence in 1945—which was hard won four years later through brutal guerilla warfare.

In 1968 Sukarno was ousted by Suharto (born Haji Mohamed Suharto), who set up a corrupt dictatorship until the country tumbled economically and protests forced him to resign in 1998. Now, the nation's leadership—which skews a lot more moderate—is working to undo the corruption schemes and structures set up by its authoritarian predecessors, while investing in education, health, and relief from recurring natural disasters.

Indonesia is modernizing at a rapid rate, and a palpable divide exists between the classes. Wealthier Indonesians are glued to their phones, much like Westerners, and the poor barely scrape by on a few dollars per day. As the biggest Muslim nation on earth, you'll always hear a call to prayer, even if you're surrounded by Hindu temples.

MYANMAR

Myanmar—renamed from Burma by the British in 1989—functioned under military rule as a completely isolated country for four decades until 2013, when a new governmental structure created the Tourism Master Plan in hopes of attracting 7.5 million visitors (and their paychecks) by 2020. The British ran Burma under colonial rule starting in the nineteenth century; the country gained independence in 1948. In 1962 General Ne Win stepped in and unleashed the world's longest-lived military regime, characterized by brutalization of citizens, imprisonment of any voices of dissent, and the sealing of the nation's borders. The current president is Win Myint, a former political prisoner of the preceding regime, but democracy activist Aung San Suu Kyi (who is barred from becoming president) really holds the reins.

Visiting Myanmar is now possible for tourists, but keep in mind the country is in deep civil unrest at the moment—as well as experiencing a brewing malaria outbreak. While modern Myanmar does not enforce a national religion, nearly 90 percent of its population is Theravada Buddhist. Somewhat surprisingly, practitioners of the historically nonviolent faith are actively cleansing the country of Rohingya Muslims, forcing millions to flee. The conflict has required many people to find refuge in Bangladesh and along the border of Thailand, where thousands of stateless Burmese refugees reside, mostly in camps with little access to services such as education.

Politically, things in Myanmar remain pretty hairy. If you do visit, one thing you will notice is that in the great scheme of scams across Southeast Asia, the Burmese are pretty honest about the price of accommodations, cab fares, and the like. Also, men make kissy faces and noises to get the attention of servers and shop owners.

SINGAPORE

It only takes a minute of being in Singapore—with its skyscraper-edged horizon and techy art parks—to understand that the culture is skewing toward industrialization and modernity. In a matter of fifty years, Singapore transformed from a string of sleepy fishing villages—brutally dominated by the Japanese during WWII—to a world superpower with modern everything and booming industry, a shift that's credited to the nation's "founding father," Lee Kuan Yew, who died in 2015. Lee's successors, up through today's leader Halimah Yacob (the first female president of the country), have maintained his vision of a thriving Singapore and continued his work to develop housing, attract tourism, and invest in industry.

Something you will most definitely notice in English-speaking Singapore is that the government—which cares deeply about the country's spic-and-span image—is all up in your business regarding a number of things, including trying to figure out how to censor Facebook by co-opting the idea of "fake news" into a narrative that fits its own ideals.

FIVE THINGS THAT ARE BANNED
IN SINGAPORE

To most Westerners, the following behaviors aren't a big deal, but in Singapore you'll get in big trouble if you:

- Chewing gum. Yep. Masticating the sticky substance was banned in 1992. Want to set up a little gum-selling business? You will be fined more than $70,000 per day until you shut it down.
- Taking a poppy-seed bagel through customs. Didn't finish your breakfast on your flight into Singapore? Tough nuts, pal. Throw that thing straight in the trash, because here, poppy seeds (in any quantity) are considered drugs.
- Getting naked . . . even if you're inside. So you're in your hostel and you need to change into something more comfortable. Better hop into a windowless room—a closet, perhaps—or face three months of jail time if some prude on the street sees you.
- Carrying durian on public transit. Good job, Singapore! We're actually okay with this one because durian smells like dead antelope stuffed with gym socks.
- Congregating in a group of more than three after ten p.m. This one is tough and is meant to discourage the disorderly conduct that apparently happens when a fourth person joins your party. Go out in numbers divisible by three, and walk in small, inconspicuous groups.

TIMOR-LESTE/ EAST TIMOR

Oil-rich nation East Timor (also known as Timor-Leste) fought long and hard for its independence, which officially began in 2002 but was followed by years of violence and rioting until a whopping decade later when things settled into a peaceful election. The entire Timor region was lazily controlled by the Portuguese for decades before the Treaty of Lisbon divided the area in half, the eastern portion of which the Portuguese continued to own and neglect. During the Asia-Pacific War (a regionalized battle of World War II), the Japanese and Australians fought it out on Timorese ground, killing about sixty thousand people in the neutral territory. When Portugal began dismantling its colonial holdings in 1975, Indonesia jumped into East Timor—even though its political party Revolutionary Front for an Independent East Timor had declared independence— as a measure to stop communism from spreading there. For several decades, East Timor was pounded by the Indonesian military, which sent militias into the area to stunt its goals toward independence. In 1999, UN forces stepped in and, to much shock worldwide, were attacked

by Indonesian forces, resulting in brutal massacre and destruction of infrastructure. Since then, the nation has been rebuilt, but it still suffers the wounds it sustained in its fight for independence.

Even though the government looks to bulk up the country's assets other than oil with side projects like tourism and agriculture, the political instability means things are still a little shaky. And visiting East Timor on a backpacker budget gets fairly expensive, because the infrastructure necessary for hanging out—like cheap hostels and bars—without dropping a wad of cash does not exist.

BRUNEI DARUSSALAM

Brunei is a wealthy sultanate that operates under Sharia law, which penalizes all citizens, Muslim or not, with corporal punishment for trespasses such as theft. The country is overflowing with gas and oil—which is estimated to run out by 2040— and citizens enjoy free health care, a high literacy rate, and one of the highest standards of living in the world. The country avoided colonization, undergoing only a brief stint as a British protectorate that ended in the 1980s.

Visiting Brunei is understandably expensive but isn't out of the question. The country is safe (remember the corporal punishment thing), its underwater adventures are much more exciting than things happening on land, and its mosques are plated in opulent gold and imported marble. Brunei is also a completely dry country because of its Muslim dominance; however, non-Muslim foreigners over the age of seventeen can bring a max of twelve cans of beer or two liters (about forty-five shots) of liquor.

Passports and Visas

SO YOU WANT TO BACKPACK AROUND SOUTHEAST ASIA? GREAT CHOICE! YOU CAN DREAM of island hopping, street-food eating, and temple meditating all you want, but without the proper documents, it'll be near impossible to get off the ground. Let's get your paperwork in order so that you can pop into every country with no issues.

PASSPORT

Flying to any part of Southeast Asia is a trek, so you'll want to spend a good amount of time there before boarding a return flight. As such, you will need to have a passport that is valid for at least six months after you land at your first destination—we recommend a full year to be on the safe side. You will also need enough pages for visa stamps, which you can get added to your passport in the States or at a US embassy when you land.

Each visa will require at least two passport pictures, so plan to get enough snaps to match the number of countries you intend to visit, plus a few more.

VISAS

People of most nationalities, US included, can travel to Brunei, Malaysia, Singapore, the Philippines, and Thailand sans visa. If you plan to visit other countries (and you should!), listen up:

Vietnam

Some visitors get a fifteen-day visa upon arrival, but not US nationals. You will need to obtain a visa prior to visiting Vietnam, either at a Vietnamese consulate in the States (which is a pain in the ass, costs a bunch, and takes about a week) or through an online visa agency such as Vietnam Visa Center, which will cost you $20 for the agent fee. The company will email you a visa that you will print and take with you to one of Vietnam's five international airports. There, you will pay the $25 fee for a single-entry thirty-day visa, or $50 for a three-month multiple-entry one. If you happen to fall in love with the country and need to stay a little longer, you can get a travel agent to extend your trip for up to ninety days for $10. Keep in mind that extending your visa will take about a week, and the best place to do it is in the city of your port of entry, or in one of the largest cities, such as Hanoi or Ho Chi Minh.

OTP Tip

Not all land and sea borders in Southeast Asia offer visas upon arrival; make sure you are entering through one that does.

Cambodia

A one-month tourist visa will cost $30 and is available for purchase at airports in Phnom Penh and Siem Reap, and also at land border crossings—the latter of which gets shady sometimes as border officials will try to overcharge you. If you're entering through a major crossing, you can get a visa in advance online at www.mfaic.gov.kh, which will cost an extra $3 and take three days to process. You can only extend your visa once for a month, or you can "cheat" the system through one of two ways: You can leave for a few days to visit Thailand, and then reenter Cambodia to purchase a fresh month-long tourist visa for $30. Alternatively, obtain a business visa from the get-go, which costs $35, lasts thirty days, and can be extended (for a fee, of course) for up to one year. Slept through your visa expiration date? You will be charged $5 per day until you get the fuck outta there.

Indonesia

US nationals are currently allowed to enter Indonesia for thirty days without a visa, but choosing this option means you cannot extend your stay. A thirty-day paid visa can be obtained at all air- and seaports (but not land borders) in Indonesia for $35 and can be renewed for thirty days. Or you can go to Singapore and come back to get a fresh start with the free visa. If you overstay your visit, you will be charged $20 per day and given a lot of shit. When obtaining your visa, you will need to show some proof that you plan to leave before your allotted time is up (a return ticket works), and when departing you will need to present your disembarkation document (that little white card you fill out on the plane)—so don't lose it or you will have hell to pay. Keep in mind that Indonesian policies change at the drop of a dime, so you should always check current guidelines before heading there.

Laos

We suggest entering through Vientiane, where you can obtain a thirty-day visa for $30 that you can extend for sixty days. If you overstay your visit, you will be fined and/or arrested. You can acquire a visa in advance, but it's not worth the trouble.

OTP Tip

Always have the exact visa amount either in local currency or in USD upon arrival.

Timor-Leste

A thirty-day tourist visa is available upon arrival for $30 at the Dili International Airport and at seaports. It can be extended for up to sixty days for $75 if you have a Timorese sponsor.

Myanmar

The best way to apply for a visa in Myanmar is through the country's Ministry of Immigration and Population website, which will cost you $50. About a month after you apply (plan accordingly), you will receive an approval letter via email that is valid for ninety days. You will present the letter at Yangon, Mandalay, or Nay Pyi Taw international airport, or at certain land crossings in exchange for a visa that is valid for twenty-eight days. You can over-stay your visa (for a charge of $3 per day), but you risk having a hard time booking accommodations as most places will not let you stay with an expired visa.

OTP Tip

Check the online resource Passport Index (www.passportindex.org), where you can read about up-to-date visa requirements to every country for US passport holders.

Health and Safety

NOTHING RUINS A TRIP FASTER THAN BEING HELLISHLY SICK OR COMPLETELY BROKE after being robbed. Get in the know about how to stay relatively healthy during your travels. In terms of safety, you will find that most issues will be associated with petty theft and low-end scams, which you can avert by staying on your toes.

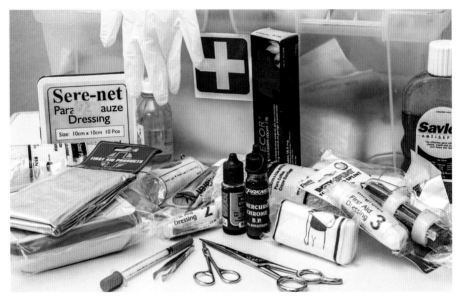

HEALTH

Life will inevitably throw curveballs your way health-wise, but taking a few predeparture precautions will help you sleep at night—likely surrounded by a mosquito net.

Bugs and Drugs

Southeast Asia is warm and humid, making it the perfect breeding ground for all kinds of bugs and bacteria. Since you are not a jungle dweller who has built immunity to these throughout your lifetime, you'll need a little help in the form of vaccinations. Currently, the only required vaccine is for yellow fever, but the World Health Organization recommends the following just to be safe:

- polio
- hepatitis A and B
- MMR (a combo shot for measles, mumps, and rubella)
- varicella
- typhoid
- adult diphtheria and tetanus

If you're staying longer than one month, you might want to tack on vaccinations for TB, meningitis, rabies, and Japanese B encephalitis. All of these are available at your local travel clinic, which you should visit about six weeks before your trip to make sure everything has time to work its magic in your bloodstream.

HYPOCHONDRIAC'S NIGHTMARE

Do you still fear SARS and West Nile virus, even though years have passed since either of those ailments has infected anyone? Well, you're in luck! Here are just a few things you can keep yourself up at night about (along with ways to prevent and treat them, because we're not total assholes).

DENGUE

A mosquito will bite you and cause your body to feel broken, achy, and weak, which is paired with severe headaches and a high fever that just does not subside.

Prevent it: Apply bug repellant, even during the day, wear protective clothing at night, and sleep under a mosquito net.

LEPTOSPIROSIS

Feel like you contracted a monster flu right after a rafting trip in Thailand? Welp, there is a chance you have lepto, a disease that can be fatal.

Treat it: You'll be so happy that you got that travel insurance, because a quick visit to the doc will score you a prescription for doxycycline, which will kick the sucker to the curb quick.

HIV

The world's least favorite STD is quite prevalent in Myanmar, Vietnam, and Thailand—where HIV kills more young people than any other illness.

Prevent it: We think you know what to do. Just do it (with condoms), and you can rest assured that you will stave off not only HIV, but herpes, genital warts, chlamydia, syphilis, and other sex nasties that are common in the region.

STRONGYLOIDIASIS

Don't ignore a rash that appears on your torso after you've been playing in the mud in Cambodia; it could be *larva currens*, a parasitic infection that may lead to the suppression of your immune system, leaving you wide open to ailments that can land you in some serious trouble.

Treat it: Visit a clinic once you notice the rash, and a doc will give you meds to clear it up before it leads to anything more serious.

TYPHOID

What may feel like a regular ol' case of upset stomach might actually be typhoid, a bacterial infection transmitted through food and water that can cause fever, headache, cough, and stomach pain.

Prevent it: Aren't you glad you listened to our advice and got yourself vaccinated? While vaccines aren't 100 percent effective—and you can treat typhoid with antibiotics—getting shot up will reduce your chances of feeling royally shitty.

Essential First Aid

Although packing your entire medicine cabinet is not necessary (and many meds can be purchased once you land), bring some essentials to keep yourself in good health.

PRESCRIPTIONS

Make sure all your medications are clearly labeled and in their original packaging, and bring more than enough to cover the duration of your trip. Ask your doc for a note for drugs that might seem suspicious to border officials (such as needles and the like).

BUG STUFF

In Southeast Asia, it's not just obnoxious houseflies that are the problem. Dangerous little buggers are everywhere, from the woods to the beach. Bug repellant (such as DEET) is super helpful, as are postbite meds such as antihistamines (cetirizine and promethazine), anti-inflammatories (good ol' ibuprofen), and antibacterial cream such as mupirocin.

BUTT AND GUT STUFF

Getting the shits is pretty much inevitable: it happens to up to 50 percent of travelers in Southeast Asia in their first two weeks on the ground. To help with the discomfort brought on by eating things that your body is not yet accustomed to, bring some Mylanta or Pepto-Bismol, loperamide (to stop the poops), and prochlorperazine (to stop the pukes). If your problem is constipation, a laxative like Metamucil will get you regular in no time. For your other end, bring some cranberry pills to keep your pisser feeling good, as you will be prone to the conditions that lead to UTIs (dehydration from the heat and/or drinking; damp underwear from whatever you get into). A Diflucan tab will keep the yeast at bay. Remember that consuming water from the tap here is a terrible idea, and ice cubes should be avoided as well. Bring water-purification tablets to avoid aquatic parasites.

ODDS AND ENDS

Packing a pair of tweezers is a lifesaver for pulling out little shards you may encounter, and having a few Band-Aids is always a good idea.

Insurance

Think about it this way: if having health insurance when you spend most of your time lying in bed watching Netflix is smart, then its importance goes up exponentially when you're diving, cliff jumping, eating things your body does not recognize, or just putting yourself in an environment far away from the safety of your bedroom. Predeparture, visit the doc to get an overall health check and to get up to date on vaccines. Make sure your insurance plan covers incidents abroad, or check out WorldNomads.com for travel insurance. Listen, if you're bitten by a monkey in some remote part of Cambodia, the Band-Aids and hand sanitizer you packed won't do shit. However, a proper insurance plan will get you emergency medical assistance, antirabies shots, and whatever meds you need to keep you from dying in the jungle.

SAFETY

Many less-traveled people assume that "unfamiliar" equates to "dangerous," which is never entirely the case. Sure, you will face some safety obstacles not found in the States—which will be amplified by the fact that you're in places where you are a target because your big-ass backpack screams foreigner. But just *being* in Southeast Asia (where people are nicer than anyone you've ever met) does not endanger your life. Still, there are certain circumstances that are unique to various countries that you should be aware of. Arm yourself with a little knowledge to avoid trouble.

Better Safe than Sorry

Get yourself a good padlock, and use it whenever you are separated from your stuff—while showering at the hostel, out for an excursion, spending the night with a stranger-turned-friend, and the like. Make sure to take photos of all your important docs (passport, visas, etc.), but also keep printed copies in your backpack in case your phone gets jacked. Keep cash and your passport out of your back pocket, and flip your pack to the front of your body in crowded situations where you may not easily feel fumbling hands on your back-side. Generally, you'll need to be a little more aware of your surroundings without becoming so paranoid that you lose sight of why you're traveling in the first place.

Theft

The chances of your being held up at gunpoint for the little cash that you may have on you are slim to none. However, you will inevitably find yourself in a few situations where you become vulnerable to petty theft. Stick to group travel if you plan to drink, and sleep with your belongings firmly attached to you on buses and trains.

Big, fast-moving cities such as Bangkok and Hanoi are notorious for snatch thieves, who can grab your stuff from their scooters while you're walking (or riding a scooter yourself). Keep everything you don't want stolen (such as your camera) close to your body, and don't put all you own into one swinging bag that can be easily grabbed.

The Po Po

As you might know from back home, cops are not always the best at keeping things orderly. The police in various regions of Southeast Asia aren't there for your safety; they see your ignorance of local laws as a way to squeeze bribes from your soft little Westerner's hands. In any location, we like to get a feel for how corrupt the police are by chatting with the locals before reporting or engaging in anything shady.

SCAMS BE GONE!

Doe-eyed tourists make perfect targets for small-scale scams in Southeast Asia. Although they don't pose any real danger, getting swindled out of a little cash will be annoying—and may bruise your "they'll never get me" ego. To help you navigate the ways in which you can get scammed, we've compiled a few common scenarios that should raise a red flag.

TAXIS

All drivers, moto or car, will always try to get a few extra bucks out of you. This low-grade scam is akin to "foreigner-pricing" schemes present in restaurants and most service establishments. In recent years, due to the proliferation of the internet, these types of swindles have died down as more travelers become aware of standard pricing. Make sure the driver turns on a meter, and if one does not exist or is "broken," negotiate a price prior to taking off, or hop out and find another ride.

BUS AGENTS

Avoid succumbing to travel agents touting great deals at bus stations for private long-distance bus rides. Your increased fare (as compared to what you would pay on a government-owned bus) will not get you great air-conditioning or some sort of VIP treatment. Instead, your shit will be stolen while you're sleeping, and you may or may not get to your desired destination.

SWINDLING STRANGERS

Friendly, well-dressed locals come up to you to spark conversation about the things you love talking about (ahem, yourself). We get it—you're in a foreign place, and you want to make friends. But think about this: how likely would you be to approach a tourist in the States to talk about their interests? This scam will lead to the type of friendship that will cause you to buy unset gemstones, pay for bottle service at karaoke joints, and treat groups of the stranger's friends to drinks you never intended to buy.

TRICKY TUK TUKS

A super-common scam in Thailand is the 10 baht tuk tuk ride, which only sounds like a great deal. You'll pay your 30 cents, hop aboard, and be driven to places where the driver can make some commission as opposed to the national monuments you were promised.

DRUG BAITING

While drug penalties in most Southeast Asian countries are severe (death sentences are more common than you'd like), enforcement of drug use and possession is often lax, creating a loophole for the ol' bait-n-bribe scam. Buying a joint off the street may result in your dealer immediately ratting you out to the cops—who will threaten you with jail time unless you line their pockets.

Conflict

Southeast Asia is a collection of somewhat interconnected countries, each with its own history of war, colonization, dictatorships, and the violence and general political unrest that result from these things.

We are all inspired to fight the patriarchy and social injustice back home, but keep your nose out of political clashes here. Things can (and have) escalated from protests to straight-up civil war, resulting in travelers needing to be evacuated or getting caught in the crossfire. Check with the various embassy sites for travel warnings to avoid conflict.

Explosives

Even though the American War (yes, same as the Vietnam War, but a more accurate name) has been over for decades, its remnants still pose a grave danger to residents and visitors of Vietnam, Laos, and Cambodia in the form of unexploded bombs and land mines. While we encourage off-trail exploration (or our name wouldn't be Off Track Planet), stepping on explosives in remote areas is a real danger, particularly in Cambodia. If you like your legs, stick to established paths there.

Sex, Partying, and Drugs

THE WIDE-EYED RUSH OF BEING IN A NEW PLACE WILL PUT YOU IN THE MOOD TO HUMP, dance, and party. Getting laid in Southeast Asia will be easy if you play your cards right. At the very least, if you get burned by backpackers, the thriving sex industry is always there to pick up the pieces of your broken heart. Drugs are illegal, kids—and finding them in Southeast Asia is not all that hard but comes with a different set of keep-yourself-outta-jail rules. When it comes to partying, Southeast Asia brings it hard with its lively beach-party scenes, laidback bars, and bumpin' clubs—not to mention all the beer pong preparties that will be in progress when you check into your hostel.

SEX

Traveling opens you up to more than just that swipe-right swagger. The screens of online dating and hooking up are replaced by the real people behind them, and you'll have no trouble at all figuring out how to get laid on the road, particularly in Southeast Asia—where sex is everywhere and the wretched heat means clothing comes off faster. Here are a few tips to help you up your game:

- First things first, you need to make sure to wrap it up, as STDs are rampant in this part of the world. Bringing some rubbers—whether you're the wearer or the, um, other person—will do you a lot of good, as finding condoms in Southeast Asia isn't always as easy as hitting the corner store at one a.m.
- Also at the top of the list is avoiding the curse of procreating by accident. Women, if you're on the pill, bring

enough to last you the whole trip, and don't you dare forget to take them on schedule. Other forms of preggo prevention, such as IUDs, are awesome while traveling because you don't have to remember a thing (except they won't prevent STDs, so again, wrap it up). Men, do your part by packing some rubbers to prevent unwanted procreating.

- Cleanliness is next to sexiness is next to . . . impossible to maintain while you're backpacking in unforgiving heat and humidity. Baby wipes, darling, are a lifesaver in more ways than one.

- If sloppy club hookups are your thing, you won't be yearning for more here. Getting wasted and making out, or more, in a dark corner will easily happen without you even trying. For something a little more substantial, remember that you have a lot of exciting, affordable activities at your fingertips and busloads of backpackers to do them with. Back home, asking someone to go scuba diving with you on a first date is super weird. Here, you can easily mingle with some hotties before hooking up in a nearby beach hammock.

- On that note, you will meet many people who are traveling alone (and maybe you're one of them). Humans, even solo travelers, have a tendency to search for companionship. Hit cafes in the morning to strike up conversation when everyone's sober. You'll likely engage in some variation on a soon-familiar exchange— *Where are you from? How long are you traveling? What is the coolest place you've seen so far?*—and that's a big advantage, because you don't really need to think about how to start small talk. A cafe chat can easily turn into bar belligerence and then a hostel hookup. Just don't expect to bring your lone rancher back home to meet ma.
- Flex. Not in the oiled-up muscle way (but it wouldn't hurt). Back home you may not be able to treat people to nice dinners or swanky resort stays, but here, where your American dollars carry a lot more value, you can. Don't buy a Rolex (which will be fake) for every person you want to bone; do treat people to meals and adventures. The bonding experience could get you laid.
- If you wake up horny in an eight-bunk room with a plan to score some action later in the night, consider coughing up a few more bucks for a private suite. The steaminess of your hookup gets sidelined once your bunkmate starts rattling the shitty metal bed when he hits his snore-stride at two a.m.
- Remember that PDA (we're talking as innocent as hand-holding) are a no-go in most countries here. Shoving your tongue down somebody's throat is all good by us, so long as it's consensual and you do it somewhere private.

PAY TO PLAY

Back home, paying for sex is seen as an act of desperation. In many parts of Southeast Asia, particularly in Thailand, the sex scene is thumpin', and paying to play is as common as pad thai. This (technically illegal) industry has its dark side, so you'll want to follow our dos and don'ts to establish the ins and outs of Southeast Asia's sexiest attractions.

YASS

- Go into a bar with confidence and cash. You must buy at least one round of drinks for the woman (who will approach you) and maybe one of her friends. Women are employees of the bar, and patronizing the pickup establishment is expected. To avoid being screwed in the ways you don't want, keep lines of communication open with the bartender about your tab.

- Determine how much you can handle. Women charge "short time" and "long time" rates, which means they will stay with you for one bone or all night, respectively. Decide what you want so that you don't get taken for a longer ride than you anticipated paying for.

- Report things that feel wrong. In backpacker areas, women will try to lure you to the girlie bars, which is normal. However, if you find yourself in some dark hole with people who don't seem like they want to be there, reporting it is your moral imperative. See the section on sex trafficking in Part III of this book for more.

- Use condoms.

NOPE

- Don't go online looking for "love." Internet prostitute searches can result in something shady that supports human—often child—trafficking. Keep your internet hookups to dating apps—which you can use here, too.

- Don't approach the bar thinking that it's an "anything goes" establishment. This isn't your unpredictable night out on the town where you may or may not get laid. This is a business, there is a menu, and the more you know about what you want, the less annoying it will be for all.

- Don't follow rando dudes into rando places. Doing so will lead you into uncomfortable situations that will scam you out of cash . . . or worse. Sex is out in the open in many locations around Southeast Asia. Red flags should immediately go up if that transparency starts to get murky.

- If pulling out and hoping for the best is your typical approach, you'll want to reacquaint yourself with Rosie Palm during of your trip to Southeast Asia, where STDs are a major issue.

PARTYING

Southeast Asia presents an endless array of places to party. The great thing about setting off on a multicountry journey is that you'll find a variety of ways to have a good time that far surpass hanging out at the same bar every night. Here are just five ways to rage the night away:

Booze Cruisin'
(Page 129)
When there's a designated driver, boats and booze are always a great mix. Find your sea legs, and party hard aboard the *SS Gonna Get Drunk* (we made that up) in Nha Trang, Vietnam, where sunrise booze cruises get the party started early.

Clubbin' x 3
(Page 126)
What "The Club" lacks in naming creativity, it makes up for with three stories of thumpin' dance floors, on-point DJs, and backpacker crowds eager to get down in da club. Find it on Khao San Road, Bangkok's main backpacker drag.

Full Moon Madness
(Page 130)
You may have heard of the monthly rager that happens during each full moon in Thailand. Well, that's not the only full moon party in this neck of the woods. Enter Sihanoukville, a feisty Cambodian island where the party is splayed across two beaches and rages all night.

Beer Hopping
(Pages 136–137)
Cambodia's craft-beer scene is poppin', and bouncing from beer to beer means visiting bars, breweries, and beer halls before melting into a night of something regrettable.

NYE Done Right
(Page 110)

Getting wet has never been wilder than at Thailand's annual Songkran celebration, where the best way to ring in the new year is to douse everyone in sight with your super soaker. Also, celebrating New Year's Eve in April means that you get to have two end-of-year ragers in one twelve-month period.

DRUGS

It is a known fact that drugs in Southeast Asia are at the same time highly illegal and easily obtained. Those two combined factors create a confusing landscape for the recreational drug user that wants to get blissfully high while at the same time

avoiding the death penalty—the punishment for drug offenses in some countries. We can't guarantee that our tips will keep you out of prison or help you score some quality narcotics; that depends completely on how slick you are.

Stoned in Paradise

What's better than visiting a stunning ancient temple? Being a little high while you saunter through to really make the pagodas pop. Countries in Southeast Asia vary widely when it comes to the penalties (and their enforcement) for possessing marijuana. In Muslim Brunei, you're better off sober unless you want to end up dead. In Laos, you will find cafes that sell joints—and dealers on the street that will sell you some herb before quickly ratting you out to police. Thailand decriminalized marijuana a bit in 2017: the country no longer assumes that all who possess it are drug dealers, meaning that mere possession comes with a lighter penalty if you get caught. If you prefer to bring your own reefer, know that you won't be considered a "trafficker" if it's under seven ounces in Malaysia, while places like Singapore will throw you in jail for life for any amount.

Party Favors

MDMA, or your friend Molly, does live in Southeast Asia but may be a little more of a recluse than she is back home. We'd suggest scoping out the possibility of landing a date with Molly at your hostel (out of earshot of employees) instead of trying to score some on the street. Malaysia is known for producing a whole bunch of MDMA, some of which trickles into the party scene. Not to scare you, but some varieties are produced raw and strong—which can mean you'll see sounds and hear colors, or it can mean you'll end up in the hospital.

Shrooms for Sale

Indonesia and Laos are notorious for their milkshakes and pizzas made with mushrooms, and not the white-button variety. You can order them on the beach in Bali to make the sunsets that much more colorful, or from a shop menu in Vang Vieng, then float blissfully down the river on an inner tube turned veritable magic carpet ride. Buying them loose on the street—or possessing any amount in your pockets and not your stomach—can get you five years in prison in Vietnam.

Harder Stuff

Dismantling the Golden Triangle—an opioid trading route that connects Thailand to Myanmar through Laos—is the biggest reason behind the strict drug laws present in most of Southeast Asia. Opium dens are the stuff of legend and have, in recent years, attracted tourists. Heroin addiction is on the rise, and trafficking the stuff will get you killed by firing squad (see the box below for proof). Interestingly enough, heroin in Phnom Penh is cheaper than cocaine and can find its way into your nose candy.

Scary Shit

Yaba is the krokodil (Google it), or "madness drug," of Southeast Asia. Named after the Hindu god of death, this stuff—which is homebrewed meth with bonus toxins like lithium, high amounts of caffeine, and mercury—will get you fucked up in ways you will regret. Myanmar produces it, Thailand distributes it, and you should probably stay the fuck away from the little red pill at all costs.

THE BALI NINE

Around these parts, execution by firing squad is the standard sentence if you're caught with a substantial amount of heroin. In Indonesia, attempts to traffic nineteen pounds of smack got most of a group of nine young Aussie dudes (dubbed the "Bali Nine") killed in 2015. The group tried to orchestrate a complicated smuggling deal. Once arrested, they lied about knowing each other in front of an Indonesian judge while being cocky shits to the media. The interesting part of this case is that many, including journalist Cindy Wockner, believe that members of the Bali Nine could have spared themselves the grisly execution if they had been a little less smug—an indicator of how drug laws operate in Indonesia and many parts of Southeast Asia. It's a principle that revolves around paying respect to the society, even if you're caught breaking the law. Take note; there's a lesson in there.

PART III

MAKE YOURSELF USEFUL

Beach parties, gorging yourself on street food, and all-night ragers have their place in backpacking across Southeast Asia. But the more you travel these beautiful lands, the more you will realize that you can go a little further than just spending your tourist dollars (which, we might add, do support the region's economy). Add some value to your trip by committing to a cause that moves you. We're here to help inspire you to find a volunteer program, internship, or study-abroad opportunity—be it saving animals from extinction, helping kids find lifelong inspiration in places where education is scarce, fighting human-rights violations, learning (and teaching) sustainable environmental practices, or lending a helping hand to people still suffering from the effects of war. Often for very reasonable program fees (which usually pay for accommodations, orientation materials, and some meals), you can both extend your trip and meet people you wouldn't otherwise. Doing something about the atrocities you encounter during your trip will not only feel good; it can make a lasting positive impact.

Kids

CHILDREN ARE OFTEN THE MOST VULNERABLE CITIZENS OF IMPOVERISHED POPULATIONS, a fact that rings true around many countries in Southeast Asia. Kids here are exploited, trafficked as laborers, and forced into sex work more often than you can imagine. You have more to offer young people than you think, particularly if you have a great grasp on the English language. Being a role model comes with many rewards, the smallest of which is feeling like you're finally adulting.

FRIENDS OF ASIA

Friends of Asia, which has been around since 2007, is a good bet for getting (and giving) the most out of your trip if you're looking to help kids in Southeast Asia. This volunteer organization is an independent company that actively works to keep pricing low (but still high enough to help it cover costs) while promoting positive change within the communities where it runs its projects—an important distinction, because some companies will take advantage of your interest in volunteering and pocket a good portion of your inflated fees. Orphanage tourism is a big issue in Southeast Asia, where travelers who hope to pull at their own heartstrings will stop in for a day visit, a phenomenon that has actually created a demand for orphans. This has resulted in children being pulled from school only to play the part of an orphan for onlookers' sake. Volunteering with Friends of Asia for any of the projects listed below is a good bet to avoid exploiting children and actually help them. Friend of Asia screens all volunteers by running a police background check, a quality you should look for in any program involving kids.

Kindergarten Volunteer
(Bangkok, Thailand)

This program places volunteers in kindergartens in slums around Bangkok, where staffing tends to be insufficient, kids (ages three to five) are full of energy, and government aid is almost nonexistent. You will spend time playing games, singing songs, and helping kids imagine a future outside of poverty—simply by speaking your native tongue. A hidden perk of this program is that you'll pick up a lot of Thai, because when you're interacting with kids you won't be so nervous about getting your pronunciation and grammar right.

OTP Tip
The program has a two-week minimum, but try to stay for at least a month (if not longer). You will be working directly with children, so committing to developing real relationships, rather than just feeling like you put in your two weeks, is important.

Teaching English
(Chiang Mai, Thailand)

This low-cost program—which runs a minimum of two weeks ($399) and costs only $80 per week thereafter, covering accommodations, some food, and an orientation program—is a great way to get some teaching experience in a place (about an hour outside of Chiang Mai) where native English speakers are rare. Your simple language skills are valuable to children here, giving them a big boost later in life. You can choose a grade level to teach (between kindergarten and twelfth grade) and will be paired with a Thai teacher, whom you will assist to create lesson plans and eventually teach a class of your own.

Victims of Agent Orange (Hanoi, Vietnam)

Located in a wellness-oriented village near Hanoi, this program is specifically focused on children and veterans who have been affected by Agent Orange—an herbicide used by Americans during the war that continues to lead to birth defects in Vietnam. Friends of Asia specifically seeks volunteers with experience in medical work and in caring for those with disabilities to help create fun environments so that kids can lead happy, normal lives. Volunteers, who are required to make a one-month commitment, will participate in playing with and caring for the kids, assist with feeding during lunch, and write proposals for grants and donations. You will also help care for the program's organic garden, which supplies the majority of the produce to the surrounding village.

WHAT REMAINS OF THE WAR?

Although the American War (known to us conveniently as the Vietnam War) has been over since 1975, it has left a lingering trail of suffering to this day. During the course of the war, American troops sprayed more than ten million gallons of the defoliant Agent Orange in southern Vietnam to clear forests and thus reveal opposing Viet Cong forces. The chemical had not been adequately tested to ensure it was safe to drop over a large population of humans. What remains is an absolute disaster. Millions of people experienced liver damage, heart conditions, cancer, and severe birth defects—which are still quite prevalent. Children are born with physical and cognitive disorders into poor families that do not have the means to provide them with the extra care they need. To make matters worse, land mines that were not detonated during the war have killed more than forty thousand Vietnamese people, many of them children, and have mangled the bodies of many more.

SLAVES OF THE SEX INDUSTRY

Prostitution (which is technically illegal in Southeast Asia) can be a great thing when it's between two (or more) consenting adults. It is a profession that can empower prostitutes while helping those looking to pay for a no-strings-attached quickie to get off and move on. However, the global sex industry has a morbidly dark underbelly, the festering guts of which are strewn about Southeast Asia, where millions of people (many of whom are children) are slaves to the trade.

Poverty Poachers

Although it's an issue in most areas of Southeast Asia, sex trafficking is most prevalent in Cambodia, Vietnam, and Thailand. In Thailand alone, about thirty thousand children are slaves of the sex industry. Demand in these countries (referred to as "sex tourism") fuels the constant supply of sex workers and slaves. A wide network between countries connects predators to children, feeding on those that are most vulnerable. Extreme poverty in these regions makes relatively highly paid sex work attractive to of-age women—but also to those looking to exploit them and their younger (sometimes wildly underage) siblings. Networks of pimps lure families that are desperate for cash to sell their children into the trade under the promise of an education or career advancement. Instead, the children are sold into the sex trade, where they are used, again and again, for profit in brothels, bars, massage parlors, and private residences. Human-rights organizations have exposed child-sex trafficking networks in Cambodia, where children as young as seven are locked in dark rooms waiting for some Western pedophile to pay to rape them.

Tricks of the Trade

A child forced into sex work early in life will eventually grow into an adult—one with deep psychological issues—who can continue to be exploited by those who control her income in bars that seem totally legit. This goes to say that choice is a relative concept, and factors such as poverty and lifelong exploitation add a complex layer to prostitution that blurs the line between choice and force. As has been shown in recent sex-ring busts in Thailand, child prostitution is often concealed (and fueled) by corrupt local officials who take a little chump change to keep quiet. Because these officials also engage in having sex with the child slaves, relying on them to crack down on the industry—which brings billions of Western dollars into the country annually—is impossible.

In recent years, the Thai government has made some strides in exposing and raising awareness about the child sex trade by posting phone numbers someone can call to report exploitation in tourist-heavy areas such as airports. And while this is a great thing, sexual predators don't just go away like the common cold. They spread like gonorrhea. Places such as Laos and politically vulnerable Myanmar are turning into sex-tourism destinations, and without the proper government action in place, women and children there are becoming more vulnerable to sex slavery. The proliferation of the internet has created yet another way for child predators to find what they're looking for in Southeast Asia—from child porn to arranged rapes—often without consequence.

What You Can Do

Organizations around the world are working to end sex slavery through various initiatives, from on-the-ground guerilla-ring-busting tactics to creating opportunities for people in vulnerable situations so that shady pimps can't coerce them into the trade so easily. You can connect with the database of volunteer opportunities (where you will be vetted yourself) through the do-gooder platform End Slavery Now and explore resources through the Bangkok-based organization End Child Prostitution and Trafficking (ECPAT).

What you *can't* do is ignore human-rights violations when you are in places where sex slavery is prevalent. As Westerners, we find the idea of having easy access to cheap sex in Southeast Asia fascinating. But remember that there is no magic wand that can tell you if a prostitute is selling her (or his) services by choice or as a victim of lifelong sexual exploitation. If something feels wrong, report it. In Thailand, you can do so by calling or texting the following number: +66 99 130 1300.

MOBILE SUMMER CAMPS (MYANMAR)

Myanmar—known as Burma until 1989—is currently in a state of scary, violent transition. The nation is made up of more than one hundred ethnic groups, and many, particularly the Rohingya Muslims, who are actively being exterminated, fear that the government (technically now a democracy but with heavy military undertones) will continue to turn on them. Refugees, many of whom are children, are fleeing to the border between Myanmar and Thailand to find safety. This idyllic, mountainous region, the Nong Khai Province, is where the organization Openmind Projects has set up mobile camps to ensure that victims of political tragedy have access to education. Volunteering here—half summer camp, half traditional school—will make you feel like a kid again.

The School Part

The organization, built on the idea of learning by doing, aims to empower children by showing them how to access knowledge on the internet—a way to learn that doesn't end with the last page of a textbook. In-class discussions are purposefully open ended so that students can learn to think critically while practicing their English-language skills. Topics covered are hyper-relevant to the kids' lives and include health and nutrition, environmental issues particular to the region, technology, and how to get a job. Students are challenged to debate about what they learn and to create videos to share on social media. Children discuss the things they learn with volunteers, which offers an extra layer of English-language interaction.

The Camp Part

At the day camps, which usually run six to eight days in either April or October,

each volunteer helps lead a small group of campers to keep interactions personal. Free time is factored into the curriculum, and you get to spend it with the kids, sharing Thai and Burmese food in the remote border mountains, where waterfalls and jungle replace the concrete and car fumes of inner-city schools. Part of your responsibility is having fun and helping to create an atmosphere similar to that of the week-long summer camp you'll never forget. You'll lead creative projects, sing songs, play games, and encourage the kids to express themselves.

The Takeaway

Young children in Southeast Asian villages often forego education to begin working to help provide for their families, which pushes them away from gaining bankable skills. Obtaining even a small amount of knowledge about how to use the internet is golden to those that might find themselves otherwise disconnected from opportunities. For stateless children, engaging with people in this setting helps them gain a confidence that can aid them in breaking the cycle of poverty. For you, life will feel like it did back at summer camp—but with a lot more feels, because you'll be doing more than just stirring the chili in the rec room and playing tonsil hockey with fellow counselors.

GET CONNECTED THROUGH GIVINGWAY

While many volunteer websites are stuck in the nineties, the digital marketplace GivingWay feels a little more modern. Its aim is to help users sort out the many volunteer opportunities available abroad. Spanning more than a hundred countries, the platform is constantly adding new programs and engaging with the volunteer community for feedback on existing projects. All you really have to do is decide that you want to volunteer, and GivingWay will help you figure out how.

LOGISTICS

GivingWay has built a database of nearly two thousand volunteer projects around the world. You can browse all the projects listed on the platform, customize the opportunity to your country or region of preference, or sort posts based on the type of work you want to do—be it in sustainability, child care, education, animal welfare, or human rights. You can also search for specific nonprofits or connect with a group that accepts volunteers in your area of interest. GivingWay is adamantly against promoting orphanage tourism or any other exploitative practice and does not post suspicious projects. However, organizations that appear on the platform are not fully vetted by GivingWay. Instead, reviews are posted by previous volunteers (a bit Yelp-like but without the passive-aggressive garbage), allowing you to decide for yourself if the opportunity is legit.

MAKE IT WORK FOR YOU

Decide on the field you're interested in, the time period during which you are available, and the region where you'd like to volunteer, and the platform will hook you up with a bunch of options that fit your criteria. We suggest you choose from among programs that have the most reviews. Each program lists details such as a project description, expected duties, and the organization's needs. Some post their program fee (ranging anywhere from zilch to a few hundred bucks per week), and some post a stipend paid to volunteers (score!). If you're a little lost about the good you'd like to do in Southeast Asia, GivingWay has a blog that focuses solely on volunteering topics and points readers to areas of interest on the platform. Once you choose your program, you will fill out an application directly with the organization and begin what we hope is a life-changing, enriching experience.

Human Rights

THE TRUTH IS, AS SHITTY AS WE THINK WE HAVE IT BACK HOME, PEOPLE IN THIS REGION suffer egregious human-rights violations. Corrupt gender norms stack the odds against women in Southeast Asia's poorest countries, often forcing them into the sex trade and spitting them out broken on the other side. Income disparities exist across the spectrum in even the most industrious nations like Singapore. Access to English-language education is a powerful tool that helps to close gender gaps and end the cycle of poverty. And guess what? You speak English!

AWARE: GENDER EQUALITY IN SINGAPORE

If your fight for women's rights was reignited during or after the 2016 elections, you can continue to tip the scales toward gender equality for women in Singapore with the Association of Women for Action and Research (AWARE). The organization has been working to empower women since 1985, researching instances of workplace sexual harassment, helping to alleviate poverty among older women, advocating for stricter domestic-abuse policies, and making strides toward creating a country where women have access and opportunities that are equal to those of their male counterparts. Singapore's economy and industry are booming, and AWARE aims to remove roadblocks to women having a fair piece of the pie. As a volunteer at AWARE's center in Singapore, you can be a crucial part of its work in a number of areas.

Helpline Volunteer

If you've ever volunteered for a suicide-prevention line or other type of helpline, you'll have a bit of an advantage for this intense assignment. The program lasts an entire year, a necessary commitment to both make an impact and understand how to be an effective phone counselor. You will be given an invaluable three-phase training course that will instruct you in counseling skills, sexual assault, abuse and violence, family law, and Sharia law so that you can handle all kinds of callers. You will have the ability to work with individuals to triage their concerns, connect them to available services, and identify advocacy issues. Once your training is complete, the position requires a commitment of three to six hours per week, which means that if you live in Singapore for a full year, you can engage in something tangible that'll help women in the region.

Research Volunteer

If you love to figure out exactly what kind of change is needed, and if writing persuasive reports to push for that change is your forte, this volunteer opportunity is right up your alley—and you must be super committed to get shit done. You will be assigned an accountability partner to help keep you motivated. You will also be part of a project team that meets once every month. The opportunity will challenge you to oversee advocacy activities, create reports regarding policy changes, and implement surveys to better understand where and how AWARE's advocacy is needed in Singapore.

Intern

The organization also offers a number of year-round, structured, résumé-building internships in four departments. Through the Advocacy, Research, and Communications arm you can learn how to get gender-equality initiatives into the mainstream using social-media resources. The Community Engagement department hosts workshops, events, and campaigns that inspire local women in Singapore to effect their own ideas. The Support Services and Sexual Assault Care Center provides counseling services for victims of abuse, and the Secretariat department engages in fund-raising to keep the organization afloat.

Do Your Own Thing

AWARE also considers collaborating on projects that you feel passionate about. Now, they won't just accept any dumb thing. Your project will have to be well thought out, effective, and in line with the work that AWARE does. You can propose new programs within AWARE's existing projects, such as raising awareness about sexual assault in Singapore through public campaigns, creating safe spaces to report abuse, and promoting initiatives that support survivors. Another option is thinking about ways to drive a more gender-balanced narrative through AWARE's Gender Equality Is Our Culture (GEC) program, which elevates women's voices in a male-dominated society; it has sponsored projects like one that invited female authors to write essays and poetry related to their experiences, and then helped them publish the works.

TEACHING ENGLISH IN SOUTHEAST ASIA

Although being an English teacher in the States might not feel like you're tackling a human-rights issue, in many parts of the world that is exactly what it is. English-language knowledge, especially when acquired from an early age, is a major asset that can help people break out of the cycle of working low-wage jobs. English speakers can seek opportunities abroad or be better equipped to open businesses in their native countries. If you struggled to learn Spanish in high school, you know that learning a second language is best done when you're young. Here are a few programs that will turn your knowledge of English into an important stepping stone for people around Southeast Asia. Many of these organizations offer other volunteer opportunities in addition to teaching English.

The Bumi Sehat Foundation (Indonesia)

This organization runs an after-school youth-enrichment program in Bali that helps kids ages ten and older really nail their English. Volunteers work with students (from three p.m. to six p.m.) and with Balinese teacher aides to create impactful curriculums. You will wake up each morning to fresh bread and fruit in a sunny house shared with other volunteers, and you are free to explore the island from Friday to Sunday when school's not in session. You'll need to commit to a four-week minimum stay, but we recommend devoting a few months to really make a difference.

We Are Bamboo (Thailand)

This volunteer program will put you face-to-face with the economic disparities present in Thailand, where, as a typical example, the tropical island of Koh Samui is split into two regions: a thriving tourist-resort destination on one side and communities struggling to make ends meet on the other. The Thai government gives little funding toward education, and the children living on the poor side of the island (where you will be located) are all but forgotten. You will work with children ages six to thirteen throughout the school day, mostly teaching English but also engaging in arts and crafts to promote creative thinking. The program accepts eight volunteers per two- to four-week session, which are offered twice per month. Registering early will score you a discount on the program fee. Since 2013, this program has set a thousand kids on the road toward becoming successful adults.

International Volunteer HQ (Malaysia)

Founded by *Harry Potter*'s Daniel Radcliffe, this organization is known for its super-affordable programs, which cost just $395 for two weeks in Malaysia. The English-language course takes place in a library in Taiping (located in northwest Malaysia), where you will play an instrumental role in running an after-school program from two p.m. until five p.m. for children ages four to twelve. Teaching resources are kind of scarce here, and volunteers will be challenged to get creative about visual aids and the like. IVHQ also operates a program for special-needs children and adults up to age thirty; volunteers (who must have special-needs training) are tasked with providing support to permanent staff in mobilizing students, helping to feed them, and organizing engaging activities.

Workaway (Cambodia)

Two hours outside of Phnom Penh lies Takeo, where the volunteer organization Workaway has partnered with a Khmer-run NGO to serve a very poor, rural population. Kids sleep on floor mats at the school and wake up at five a.m. to start their day. Your job will be to lead simple English-instruction classes for two to three hours per day. Kids in this region do not have many chances to interact with English speakers, so by just being a native speaker you're already doing a lot to help them get comfortable with the language. In addition to teaching English, you will help engage the kids in supplemental activities that aim to boost their self-esteem, leadership skills, and self-discipline. As a bonus, the school can arrange for a free Khmer-language class to help you be a better educator and world traveler.

HOW TO BE A RESPONSIBLE VOLUNTEER

Volunteering in a place like Southeast Asia involves a lot more than merely showing up. If you're looking to put a few lines on your résumé or bulk up that college application, this region—which comprises many developing countries with volatile issues—is not the place to do it. Volunteering will be life-changing for you, but it also needs to benefit those you serve. Keep these tips in mind to maximize the time you donate:

- Evaluate the skills that you can contribute. Speaking English is a good start, but if you don't have the communication skills to help someone learn your native tongue, you might consider offering more labor-oriented work like construction or gardening.
- Connect with the organization you plan to work with well in advance so that you can feel out what to expect and what they will need from you.
- Not every organization is doing good for its community. Some organizations pose as volunteer organizations simply to use your free labor instead of hiring a local. Ask about their responsible-tourism policies to make sure nobody gets screwed over.
- Most programs charge a project fee, and that shouldn't be a red flag. However, some hike up the price to profit from your stay—with little of the actual fee going to program necessities. Ask about that, diligently.

- If you are working with children, the organization should screen you. If it doesn't, that's a big red flag. A lack of background screening leaves an open door for sex offenders and others who don't have the kids' best interests in mind.
- If you're shy, consider stepping out of your shell. You will be in a place where people may not have much interaction with Westerners aside from a shitty tourist now and again. Engaging in meaningful interactions across language barriers may be tough for you if you're introverted, but consider this an opportunity to better yourself in a way that matters.
- Volunteering gives you an opportunity to become a quasi local. Make an effort to shop, eat, and hang out in places that support the local economy, and encourage other volunteer friends you make along the way to do the same.

BUILDING CLAY HOUSES (THAILAND)

Everyone knows that Legos were the best toys (well, next to Transformers). Add a little mud and a lot of purpose to the mix, and you've got an eco-clay community-building project that's well underway in western Thailand. You can get in on the action with the volunteer company Involvement Volunteers International.

Dirty Deets

This project, located in the remote town of Singburi, offers programs that start at a minimum of one week or can last up to several months. Volunteers—who must be over eighteen and able-bodied—are constructing affordable and practical housing and infrastructure, including a large school complex, in the area. The program fee ($235 per week) includes airport pickup, all weekday meals (and some on the weekends), and insurance. Volunteers participate in all aspects of turning clay into naturally temperature-controlled buildings. Accommodations are hostel-style, with bunk beds, an in-suite shared bathroom, and good Wi-Fi. Alcohol is not allowed to be consumed on premises, which gives you good reason to head out to the local bars, where you will meet many volunteers from other programs around town.

Clay All Day

The great thing about this program is that you will have to erect the houses from the ground up, in the most literal way. Building materials are not just handed to you. Clay needs to be extracted from the ground, blended with water, and rigorously mixed (with just your little feet). After all that, it has to rest for a day—which means you get to play with more clay. Once the mixture is ready, you will pour it into brick molds, which take two weeks to mature into clay bricks. Once the building blocks are ready, construction can begin. That entails utilizing rickety handmade scaffolding for building vertically. The entire process is slow, laborious, and, in the end, very satisfying.

Downtime

Rainy days are a no-go for building houses, as the clay needs sun to dry. Additionally, the latter part of Wednesdays, along with weekends, are allotted for free time. Spend it biking around town to visit local temples, explore colorful architecture, and dine at roadside restaurants that serve the kind of food your grandma would make if she were Thai. Attractions in town include the Wat Phikun Thong, a temple that houses one of the largest golden Buddha statues in Thailand; Pak Bang Market, which has been hustling fresh food for more than 150 years; and the artifact-packed Inburi National Museum. One of the biggest perks is that you get to live in a community full of Thai culture that's not geared toward attracting tourists, but it's only ninety miles to Bangkok. Life here moves a lot slower, so enjoy the pace while the clay does its thing.

OTP Tip

Plan a return trip to Singburi in a few years, when the village you helped to build is fully operational. We imagine it'll be a uniquely rewarding experience.

STUDY ABROAD IN VIETNAM WITH IPSL

Studying abroad always has a purpose, but it's usually motivated by your desire to discover a new culture, food, or adventure while racking up class credits. Service-learning is a concept that has *something* to do with uncovering novel, worldly experiences, but it is mostly focused on what *you* can do for the world around you. International Partnership for Service Learning (IPSL) is a well-established,

respected organization that helps travel-minded people turn into social-justice advocates through a number of programs aimed at different study levels. IPSL's program in Hanoi offers a valuable learning experience that will help you understand the often tense crossroads of latent communism and thriving new development.

institute for global learning

Service-Learning

The IPSL program requires three core classes, one of which is Vietnamese-language instruction, and the other two of which focus on COSA (or Community Organizing and Social Activism). The latter is an in-depth study of social-justice activism that analyzes the successes and failures of movements in history. You will acquire the skills to understand how to ethically approach community organizing, engage in effective advocacy, and inspire others to follow—skills that you can use wherever you choose to effect change, even back home in the States. You will also choose from a wide range of electives to supplement your core classes, among them Sustainable Tourism, Globalization and Social Justice, and Politics and Policy of Development.

Service-Doing

Along with the academic curriculum, you will volunteer for approximately fifteen hours per week in the local community to put your service skills to the test—and to learn a thing or two outside the classroom. IPSL offers opportunities in a number of fields relevant to fighting for equality and equity in Vietnam, including women's empowerment and microfinance projects, poverty alleviation, eco-tourism

development, and youth programs. Although your interests in a particular field are considered, the main motives behind your placement are your language-proficiency skills and the needs of the community or agency where you will volunteer. This is a tenant of service-learning: the outcome of your work for the community is as important as the résumé-building benefits and learning experiences you acquire. IPSL is also careful about separating English-speaking students by placing them in different agencies so that they can get the full immersive experience.

Why Vietnam?

Vietnam is a unique destination in that communism is still alive here while new technology and Western ideals continue to penetrate everyday life. You will learn about social systems, politics, history, and culture through IPSL and will become more aware of how to impart real social change through the COSA core classes. The service portion will bring you face-to-face with the country's most pervasive issues and the people who are affected by them daily. With these tools, plus a basic knowledge of the Vietnamese language, your interactions with locals and your engagement in day-to-day life in Vietnam will be hyperfocused and -informed—with a little partying on the weekends, of course.

How Much?

These accredited courses will give you up to eighteen college credits for a three-month semester or six credits for a month-long summer program (which eliminates the electives requirement). It will cost you about what a typical semester in college costs: $15,000 (which includes dorm-style accommodations, three meals per day, health insurance, and a few other costs) plus in-country expenses. You can apply for scholarships or grants. Since IPSL is highly regarded, the course will get you more than bragging rights; it is a huge boon to your graduate-admissions materials and your résumé.

Sustainability

IT'S NO SECRET THAT OUR NATURAL RESOURCES ARE ON THEIR WAY TO HELL. PEOPLE IN Southeast Asia are disproportionately affected by the world's demand for palm oil (found in everything from soap to cereal), which has led to disastrous consequences in Indonesia. Not to mention the fact that plastics are clogging up the region's beaches and waterways. You can continue to sit on your ass and recycle, or you can up your game by volunteering and doing some real to save the earth.

PHUK PALM OIL

Indonesian forests are being destroyed for pizza dough. Crazy, right? Peep this: the production of palm oil—which is used in 50 percent of all household items, including shampoo, lipstick, baked goods, and, yes, pizza dough—directly contributes to the habitat depletion of lovable, too-close-to-humankind orangutans; clears forests at lightning speed; and presents some real-deal human-rights issues. Native to western Africa, palm fruit trees thrive in rainy, tropical climates like Indonesia. For

this reason, football-field-sized indigenous forests are being cleared in the region to plant palm oil trees, which is leading to mass-scale deforestation. Clearing biodiverse forested land exposes animals to poachers, disrupts the ecosystems they maintain, and is just plain rude.

Palm Problem

In addition to creating a giant spewing mess of pollution (the smoke clouds of which spread across whole countries), palm oil production also royally screws the people—and wildlife—who occupy

palm-oil-producing lands. Corporations come in under the guise of boosting local economies, but they clear indigenous populations that rely upon the forest for diversified food and medicine, and force them—including young children—to work on palm oil plantations for little pay. People who were once rich with resources become marginalized, impoverished, and slaves of the industry, all for the sake of making processed party foods.

In the last thirty-five years, illegal logging for palm oil has led to the depletion of 50 percent of the tropical rainforest in Sumatra. As a result, wild orangutans are predicted to be extinct in the next decade, and Sumatran tigers in less than three. The rate of deforestation is massively outpacing that of the progress made to remedy the various issues tied to the palm oil industry. The nonprofit group Roundtable on Sustainable Palm Oil (RSPO) was formed in 2004 to address the exploitative system. RSPO issues Certified Sustainable Palm Oil (CSPO) labels to producers that follow a (pretty lenient) set of standards, which do not include abstaining from the clearing of forests or the planting of trees in biosensitive areas. So what can you do?

Help the Hurt

Go Abroad—one of the best volunteer organizations in the world—sponsors the Indonesia Orangutan Conservation program in Sumatra, which is dedicated to helping the animals most greatly affected by the global demand for palm oil. The work involves small groups that keep track of animal populations in the region, provide the apes with prepared meals, and help to restore their habitat through reforestation efforts. The thirteen-day program costs $1,045 for students ($1,395 for nonstudents), plus an $85 registration fee. Charges cover ground transportation, food, and accommodations. Volunteers can opt for add-ons such as visiting local villages, hanging with elephants at sanctuaries, and river rafting.

DIVE DEEP: MARINE CONSERVATION

Southeast Asia has a tumultuous relationship with the sea that surrounds it. The humans that live here have long depended on the oceans for food, but marine life has suffered due to a number of things—including shitty tourists that love to throw their Red Bull cans and McDonald's wrappers whereverthefuck because they're on vacation and can't be bothered to be decent. Globalization has also played a part in disrupting one of Southeast Asia's most valuable resources. If you're a fan of water and everything that exists beneath and above it, here are a few ways you can dive deep into marine conservation in Southeast Asia.

Professional Association of Diving Instructors (PADI) scuba course to get them ready for work. If you're a beginner, you will be able to dive after the first week in the program. Those with existing certification will be administered an advanced course, and experienced divers will take a shark-conservation course, allowing them to do the big-kid work. The aim of the program is to remove waste from coral reefs, keep track of native species of fish and marine life, and replant mangroves and forests—which are often where native marine animals start their life cycles. Work is a five-day-per-week endeavor, but accommodations are private bungalows (each with a bathroom!), where you can chill and think about how your work matters to the local communities that depend on the ocean.

Projects Abroad (Thailand)

Along the Andaman Sea in the Krabi Province—where some of the country's oldest mangroves and lowland forests live—you will be exposed to an underwater world that's in dire need of conservation. All volunteers are required to pass the

Marine Conservation (Cambodia)

The National Geographic Society awarded this program a Marine Protection Prize, so you know it's überlegit. Located on the private island of Koh She, which neighbors six other islands, the program focuses on ten key conservation initiatives, including

identifying fish, invertebrate, seahorse, and mammal populations; helping to manage marine fisheries resources; and engaging in policies that defend the island and its inhabitants. You can get scuba-certified on the spot and start diving in no time, and the data you collect will help researchers plan targeted conservation strategies. Weekends are for tanning, so bring a book.

LAMAVE (Philippines)

The Filipino organization LAMAVE (Large Marine Vertebrates Research Institute) is all about helping specific species of ocean animals survive in our not-so-great world. Each program is led by a local scholar who is chosen based on his or her passion for ocean conservation, particularly in the Philippines. Each project varies in duration (between one and three months), and some require prior diving experience and certification. Located at the center of the Coral Triangle, the waters surrounding

the Philippine islands are some of the most diverse in the world. LAMAVE gets you into the thick of it with projects that focus on tracking previously identified whale sharks to monitor their behavior around Honda Bay, collecting baseline data using photo-identification of the green turtles of Apo Island, and identifying the key migratory and living areas of manta and devil ray populations, which have been decimated by illegal hunters in recent years. Participating in any of these experiences means you will need to put your phone down and focus on the real world for a while, which is a win in our book.

LARGE
MARINE
VERTEBRATES
RESEARCH
INSTITUTE
PHILIPPINES

Gili Shark Conservation (Indonesia)

If living in pure paradise while helping adorable sharks is your idea of fun, the Gili Shark Conservation program has got the goods. The project mostly takes place on the island Gili Air but also helps conservation efforts on nearby Gili Trawangan and Gili Meno. Volunteers spend time with experienced researchers taking underwater video, conducting roaming dives, performing water and beach cleanups, and interacting with local schools in educational sessions to help students be more conservation-minded. You'll live at the project villa, where you'll have access to a pool and organic meals, and you'll get to breathe the clean air (unadulterated by motor vehicles, which are not allowed on the island) while watching the rainbow-hued sunset every night. Weekly language lessons expose you to the *bahasa*, the official language of Indonesia. As a bonus, Bali is only twenty-five miles away—an easy weekend trip if you need even more island paradise in your life.

TRACC (Malaysia)

This program, with the full name Tropical Research and Conservation Centre, is all about restoring the health of coral reefs. TRACC volunteers have revived a great portion of Pom Pom Island by planting more than seventy-five hundred reef fragments over the years. It takes time to familiarize yourself with the project at hand, so each requires a minimum two-week commitment. The work week runs from Tuesday to Saturday, when most of the diving takes place, with a free "Funday" Sunday and a "dry" Monday—so you can get your ears nice and unclogged and your lungs free of nitrogen. Local cooks dish up a breakfast and buffet-style lunch every day. TRACC is actively reducing the amount of meat it uses in meals to cut down on its environmental footprint and asks that you practice what you preach by sticking to reusable containers for all that you bring. You will sleep in a tent, share a shower, and wake up daily with a new sense of purpose.

OTP Tip

If you're currently studying in the field of marine conversation or biology, you can score some class credits with TRACC's A-Level, world-recognized program, which allows you to put in 360 hours of marine-science study, with a focus on tropical ecosystems, in fourteen weeks.

MO TRASH, MO PROBLEMS

Before you visit Southeast Asia, you might have an image in your mind of bright blue waters, rolling emerald rice paddies, and serene islands with sand that's as pure as fresh-fallen snow. And while all of these images will be fulfilled on some level, one thing you will notice once you get there is a fuckton of trash. Instead of just chalking it up to humans being assholes, you can change your perspective and do something about it.

WTF Is Trashpacking?

On a super-simple level, trashpacking is exactly what it sounds like: picking up trash while backpacking. However, the concept is actually a way of life that has a ripple effect. Becoming a trashpacker means acknowledging the damaging effect tourism has on those beautiful beaches you imagined predeparture and committing to picking up a piece of trash, even if you weren't the one who threw it on the ground. It's about shifting that "vacation" mindset into one that acknowledges that the places tourists visit have to bear the impact of thousands of people treating them like dumps.

Ready to Trashpack?

To start, all you need is a reusable bag. Whether you're picking up a piece of trash or dedicating an hour to cleaning up a portion of beach, trashpacking will soon become a way of life. Along the way, you'll notice that what you think is a solitary act of awareness will inevitably become an inspiration to others to do the same—or at the very least, cause others to ask you what the hell you're doing. If you've ever lived in a messy room for a prolonged period of time (oh, we know you have), you know that once you pick up one corner of it, the rest starts to stand out for the mess that it is. It's a game of awareness, and the same applies to every piece of trash you see on the ground. Many trashpackers are now part of larger cleanup organizations across Southeast Asia, with support from both fellow travelers and locals.

Now What?

The issue of what to do with the large amounts of trash you've collected is more complex than just finding the nearest recycling bin (which may or not exist). The truth is, a lot of trash here is either burned or dumped into an out-of-sight landfill, which just turns one problem into another. You can link up with organizations such as Trash Hero, which hosts cleanups around Southeast Asia and also works with local organizations to turn bottles, caps, broken flip-flops, and nonbiodegradable materials (those damn KitKat wrappers) into new items—like eco-bricks, which are used as building blocks for schools.

Cycle of Trash

To bring trashpacking full circle, do not engage in practices that add to the garbage problem. Avoid single-use plastics like the plague that they are. Sip from reusable cups, don't use straws, refuse excessive napkins and utensils from street vendors, carry your own bags to supermarkets, and don't throw anything on the ground—unless, of course, you plan to pick it up as trashpacking practice.

Animals

CLIMATE CHANGE AND OTHER MANMADE DISASTERS ARE MAKING THIS WORLD A LOT less habitable for animals. Southeast Asia is home to some of the most diverse animal species in the world, many of which are losing their homes in the name of careless modernization. What's more, wild animals such as elephants and monkeys are abused for the entertainment of tourists. The dog-meat trade is a cruel reality for man's best friend— and a practice that might make you think twice about all animals that are exploited for food. You can be the voice of the voiceless here—and have a lot of fun along the way.

DOG EAT DOG

While China is most commonly known for its penchant for dog meat, areas in Southeast Asia, particularly Cambodia, also see dogs as food and not friends. Dog flesh is purported to be a cure-all for a host of ailments, such as erectile dysfunction, insomnia, and skin rashes. It is also said to be a "hot meat," which helps spike the internal temperature of the consumer, making it a go-to food when the thermometer drops. An estimated 60 percent of Cambodians have eaten dog meat, and its appeal is on the rise. Additionally, many Chinese and Korean citizens frequent Cambodia and eat dog while they sightsee, making the industry a favorable one for attracting tourists. If you're hoping to save Old Yeller, you've got a long road ahead.

Play Dead

As opposed to pigs and cows, dogs are not often raised on factory farms. Instead, strays are wrangled from the street with lassos or are stolen from residents who keep them as companions, then thrown in

and cows form incredible social bonds that are similar to what you and Lassie had growing up. This means that shoveling down bacon or chomping on a burger isn't all that different from eating dog stew. If you're of the mindset that eating meat across the species spectrum is pretty fucked up, then working to end Cambodia's dog-meat trade is a good place to continue your activism.

What You Can Do

The most obvious step is to abstain from eating dog meat. A key difference between other farmed animals and dogs slaughtered for meat in Cambodia is that the former have some (albeit rarely enforced) protections that are meant to ensure they don't live a life of agony before being killed. Because no laws actually govern the way dogs are treated (and abuse is actively worked into the slaughter practice), reporting animal cruelty falls on deaf ears. In fact, the Cambodian government campaigned in 2003 to convince people to eat more dogs to help the country control its stray population. So where does that leave you? Well, yelling about how shitty people in Cambodia are for eating dogs isn't going to do much—except make you look like a racist asshole. You can, however, tap into the core and volunteer at shelters to help control the dog population (and do a little advocacy work on the side). The Phnom Penh Animal Welfare Society (adorably, PPAWS) welcomes volunteers (particularly those with veterinary experience) to help with its mission to provide medical treatment, vaccinate, and spay and neuter stray dogs and cats in Cambodia. PPAWS works with monks in pagodas to help them care for animals and partners with other organizations to help rehome animals and take them off the streets and away from the dog-meat trade.

packed cages where they await slaughter. It is believed that dog meat has the best flavor and medicinal qualities when the animal is tortured before slaughter, as fear releases endorphins. This is achieved by hanging the dogs by their necks and dismembering or skinning them alive, beating them repeatedly, and/or burning them to elicit maximum panic. When it comes time to eat, dogs are often flame-grilled whole and served as part of curries. Because many Westerners see the practice of turning Toto into a kebab barbaric, the dog-meat trade is moving away from being out in the open to more obscure culinary corners, making it harder to tackle and a bit more like other closed-door animal-slaughter industries.

Blame Game

Calling out locals for eating dog meat is a slippery slope of hypocrisy. It may seem completely foreign and grotesque to you that Cambodians consume canines. But before you point fingers, consider this: a pig is about as intelligent as a toddler,

ELEPHANT SANCTUARIES

Elephants are gentle giants that we can't help but love. However, because of their kind and trusting nature, many have been exploited for their ivory tusks, as forced entertainers in zoos, and for tourist attractions, particularly in Southeast Asia. An elephant ride might sound exciting—something epic that cannot be experienced back in the States—but these wild animals endure hell for your hour-long excursion through their jungle.

Why Do Elephants Need to Be Saved?

In nature, elephants do not work to serve humans. They graze on plants, take care of their young, and bathe. Elephant-ride operators "coerce" the animals—often in violent ways. The truth is, in order to "tame" an elephant enough to let you ride it, trainers must start breaking them at a very young age—in Thailand the word for this practice is *phajaan* (or "the crush"). Babies are taken from their mothers and confined, beaten, and starved until they are forced into submission. During elephant rides, operators sometimes use bull hooks to control the large animals, but even if they don't, elephants are too scared to disobey their trainers because they have incredible long-term memories of the horrors they endured as youngsters.

Sanctuaries

There are better ways to get close to these majestic beasts—whose spines are not meant for bearing the weight of humans.

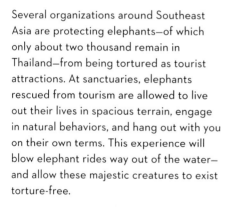

Several organizations around Southeast Asia are protecting elephants—of which only about two thousand remain in Thailand—from being tortured as tourist attractions. At sanctuaries, elephants rescued from tourism are allowed to live out their lives in spacious terrain, engage in natural behaviors, and hang out with you on their own terms. This experience will blow elephant rides way out of the water—and allow these majestic creatures to exist torture-free.

Save Elephant Foundation

This organization runs several accredited animal sanctuaries in Thailand, Cambodia, and Myanmar, most notably the Elephant Nature Park—which sits in a lush, expansive jungle in northern Thailand. The foundation rehabilitates elephants that it rescues from tourism—who often come to them emaciated and afraid of human interaction. Volunteers can choose between a short

visit and a full overnight slumber party (two days and one night). So what can you expect? Depending on the length of your visit, you will be able to feed elephants fruits and vegetables, take a hike with them through the area's lush mountains, watch (and help) them take mud baths—and help the lovable creatures rebuild trust in humankind with lots of snuggles along the way.

Tides Are Changing

As more tourists become aware of the dubious practices surrounding elephant rides and begin to steer clear of companies the minute they see a bull hook, the practice itself has begun to shift. Elephant rides are becoming less fashionable, and interacting with elephants in a sanctuary-like setting is becoming more selfie-worthy, forcing companies that mistreat animals to change their ways to follow the dollars. If you want to hang with elephants, make sure you're pushing the ethical needle in the right direction. Bring peanuts.

SAVING ANIMALS YOU'VE NEVER HEARD OF

We're all aware that many species of bears and big cats are endangered, but many lesser-known critters have it pretty bad, too. Aside from being captured and tortured for the sake of selfies, many animals in Southeast Asia are poached for their parts, illegally traded to other countries as exotic pets, and farmed for their fur, scales, or meat. Here are a few animals you may not know need saving.

Malayan Sun Bear (Malaysia)

The closest thing to an actual teddy bear in the wild, these are the smallest bears on the block (about the size of sheep dogs). Sun bears have it bad for two main reasons: they're farmed for the bile in their gallbladders, which is thought to afford some medicinal purpose, and they like to munch on coconut palms and bananas, so their habitat is at odds with loggers' clearing of forestland. The Borneo Sun Bear Conservation Centre welcomes volunteers for fourteen to twenty-eight days to its giant forest compound, where bears get to hang out freely, doing their bear things. Volunteers work alongside experienced researchers, help take care of bears, and educate the community about conservation.

Tarsier (Philippines)

If you've ever seen the eighties classic *The Gremlins*, you know what a tarsier looks like. The shy, big-eyed primate spends a lot of its time cuddled high up in trees, eating insects and being adorable. As the trees they love disappear, so do the tarsiers. Luckily, Carlito Pizarras—known locally as the "Tarsier Man"—set up the Tarsier Research and Development Center on the island of Bohol to conserve their diminishing populations. The sanctuary has volunteer opportunities based on its needs, which can range from planting tree seedlings in barren forest areas to supporting wildlife rejuvenation to being a guide for tourists who just want to take a quick pic of a tarsier before buying a fake stuffed one at the gift shop. If you do land here, know that you'll be living in the middle of a jungle—which, to us, is quite all right.

Gibbon (Thailand)

Furry-faced gibbons are not monkeys; they're apes—lesser (as in, not great) apes, to be exact. Gibbons in Thailand have been dealt a shitty hand. In addition to habitat loss, adults are vulnerable to poaching, and their orphans are often enslaved to perform in touristic parts of Thailand. The Gibbon Rehabilitation Project aims to stop these apes from being driven to extinction for the purpose of entertainment. The project's center is split into two sections: one where gibbons who need lifelong care reside, and another where the apes are rehabilitated to be returned to the wild (and where human contact is kept to a minimum). Volunteers can help on both sides with feeding and cleaning the animals and collecting tracking data on those that are released.

Pangolin (Vietnam)

A pangolin looks like an anteater (a type of which they are) and an armadillo *Freaky Friday*–ed their way into each other. When they get scared they turn into giant roly-polies, curling into a scaly ball to protect their sensitive parts. It's a little-known fact that pangolins are the world's most trafficked animal, coveted mostly for their scales, which are made of keratin—the same substance found in rhino horns. The Carnivore and Pangolin Education Centre, which rescues pangolins from the illegal wildlife trade, welcomes volunteers for a week or longer to help feed them and monitor their behavior. The center also rehabs and releases other carnivores you've never heard of, such as the Owston's palm civet (a zebra-patterned, shrew-like dude), the binturong (pretty

much a bear and cat hybrid), and the hairy-nosed otter (which is surprisingly smooth-nosed in appearance).

Dhole (Thailand)

Not much is known about the dhole (also known as the Asiatic wild dog) except that they do wild-dog-like things (i.e., hunt in packs and make whistling doggy noises). There aren't many in the wild, and they are seen as pests, which means they are trapped and killed often. The environmental nonprofit Earthwatch is currently conducting a research project in areas of Thailand where the dogs have been spotted. Volunteer opportunities last one to two weeks and involve fitting dholes with tracking collars and gathering data about what they do in the wild. Kind of like putting a GoPro on your Labrador, but probably a lot trickier.

Slow Loris (Indonesia)

You may have seen these wide-eyed creatures in a few viral tickle videos. Sadly, those clicks on YouTube have actually contributed to this sweet little primate's demise. First, the "hands-up" reaction to tickling is a stress response, which is not enjoyable for the slow loris. And because so many people thought that a loris would make a perfect pet after the slew of videos, illegal trade of the cute critters has skyrocketed. Once the slow loris is in your house and not just on a screen, the animals are wild AF and have the teeth to prove it—which illegal traders often clip or remove to make them more docile, resulting in potential death or severe infection. On top of everything, several parts of their bodies are ingredients in traditional medicine. It's all pretty fucking ugly, but luckily there is something you can do. You can volunteer with International Animal Rescue in Indonesia, which actively busts illegal traders with the help of law enforcement, and rescues, rehabs, and releases the nocturnal creatures back into the wild.

Giant Ibis (Cambodia)

Through nesting projects and supplemental feeding programs, the Sam Veasna Center in Cambodia works hard to make sure the giant ibis (a long-billed water bird that's on the critically endangered list), along with its feathered and furry friends, doesn't go extinct. While the center does not offer volunteer programs, booking a conservation tour—which allows you to take a half-day stroll through the wild or embark on a "supertour" that lasts several weeks and visits various biodiverse parts of the country—helps support Sam Veasna's assorted efforts to protect wildlife. Tours offer a unique look at Cambodia's native species, such as white-rumped vultures, a bunch of monkeys, and constricting snakes. The funds generated go toward supporting local communities, building infrastructure, aiding in direct conservation needs, and expanding the organization's ecotourism endeavors.

Disease and Disaster

POVERTY IS INEXTRICABLY TIED TO DISEASE, INCLUDING AIDS. FURTHERMORE, OTHER factors such as earthquakes, cyclones, and unexploded land mines impact poor communities at a disproportionate rate. Able-bodied people like you are a great asset to those with little access to health care and disaster relief. If you're looking to join the medical profession for the long run, honing your skills in Southeast Asia is an invaluable experience. You will navigate sometimes subpar hospital equipment and conditions that will make working in the States much easier.

DESTIGMATIZING HIV IN CAMBODIA

Cambodia's first reported case of HIV—the virus that leads to AIDS—was in 1991; as in much of the rest of the world, the auto-immune disease became an epidemic by 1995. Since then, Cambodia has been touted as a leader in halting the spread of AIDS, but at least fifteen thousand of its poorest people are still suffering from both the physical symptoms and the emotional toll of having a chronic sexually transmitted disease in a culture that stigmatizes HIV-positive individuals, even children, as outcasts. Global Crossroad's HIV/AIDS program in Cambodia aims to address the underlying—and lasting—effects of the illness through a low-cost program that makes a big difference in the lives of individuals and their families.

Progress

Cambodia has lost an estimated 115,000 people to AIDS since the first reported case; approximately 70,000 people are currently living with HIV/AIDS. In 2013, Cambodia committed to the global "90-90-90" initiative, which seeks to diagnose 90 percent of the people living with HIV, treat 90 percent of those diagnosed with antiretrovirals, and ensure that 90 percent of those on treatment are virally suppressed by 2020. Since then, the country has been active in addressing issues related to the spread and treatment of HIV; its efforts helped to slash new infections by 96 percent in 2015. Although these numbers are amazing, Cambodia's prevalence rate remains at 0.5 percent—with HIV being one of the two leading causes of death among sex workers and their children (the other is botched abortions). Those who contract or are living with the disease face a sad reality.

Karma

The idea of karma is prevalent throughout Cambodian culture, and it applies to those infected with HIV in an alarming way. People are ostracized, discriminated against, and stigmatized, with children feeling the brunt of the intolerance because they are often unable to reach necessary medical services. Cambodia is one of the poorest countries in Southeast Asia, and for many women sex work is the only way to pay the bills. Many sex workers do whatever it takes to make a living (e.g., not insisting that a condom be used) and thus contract HIV, which they may pass on to their unborn children. The child-sex and trafficking industry is rampant in Cambodia, compounding the issue further.

Doing Your Part

Volunteering with Global Crossroad's HIV/AIDS program is almost guaranteed to be a rewarding experience—and one that only costs $400 for two weeks, with meals, airport pickup, and accommodations included. Volunteers help children orphaned by AIDS deaths (and sometimes infected themselves) to access services. Volunteers also help treat related ailments—such as headaches, stomachaches, and skin diseases—to help patients lead a more comfortable life. The simple positive human interaction offered by kindhearted volunteers betters patients' lives. Another part of the program involves outreach education in the surrounding community, which aims to foster the acceptance of those living with AIDS, prevent further spread of the disease, and create a safe space where diagnosis and treatment are immediate and effective.

RED CROSS DISASTER RESPONDERS

The Red Cross is the kind of organization you don't really think about until things go horribly wrong. If your house burns down, the Red Cross will be there with a little bag of toiletries and solid advice about what to do next. If there's a big-ass earthquake, the organization rallies its troops to triage the damage and lend a hand. (Dropped your phone in the shitter again? Sorry bud, that's all you.) If you want to be *that* person for someone in distress, joining the Red Cross is a life-changing experience. Founded in 1859, the combined divisions of the Red Cross and Red Crescent—which include two international committees and 188 individual societies—make up the largest aid network in the world, and volunteering with it will be a major asset should you choose a career in humanitarian work.

To Start

To qualify as an international volunteer, you will need to get your bearings at your local Red Cross Society. Local factions provide global disaster-relief training, which includes education about effective strategies used in the past by disaster responders in 190 countries. To become a deployable volunteer, you will need to gather at least two years of field experience, be available on short notice (and be able to travel for a minimum of four weeks), possess diplomacy and problem-solving skills, and maintain excellent physical health. The Red Cross only deploys responders that are proficient in one or more core technical skills, all of which can be attained through dedicated volunteer work at your local chapter. Active recruitments happen once or twice per year, and prospective responders must undergo a background check and a series of interviews.

On the Ground

Local Red Cross offices typically handle their own disaster-relief efforts, except when things become overwhelming. Recurring earthquakes in Indonesia, cyclones in Laos, flooding and landslides in the Philippines, and the brewing genocide of the Rohingya Muslims in Myanmar all require a lot of backup from American Red Cross volunteers, about twenty to thirty of whom are deployed globally every year. Being deployed during a disaster is not the kind of easy ride offered at a cushy program complete with an air-conditioned volunteer house. Deployment means spending your days engaging in hard physical and emotional labor and your nights sleeping in tents, while managing teams and coordinating multiple initiatives to lead the mission in a way that creates the biggest impact for incredibly vulnerable populations. The reward is immense, however, as you will have the great satisfaction of knowing that instead of sending thoughts and prayers when disaster strikes (and then scrolling to the next thing on Facebook), you will be on the ground helping families find food, water, medical care, safety, and each other.

EAST MEETS WEST: MEDICAL VOLUNTEER OPPORTUNITIES WITH PROJECTS ABROAD

Projects Abroad is a well-known volunteer and internship network with placements all over the world. Its top-notch medically focused programs in Southeast Asia help prospective doctors and other medical professionals understand what it's like treating patients under suboptimal conditions—a circumstance that's true in more parts of the world than not. In addition to doing satisfying work, you will bolster your résumé with experience that's hard to come by in the United States medical industry, where internship competition is stiff. Pull up your sleeves, wash your hands to the elbow, and step into places where your help will be emphatically appreciated.

Medicine (Vietnam)

You'll need a year of premedical undergraduate study before taking on this internship, where you'll work in some of the best hospitals in Hanoi. To get your bearings, you will shadow medical professionals in fields such as internal medicine, pediatrics, oncology, and surgery. The program (which has a two-week minimum commitment) also offers a unique opportunity to work with doctors who provide acupuncture to autistic children from northern Vietnam. You can choose the hospital in which you wish to complete your internship. If you're hoping to one day be a surgeon, this opportunity offers an extensive surgical-procedure immersion program, where you can witness anything from orthopedic surgery to emergency lifesaving procedures. Here, you'll fill syringes with the best of them.

Dentistry (Cambodia)

We never understood why anybody would purposefully decide to dig around in other people's mouths, but if that's your cup of tea, we salute you. If you're going to commit to dentistry, a great place to start is in Phnom Penh, where you'll be placed at the state hospital and also at a private clinic to get the feel of both. You'll assist with diagnosis and treatment of common dental ailments, as well as mouth disorders, jaw deformities, and specific dental-surgery procedures. You'll need to commit to at least four weeks and have three years of dental study completed prior to arrival. Many of the dentists you'll be assisting speak English, but it's a big plus if you *parlez Français*.

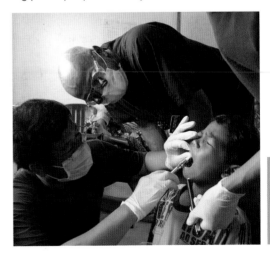

Physical Therapy (Vietnam)

The residents of Vietnam, young and old, have been (and continue to be) tremendously affected by the American War, and their basic needs are often overlooked. In this program, you will work alongside local physical therapy professionals; once you've proven your abilities you may be assigned your own patients or independent work with groups. You will learn a number of techniques, including Eastern massage therapies, to help patients recover from paralysis or other physical limitations. Several rehabilitation centers focus on helping children who suffer from the lasting physical and mental effects of exposure to Agent Orange. These kids don't get a lot of visitors, and your time and assistance will be reciprocated with intense gratitude. You must stick around for at least two weeks, and the longer you stay the more satisfying it will be to see patients continuing to improve with your help.

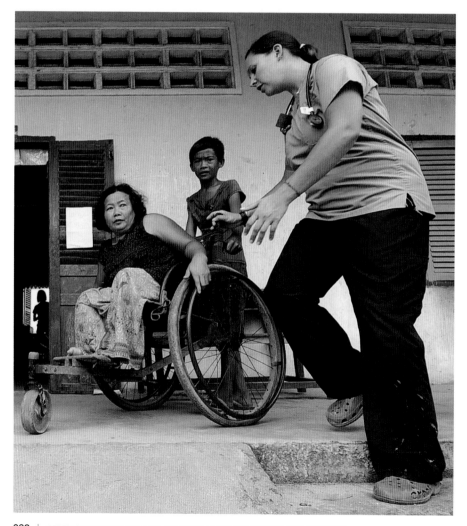

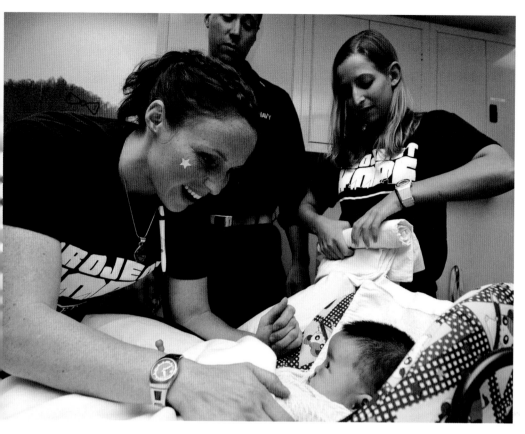

Special-Needs Care (Cambodia)

Although you can intern with special-needs babies, children, and adults as a beginning occupational therapist (with one year of experience), the program is severely short of staff who have a little more experience (three years or more working or studying in the field). Opportunities include working with children that have survived meningitis, patients that are living with cerebral palsy and other muscular disorders, and HIV-positive patients. The mission is to improve their quality of life through physical mobility and emotional support. The facilities offer fairly well-equipped therapy rooms. Cambodia's arm of Veterans International is in particular need of interns to help patients cope with the remnants of war, including the effects of existent land mines.

Public Health (Philippines)

In the Philippines, seven of the ten leading causes of death are attributed to diabetes, heart disease, and cancer, all noncommunicable diseases (NCD) that are closely related to lifestyle choices such as diet, smoking, drug addiction, and alcohol abuse. As a public health intern here, you will be paramount in helping to turn the tide for Filipinos who don't have access to preventive health care. In the community where you are placed, you will be part of a data-collection team that surveys health metrics such as blood pressure, cholesterol, and BMI. Data are turned into a plan to help individuals (and their families) at risk of developing NCDs address issues—through nutrition education and addiction support—before they become chronic illnesses.

WRAPPING UP

FOR US, TRAVEL HAS ALWAYS BEEN A WAY TO BURST OUR COMFORT BUBBLES TO BECOME better world citizens. We hope that this book inspires you to explore the unknown with fervor and excitement, while leaving a positive mark in every place you visit. Trading your warm bed for a metal hostel bunk and your abundant closet for a backpack will not be easy, but it will be worth it.

You will find that fear and fun often go hand in hand once you learn to confront new experiences—from deep-fried bugs to unfamiliar celebrations—head on and let them transform you. Because, let's be honest, one of the scariest things in the world is living with the regret that you never got to explore it.

THE AUTHORS

FREDDIE PIKOVSKY

Freddie created Off Track Planet with Anna in 2009 from a passion to inspire more young people to travel the world and gain perspective on our planet, empathy toward people, and a desire to improve themselves. After spending nearly ten years producing Off Track Planet—jaunting around the world to seek inspiration in new places, cultures, food, and friends—Freddie hopes this book continues to fulfill that mission. He would like to give a special thanks to Anna for her talent and commitment, to Adam Silver for his constant friendship and support, to Jennifer Herrera and the David Black Agency, and to the friends he made at Lazycrazy Homestay in Sapa.

A cold beer and a spicy bowl of hot soup sitting on a little plastic street-side table in Vietnam were had many nights in your honor, Anthony Bourdain, and Off Track Planet wouldn't exist if you hadn't been there to serve as our inspiration. You are greatly missed.

ANNA STAROSTINETSKAYA

Anna was born in the former USSR and raised in Los Angeles. She moved to New York, where she learned the value of a good winter coat. She now resides in San Francisco, a place where summer only happens for one week in February. Since the last election, Anna has been looking to get rid of her winter coats for good by escaping to the Philippines, where she would perpetually island-hop with a coconut water in hand.

Anna would like to thank her best friend of more than twenty years (and fellow USSR immigrant), Vera Bakman, without whom Anna's life would be incomplete. Anna plans to grow old with Vera, eventually turning into the loudly dressed cat ladies the universe has always intended them to be. In Soviet Russia, future plans you!

PHOTO CREDITS

p. 6: "Takeaway"; p. 8: Marcello Rabozzi; p. 9: Freddie Pikovsky; p. 10 (top left): Putu Andika Panendra; p. 10 (top right): Freddie Pikovsky; p. 10 (middle left): Freddie Pikovsky; p. 10 (bottom left): Adam Silver; p. 10 (bottom right): "pen_ash"; p. 12: Opick Mataram Web; p. 13 (top):Freddie Pikovsky; p. 13 (middle): Adam Silver; p. 13 (bottom): Adam Silver; p. 14 (all): Freddie Pikovsky; p. 15: Freddie Pikovsky; p. 16 (all): Freddie Pikovsky; p. 17 (top left): Nicolaus Erwin; p. 17 (middle right): Sherra Triarosdiana; p. 18 (top right): Peggy und Marco Lachmann-Anke; p. 18 (middle right): "Lemon mintmint"; p. 18 (bottom): Phongsak Manodee; p. 19: Pixabay; p. 20: Tigitmotorbikes; p. 21: Quang Nguyen vinh; p. 22 (top left): "Lelong"; p. 22 (top right): Dave Bunnell; p. 23 (top left): Doug Knuth; p. 23 (top right): "Peacefulday"; p. 24: Freddie Pikovsky; p. 25: Freddie Pikovsky; p. 26 (top left): Roger Price; p. 26 (top right): Khoa Huynh; p. 27 (top right): "EladeManu"; p. 27 (bottom right): "wavehavenbali"; p. 28 (top right): Kahunapule Michael Johnson; p. 28 (bottom right): "Arabsalam"; p. 28 (bottom left): Kars Alfrink; p. 29 (top): Sasin Tipchai; p. 29 (bottom right): "Alit Design"; p. 30: Albert Dezetter; p. 31: Sasin Tipchai; p. 32 (top left): Freddie Pikovsky; p. 32 (right): Ronnie Rey Manjares; p. 33 (top left): Oliver Sjöström; p. 33 (top right): "P.A.V. Mahusay"; p. 34: Levi Morsy; p. 35: Made agus devayana; p. 36 (top): "Opick Mataram Web"; p. 36 (bottom left): Simon Bardet; p. 37: Simon Bardet; p. 38 (all): Freddie Pikovsky; p. 39: Freddie Pikovsky; p. 40: Freddie Pikovsky; p. 41: Alain Berger; p. 42 (top right): Abe Khao Lak; p. 42 (bottom left): Christian Jensen; p. 43: Alit Suarnegara; p. 44: Jorge Láscar; p. 45: "kallerna"; p. 46: Freddie Pikovsky; p. 47 (top left): Yusuke Kawasaki; p. 47 (bottom right): Tara Angkor Hotel; p. 48 (top right): "Robrrb"; p. 48 (middle left): "mollyali"; p. 49: Thomas Quine; p. 50: Patrick Liu; p. 51 (top): "upsidedown.com.ph"; p. 51 (bottom): Ho Chi Minh Mausoleum; p. 52 (top right): "tefl Search"; p. 52 (bottom left): "plusgood"; p. 53: "matham315"; p. 54 (bottom left): Dean Moriarty; p. 54 (bottom right): Daniel Nebreda; p. 55 (top left): Pixabay; p. 55 (top right): Adam Silver; p. 56: Freddie Pikovsky; p. 57: Michelle Maria; p. 58: "vincentc"; p. 59 (top): Deny Sabri; p. 59 (bottom right): Joachim Engel; p. 60: Sasin Tipchai; p. 61: Marco Zanferrari; p. 62: "Arul"; p. 63: Pixabay; p. 64 (bottom left): "chinsoontan"; p. 64 (middle right): Adrian Lim; p. 65 (top): "jet sun"; p. 65 (bottom left): Kullez; p. 66 (top): Jorge Láscar; p. 66 (bottom): Bernard Spragg; p. 67: Alan Wat; p. 68: Alan Wat; p. 69 (middle left): Freddie Pikovsky; p. 69 (bottom right): Aussie Assault Follow; p. 70: "kamodayz"; p. 71 (both): Jason Goh; p. 72 (top left): Marco Nürnberger; p. 72 (right): Freddie Pikovsky; p. 73: "Franzfoto"; p. 74: Pixabay; p. 75: "Anne and David"; p. 76 (top left): Freddie Pikovsky; p. 76 (bottom): "sowrirajan"; p. 77 (top): Freddie Pikovsky; p. 77 (bottom): Jacob French; p. 78 (top): "kuujinbo"; p. 78 (bottom right): Freddie Pikovsky; p. 79: "goomba478"; p. 80 (all): Freddie Pikovsky; p. 81: Allie Caulfield; p. 82 (top left): "naturepost"; p. 82 (right): Madeleine Deaton; p. 83 (top): Vee Satayamas; p. 83 (bottom right): Katherine Lim; p. 84: Adam Silver; p. 85: Adam Silver; p. 86 (top right): phuongkim1981; p. 86 (bottom): David Loong; p. 87 (top): kenji ross; p. 87 (bottom right): Maggie Chai; p. 88: Australian Embassy Jakarta; p. 89 (top left): Kedai Joni; p. 89 (bottom): chee hong; p. 90: Charles Haynes; p. 91 (left): Marion Paul Baylado; p. 91 (right): Gerald Mendoza; p. 92: Shubert Ciencia; p. 93: Rob Bertholf; p. 94: NuCastielFollow; p. 95: Basil Strahm; p. 97: Adam Silver; p. 98: Thomas Schoch; p. 99 (left): Oskari Kettunen; p. 99 (right): Anne and David; p. 100: secretlondon123; p. 101 (bottom left): Hajime Nakano; p. 101 (right): "Alpha"; p. 102: Pandora Voon; p. 103: Freddie Pikovsky; p. 104: "xiaolinzi821";

p. 105 (top left): Françoise GISBERT; p. 105 (top right): "志輝 馮"; p. 105 (bottom right): Françoise GISBERT; p. 106: Brian Jeffery Beggerly; p. 107 (top left): John Shedrick; p. 107 (top right): Freddie Pikovsky; p. 107 (bottom): Freddie Pikovsky; p. 108: Freddie Pikovsky; p. 110: helmi099; p. 111 (top): John Shedrick; p. 111 (bottom): Phuket@photographer.net; p. 113 (both): Phuket@photographer.net; p. 114 (both): Phuket@photographer.net; p. 114 (bottom): Sam Sherratt; p. 116 (both): "GETaiwan NTU"; p. 117: Pixabay; p. 118: "Sakyant"; p. 119: Michelle Hamilton; p. 120: Pixabay; p. 121: "Sakyant"; p. 122: Freddie Pikovsky; p. 123: Adam Selwood; p. 124 (top right): Vasenka Photography; p. 124 (bottom): "Soi Cowboy"; p. 125 (both): John Shedrick; p. 126 (top): "Sergey"; p. 126 (bottom): "Steve Upton"; p. 127 (top): Anita "kolibri5"; p. 127 (bottom right): Jan Seifert; p. 128: Reinardt Gilfillan; p. 129 (top): Quang Nguyen vinh; p. 130 (top left): "Bleeding Mole"; p. 130 (bottom): Adam Silver; p. 131 (both): Freddie Pikovsky; p. 132: Freddie Pikovsky; p. 133: "White Party BKK"; p. 134: "White Party BKK"; p. 136: "Marie"; p. 137: Yohann Legrand; p. 138: Sam Walker; p. 139 (top): "onono"; p. 139 (bottom): Timothy Subroto; p. 140: Agustina Sulistio; p. 141: Rob Young; p. 142 (top left): Christian Haugen; p. 142 (bottom): Nick Hewson; p. 144 (top left): Freddie Pikovsky; p. 144 (top right): Freddie Pikovsky; p. 144 (middle top left): Thomas Ulrich; p. 144 (middle bottom left): Freddie Pikovsky; p. 144 (middle right): Pixabay; p. 144 (bottom): Sasin Tipchai; p. 146: "tk tan"; p. 147 (left): Aleksandr Zykov; p. 147 (right): Mills Baker; p. 148 (both): Freddie Pikovsky; p. 149: Dennis Wong; p. 151: Freddie Pikovsky; p. 152: Pixabay; p. 153: "cmor15"; p. 154: Pixabay; p. 155: Freddie Pikovsky; p. 156: Dennis Jarvis; p. 157: Pixabay; p. 158: Adam Silver; p. 159 (both): Freddie Pikovsky; p. 160 (left): Allie Brown "@downtownalliebrown"; p. 160 (right): Pixabay; p. 161: Freddie Pikovsky; p. 162: Phuket@photographer.net; p. 163: Maung Ne Lynn Aung; p. 164: Thomas Ulrich; p. 167: Pixabay; p. 168: "pereslavl"; p. 169: "cytis"; p. 170 (all): Freddie Pikovsky; p. 171 (left): Sasin Tipchai; p. 171 (right): "Jnzl's Photos"; p. 172: "pittaya"; p. 173: "ingo66"; p. 174: Sasin Tipchai; p. 175: Anita "kolibri5"; p. 176: Adam Silver; p. 177: Freddie Pikovsky; p. 178 (both): Freddie Pikovsky; p. 179: Freddie Pikovsky; p. 180: Freddie Pikovsky; p. 181: Adam Silver; p. 182: "igormattio"; p. 183: Jah Cordova; p. 184: Carina Chen; p. 185: Pixabay; p. 187: Ellen Forsyth; p. 188: Freddie Pikovsky; p. 190: "Azchael"; p. 191: Steve Buissinne; p. 192: John Tann; p. 193: Quinn Comendant; p. 194: "runran"; p. 195: Michael Coghlan; p. 197: Freddie Pikovsky; p. 198 (top left): "Saigon Soul"; p. 198 (top right): "Saigon Soul"; p. 198 (bottom): David Shankbone; p. 199 (bottom): "Kojach"; p. 201 (top left): Freddie Pikovsky; p. 201 (top right): Aiko Konishi; p. 201 (bottom left): Freddie Pikovsky; p. 201 (bottom right): "tausend und eins"; p. 202: Freddie Pikovsky; p. 204 (top left): "Frontier official"; p. 204 (top right): Steve De Neef / LAMAVE; p. 204 (middle left): UK Department for International Development; p. 204 (middle right): UK Department for International Development; p. 204 (bottom left): "Frontier official"; p. 204 (bottom right): Freddie Pikovsky; p. 206: "tajai"; p. 207 (top left): Freddie Pikovsky; p. 207 (top right): Adam Silver; p. 207 (bottom left): "ND Strupler"; p. 207 (bottom right): Justin Vidamo; p. 208: "jh_tan84"; p. 211: UK Department for International Development; p. 213: Nguyen Hung Vu; p. 215: "COMSEVENTHFLT"; p. 216: Nguyen Hung Vu; p. 218: Brian Hoffman; p. 219: "IPSL institute for global learning"; p. 220: "tajai"; p. 221: "Charles EYES PiX"; p. 222: "Takver"; p. 223: Benjamin Hollis; p. 224 (top): Benjamin Hollis; p. 224 (bottom right): LAMAVE; p. 225 (top left): Gili Shark Conservation; p. 225 (top right): Gili Shark Conservation; p. 225 (bottom left): Gili Shark Conservation; p. 227: "plusgood"; p. 228: Mark Fahey; p. 229: Freddie Pikovsky; p. 230 (both): Freddie Pikovsky; p. 231 (left): "cuatrok77"; p. 231 (right): Niek van Son; p. 232: Chris Phutully; p. 234: "COMSEVENTHFLT"; p. 235: Military Sealift Command; p. 237: Cooperation Afloat Readiness and Training; p. 238: "COMSEVENTHFLT"; p. 239: "COMSEVENTHFLT"; p. 240 (left): Oliver Sjöström; p. 240 (top right): Robert Nyman; p. 240 (bottom right): Freddie Pikovsky; p. 241 (top left): Adam Silver; p. 241 (top right): William Cho; p. 241 (middle top right): Andrea Schaffer; p. 241 (middle left): Bernard Spragg; p. 241 (middle right [fruit]): "16:9clue"; p. 241 (bottom left): Pixabay; p. 241 (lottom right): "Manuae"

INDEX

F

G

K

L

M

X

Y